GW00691306

A Sense of the Past

Studies in current archaeological applications of remote sensing and non-invasive prospection methods

Edited by

Hans Kamermans
Martin Gojda
Axel G. Posluschny

HERITAGE · DATA · KNOWLEDGE

BAR International Series 2588
2014

Published by

Archaeopress
Publishers of British Archaeological Reports
Gordon House
276 Banbury Road
Oxford OX2 7ED
England
bar@archaeopress.com
www.archaeopress.com

BAR S2588

A Sense of the Past: Studies in current archaeological applications of remote sensing and non-invasive prospection methods

ISBN 978 1 4073 1216 3

Front cover illustration: DTM of a set of artillery forts (a later addition to the great fortified town of Terezín (north-west Bohemia, Czech Republic) which was constructed across the Labe river in the mid 19th century), a result of ALS (March 2011). The current state of the monument which has been partly levelled (forts 1 and 4) is well illustrated by this way. Also, a dense network of former trackways and linear earthworks of which some may have been connected with the fort system is apparent.

Back cover illustration: Vladař (western Bohemia, Czech Republic) DTM of extensively fortified Iron Age hillfort produced from airborne laser scanned data acquired in March 2010. The image displays perfectly the current state of the site and its individual components, such as the so-called acropolis situated in the highest part of the hillfort (coloured blue) and the fortification system of ramparts and ditches in the western and northern parts of the flat table hill.

The project ArchaeoLandscapes Europe has been funded with support from the European Commission (Culture Programme 2007–2013–CU7–MULT7 Agreement Number 2010-1486 / 001-001). This publication reflects the views of the authors, and the Commission cannot be held responsible for any use which may be made of the information contained therein.

Printed in England by 4edge, Hockley

All BAR titles are available from:

Hadrian Books Ltd
122 Banbury Road
Oxford
OX2 7BP
England
www.hadrianbooks.co.uk

The current BAR catalogue with details of all titles in print, prices and means of payment is available free from Hadrian Books or may be downloaded from www.archaeopress.com

TABLE OF CONTENTS

LIST OF CONTRIBUTORS

A. Agapiou: *Department of Civil Engineering and Geomatics, Cyprus University of Technology, Limassol, Cyprus.*

Ian Armit: *Archaeological Sciences, School of Applied Sciences, University of Bradford, UK.*

Michał Bugaj: *National Heritage Board of Poland, Warsaw, Poland.*

James Bonsall: *Archaeological Sciences, School of Applied Sciences, University of Bradford, UK.*

Richard Ciolek-Torello: *Statistical Research, Inc.,Redlands, CA, USA.*

Tom Debruyne: *Inter-Municipal Archaeological Service PORTIVA, city, Belgium.*

Sylvane Dederix: *Université Catholique de Louvain, Louvain-la-Neuve, Belgium* **and** *Laboratory of Geophysical - Satellite Remote Sensing & Archaeo-environment I.M.S - F.O.R.T.H., Rethymnon, Greece.*

François Djindjian: *University of Paris 1 and CNRS, Paris, France.*

Christopher Gaffney: *Archaeological Sciences, School of Applied Sciences, University of Bradford, UK.*

A. Georgopoulos: *School of Rural & Surveying Engineering, National Technical University of Athens, Athens, Greece.*

Claire Goffioul: *Ministry of Wallon Region, Department of Archaeology, city, Belgium.*

Martin Gojda: *University of Kardynal Stefan Wyszynski, Warsaw, Poland.*

Lars Gustavsen: *The Norwegian Institute for Cultural Heritage Research, Oslo, Norway.*

D.G. Hadjimitsis: *Department of Civil Engineering and Geomatics, Cyprus University of Technology, Limassol, Cyprus.*

Jeffrey A. Homburg: *Statistical Research, Inc., Tucson, Arizona, USA.*

Mariza Kormann: *Kellogg College, The University of Oxford, Oxford, UK.*

Gary Lock: *School of Archaeology, The University of Oxford< Oxford, UK.*

Marc Lodewijckx: *Leuven University, Department of Archaeology and Art History, Leuven, Belgium.*

Rory McNeary: *Centre for Maritime Archaeology, School of Environmental Sciences, University of Ulster, UK.*

N. Papadopoulos: *Laboratory of Geophysical - Satellite Remote Sensing and Archaeo-environment, Institute for Mediterranean Studies (I.M.S.), Foundation for Research and Technology, Hellas (F.O.R.T.H.), Rethymnon, Greece.*

René Pelegrin: *Leuven University, Department of Archaeology and Art History, Leuven, Belgium.*

M.C. Salvi: *Laboratory of Geophysical - Satellite Remote Sensing and Archaeo-environment, Institute for Mediterranean Studies (I.M.S.), Foundation for Research and Technology, Hellas (F.O.R.T.H.), Rethymnon, Greece.*

Apostolos Sarris: *Laboratory of Geophysical - Satellite Remote Sensing and Archaeo-environment, Institute for Mediterranean Studies (I.M.S.), Foundation for Research and Technology, Hellas (F.O.R.T.H.), Rethymnon, Greece.*

E. Seferou: *Laboratory of Geophysical - Satellite Remote Sensing and Archaeo-environment, Institute for Mediterranean Studies (I.M.S.), Foundation for Research and Technology, Hellas (F.O.R.T.H.), Rethymnon, Greece.*

Gunnar Siedler: *Fokus GmbH Leipzig, Leipzig, Germany.*

Ladislav Šmejda: *Department of Archaeology, University of West Bohemia, Plzeň, The Czech Republic.*

Arne Anderson Stamnes: *The NTNU Museum of Natural History and Archaeology, Oslo, Norway.*

Sebastian Vetter: *Fokus GmbH Leipzig, Leipzig, Germany.*

Robert M. Wegener: *Statistical Research, Inc., Tucson, Arizona, USA.*

Michele Wienhold: *University of Central Lancashire, Preston, UK.*

INTRODUCTION

Hans Kamermans, Martin Gojda and Axel G. Posluschny

We will start this editorial with a warning. This book has nothing to do with the novel *The Sense of the Past* by Henry James. Both books have (most of) the title in common and the fact that they deal with the past, but that is the only resemblance. In his unfinished novel from 1917, Henry James' protagonist travels back in time. We, archaeologists, study the past with different methods. This publication presents applications of one of our techniques: remote sensing. We use remote sensing in this book in the widest sense as *a set of scientific methods that is concerned with the measurement and interpretation of electromagnetic radiation reflected or emitted by a target from a receiver at a distance from the target.* In this way remote sensing includes the study of images made from the air and from space but also the results of geophysical techniques like magnetometry, Ground Penetrating Radar (GPR) and Electrical Resistivity Tomography (ERT).

Remote sensing is a hot topic in archaeology due to, among others, the success of Google Earth, the easy availability of satellite images, and the relatively cheap and easy to apply geophysical techniques. Recently a number of books have been published on this topic like *Mapping Archaeological Landscapes from Space*, edited by Douglas C. Comer and Michael J. Harrower (2013), *Interpreting Archaeological Topography*, edited by Rachel S. Opitz and David C. Cowley (2013), and *Archeologie a letecké laserové skenování krajiny – Archaeology and Airborne Laser Scanning of the Landscape*, edited by M. Gojda and J. John (2013).

This volume groups together papers presented at a commission 4 session at the XVI UISPP World Congress in Florianópolis, Brazil (4-10 September 2011), a UISPP commission 4 session in Leiden, The Netherlands (2nd November 2012) and at a session entitled *Advanced Prospection Methods for Cultural Heritage Management – Experiences and Challenges during* the EAA Annual Meeting in Helsinki, Finland (29th August – 1st September 2012). The organisers of these sessions are also the editors of this volume.

The International Union of Prehistoric and Protohistoric Sciences (Union Internationale des Sciences Préhistoriques et Protohistoriques – UISPP) was founded on May 28th, 1931, in Bern, and integrates all sciences related to prehistoric and protohistoric development: archaeology, anthropology, palaeontology, geology, zoology, botany, environment, physics, chemistry, geography, history,

numismatics, epigraphy, mathematics and other. Research on adaptation mechanisms and human societies' behaviour dynamics are at the centre of the scientific interest of UISPP. For this aim, UISPP periodically organises a world congress of prehistoric and protohistoric sciences, on which occasion the progress of knowledge is presented and common research goals are set. For these, UISPP creates scientific commissions devoted to specialised research themes. Since September 29th, 1955 the UISPP is a member of the UNESCO associate International Council of Philosophy and Human Sciences.

The European Association of Archaeologists (EAA) is a membership-based association open to all archaeologists and other related or interested individuals or bodies. The members are working in prehistory, classical, medieval and later archaeology. In 1994 at the Inaugural Meeting of the EAA held in Ljubljana, Slovenia, the EAA Statutes were formally approved. They stipulate that the EAA was created:

- to promote the development of archaeological research and the exchange of archaeological information
- to promote the management and interpretation of the European archaeological heritage
- to promote proper ethical and scientific standards for archaeological work
- to promote the interests of professional archaeologists in Europe
- to promote co-operation with other organisations with similar aims

The session at the UISPP conference in Florianopolis was a merger of two originally planned sessions called *C23 Landscape archaeology II / GIS applications in Archaeology of Large landscapes,* a session in co-operation with CAA, of which Hans Kamermans was one of the organisers, and *C24 Landscape archaeology III / Archaeological Survey,* a session in co-operation with ArchaeoLandscapes, of which Axel Posluschny was one of the organisers. The new, unnamed session was chaired by Axel Posluschny and Hans Kamermans.

The UISPP commission 4 session in Leiden was called *New developments in the Application of Computers and Quantitative Methods in Archaeology* and organised by Hans Kamermans.

Axel Posluschny is working at the Roman-Germanic

Commission of the German Archaeological Institute as the project leader of the EU project *ArchaeoLandscapes Europe*. He is also a Steering Committee member of the international association *Computer Applications and Quantitative Methods in Archaeology* (CAA).

Hans Kamermans is Associate Professor at the Faculty of Archaeology, Leiden University in the Netherlands. His teaching and research is in computer applications in archaeology.

Martin Gojda organised the EAA session. He is Professor at the University of West Bohemia in Pilsen, Czech Republic (Head of Archaeology Department between 2005 – 2011) and at the University of Kardynal Stefan Wyszynski in Warsaw (Poland) where he teaches landscape archaeology, non-invasive methods and archaeology of Early Medieval Europe. He is also a co-ordinator of the aerial archaeology programme and curator of the archive of aerial photographs in the Institute of Archaeology, Academy of Sciences of the Czech Republic (Prague).

The book starts firmly on the ground with the application of geophysical techniques from Ireland, Norway, Greece, Poland and the Czech Republic. Then we leave the surface. The following technique is LiDAR with examples from Northern Ireland (UK), the Czech Republic and Arizona (USA). Aerial photography is presented in an example from Belgium and the use of ground spectroscopy in an example from Cyprus. The next chapter describes a German example of automated 3D-object documentation on the basis of an image set. The last two chapters are stretching the topic of remote sensing a little. The first one describes the Fuzzy Cumulative Visibility Analysis (FCVA) of Neolithic long barrows in the Danebury region in England (UK). One can argue that visibility studies are in fact part of remote sensing. We measure and interpret the electromagnetic radiation (visible light) reflected by the landscape and received by our eyes. However, whether it is still remote sensing when we do this by simulating this on a computer remains a question. The last contribution is a stranger in our midst. It describes invention and innovation processes in Prehistoric societies during the transition between the Middle and Upper Palaeolithic in Europe.

Henry James, as a writer of novels, can invent the past. In fact he knows the past; so the title of his book is *The Sense of the Past*. Scientists try to reconstruct the past but usually end up with more questions than answers. That is why our book is called *A Sense of the Past*. Maybe time travel would have given us more concrete answers on some of the topics but in the meantime these fascinating techniques give us definitely a sense of the past.

Acknowledgements

This publication is sponsored by *ArchaeoLandscapes Europe* (*ArcLand*). *ArcLand* is a large European network within the framework of the Culture 2007–2013 programme. The EU has decided to support this initiative to overcome the differences in the use and acceptance of modern remote sensing techniques and to foster co-operation between archaeological institutions. It is the aim of this network to support any kind of collaboration that enhances public awareness of the European Landscapes and their research by means of Remote Sensing techniques and aids the dissemination of aerial and remote sensing techniques.

We would like to thank Kelly Fennema for correcting the English texts, Gertrudis Offenberg for the title of the book and Till Sonnemann for his help to clarify some incomprehensible sentences in the content.

References

Comer, D.C. - Harrower, M.J. eds 2013: Mapping Archaeological Landscapes from Space. New York: Springer.

Gojda, M. - John, J. eds 2013: Archeologie a letecké laserové skenování krajiny - Archaeology and Airborne Laser Scanning of the Landscape. Pilsen: University of West Bohemia.

James, H. 1917: The Sense of the Past. London: W. Collins Sons & Co.

Opitz, R.S. – Cowley, D.C. eds 2013: Interpreting Archaeological Topography. 3D Data, Visualisation and Observation. Occasional Publications of the Aerial Archaeological Research Group No. 5. Oxford: Oxbow Books.

A Decade of Ground Truthing: Reappraising Magnetometer Prospection Surveys on Linear Corridors in Light of Excavation Evidence 2001-2010

James Bonsall, Christopher Gaffney and Ian Armit

Abstract: *1,100 hectares of magnetometer surveys assessed multiple linear corridors across Ireland as part of a wider programme in advance of road construction from 2001-2010. 67 % of the survey areas were ground-truthed via detailed excavations. A two-year research project has created, critically reviewed and reappraised this digital archive, which has provided a considerable opportunity to assess the suitability of magnetometry to map and interpret anomalies that are often the product of subtle archaeological features.*

The role of geology plays the most significant factor in the success or otherwise of magnetometer surveys. The technique is particularly successful at identifying burnt features and enclosed occupation sites upon favourable geology. Similar archaeological sites were often missed due to poor magnetic contrasts in areas overlain by peats, or obscured by strongly magnetic igneous and metamorphic geology. Sites comprising small cut features such as post-pits, post-holes (most typically Neolithic structures) and inhumations could not be identified using a standard methodology, even upon the most favourable geologies.

The academic analysis of ground-truthed geophysical data will have a great impact beyond Ireland, as it defines the limitations of magnetometer surveys in terms of geology, landscape and site type that can have applications elsewhere. The assessment of non-magnetic archaeological features or sites on unfavourable geologies, require alternative - and in some cases, more labour intensive – techniques to suitably appreciate the underlying archaeology.

Keywords: *Magnetometry - Ground Truthing - Archaeological Feedback- Ireland - Low- contrast soils - Road Schemes*

Introduction

Geophysical surveys have been used on a variety of commercial archaeological projects over the last thirty years across Europe (*Catherall et al. 1984; Dawson - Gaffney 1995; Sarris - Jones 2000; Gaffney - Gater 2003; David et al. 2008; Campana 2011; Campana - Dabas 2011; Viberg et al. 2011*). Magnetometer surveys are widely regarded as the most suitable method of geophysical assessment due to their ability to rapidly identify a wide range of archaeological deposits, including earth-cut or in-filled features, areas of burning and industry as well as occupation activity (*Clark 1996; Gaffney - Gater 2003*). Upon favourable geological backgrounds archaeological features are clear and coherently observed in magnetometer data but are poorly seen or not seen at all on unfavourable geology. This study will examine the distribution and influences of Irish geological conditions upon magnetometry data via a study of complementary ground-truthed excavations. The research utilises more than 1,100 hectares of magnetometer survey data derived from Irish road scheme projects to compare with data from subsequent excavations in order to determine (and quantify) the success or otherwise of magnetometer surveys upon various Irish soils.

A reliance on magnetometry?

Some of the most technologically advanced surveys on recent large-scale European infrastructure projects have suggested potential problems for the application of magnetometry upon low-contrast soils. The Brescia-Bergamo-Milano Motorway (BREBEMI) project in northern Italy (*Campana 2011; Campana - Dabas 2011*), surveyed 217 hectares with high resolution AMP© acquired magnetometry. In the published papers there were many successes reported, however the authors also reported noisy background data and low contrasts that occasionally hindered an archaeological interpretation.

Archaeological geophysical surveys are carried out under licence in Ireland and their use has been recorded in detail (*NMS 2008, 2012*). Magnetometry has been the favoured technique and accounts for 53 % of all archaeological geophysical licence applications (Table 1). Geophysical surveys have been regularly used on commercial projects in Ireland since the 1980s (*Cleary et al. 1987*) and extensively so since the 2000s (Fig. 1) prior to the development of large-scale linear road corridors (*DAHGI - NRA 2000; O'Rourke 2003; NRA 2005; NMS 2008, 2012; Bonsall et al. 2013b*). Based on available comparative data for the period 2001-2010 (*Stamnes - Gustavsen, this volume; Viberg et al. 2011; Visser et al. 2011; AIP 2012*), Ireland has the second highest use of archaeological geophysics in Europe after England, both in frequency of surveys and the number of surveys per square kilometre. Ireland has carried out seven times as many surveys as Sweden and the Netherlands and eleven times that of Norway. A challenge faced by geophysicists in the commercial world is the lack

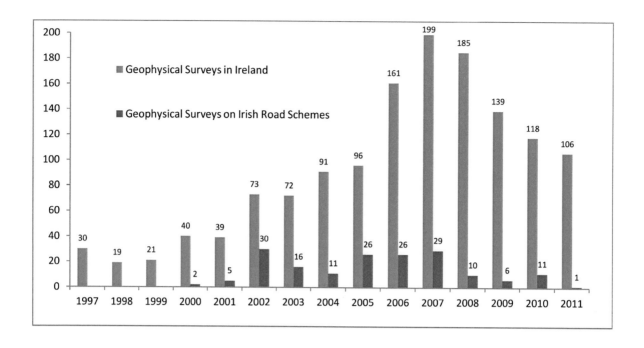

Fig. 1. Frequency of archaeological geophysical surveys in Ireland and upon Irish road schemes.

Table 1. Frequency of archaeological geophysics techniques, based on Detection Licence applications from 1997-2011.

Method	**Use**	**Number of Detection Licence applications**	**%**
Magnetometry	High	1,139	53%
Electrical Resistance	High / Mid	653	31%
Magnetic Susceptibility	Mid	199	9%
Ground Penetrating Radar	Mid / Low	102	5%
Electromagnetic	Low	23	1%
Metal Detectors	Low	17	<1%
Seismic	Low	3	<1%
Microgravity	Low	1	<1%
Total 2,137			

of feedback from subsequent phases of investigations such as intrusive excavations. If it exists at all, feedback is often anecdotal (i.e. "it worked / it didn't work") rather than evidence based empirical data.

Archaeological Investigations in Ireland and opportunities for feedback on Road Schemes

The National Roads Authority (NRA) is an independent statutory body in Ireland with the primary function for securing the provision of a safe and efficient network of national roads (*O'Rourke 2003*). Since 1993 the NRA has overseen the management of 173 road schemes across Ireland, including the completion of 82 schemes, six currently under construction and a further 33 at the planning stage. Archaeological investigations along new road corridors are carried out by the NRA (*Kirwan 2003*) as part of Ireland's obligation as a signatory state to the *European*

Convention on the Protection of the Archaeological Heritage, known as the Valletta Convention (*Council of Europe 1992*). Whilst there is a preference for preservation *in situ* of archaeological deposits, it is recognised that some archaeological features cannot avoid the impact of large developments and that those must be investigated and recorded in a scientific manner.

A number of regional NRA Project Archaeologists oversee all aspects of cultural resource management with respect to Irish national legislation and codes of practice established between the government and the NRA (*DAHGI 1999; DAHGI - NRA 2000*). These documents go further than the requirements of the Valletta Convention: there is a strong emphasis on obtaining the "fullest possible level of pre-development archaeological assessment, both in respect of known sites and as yet unidentified ones" (*Kirwan 2003*). Under these circumstances, geophysical survey has a

Table 2. Typical examples of timescales for archaeological investigations used on road schemes. Earlier stages of assessment (route selection, desktop-analysis and walkover surveys) always precede the use of geophysical survey, often by many years.

Method of Assessment	Road Scheme Name					
	M3 Clonee-Kells Motorway	M18 Ennis Bypass	M25 Waterford Bypass	M4 Kinnegad-Enfield-Kilcock Motorway	M18 Oranmore-Gort Motorway	M18 Gort-Crusheen Motorway
Geophysical Survey	2001-02	2001-03	2002-04	2002	2004	2004-07
Test Trenching	2004	2002-03	2002-03	2002	2007	2007
Resolution Excavations	2005-07	2004	2004-07	2002	2008-10	2007-08
Final Report (grey literature)	2008-10	2006	2008-09	2004	2010	2010
Publication (scheme monograph)	2009-13	2012	2011	2008	2011	2012

strong role to play in determining the presence/absence of unidentified sites. Irish legislation also requires preservation by record of archaeological objects and deposits for those scenarios where preservation *in situ* is not possible: archaeological features are excavated and recorded in their entirety (i.e. a 100 % recovery or retrieval rate, without sampling). These result in often large-scale excavations carried out for the NRA that have created a large corpus of more than 800 excavations between 1992-2008 that may be used to study the effectiveness of the earlier geophysical assessments.

In contrast to other countries (such as the experience of *Stäuble 2012* in Germany), the NRA in Ireland are afforded a significant amount of time to discover, identify, mitigate, excavate and resolve all of the archaeological deposits that are encountered on new road schemes, a timescale that may last several years and in some cases more than a decade. Geophysical survey is one of a number of methods used to achieved this, most of which are procured from commercial archaeological contractors via a competitive tendering process. Archaeological contributions in the form of desk-based assessments (DBA) and field-walking are made to Constraints Studies, Route Selection Reports and Environmental Impact Assessments (EIAs). Geophysical surveys have in the past occurred after the EIAs, but are now used to form part of these documents when seeking planning permission to build a new road. Extensive test (or 'trial') trenching occurs in a standard testing pattern across the entire road scheme (a central continuous trench with regular perpendicular off-shoots) and at locations highlighted by earlier investigations, e.g. areas of archaeological potential identified by the DBA or anomalies highlighted in the geophysical reports (*O'Rourke 2003*). Such extensive background investigations allow for the identification of many archaeological features and reduce the need for monitoring and topsoil stripping. Once an archaeological feature has been identified, resolution (or 'final') excavations are carried out at clearly defined locations. Post-excavation work is carried out by the resolution excavation contractor and the findings are disseminated to the public in a published monograph for the road scheme.

Publishing the results of archaeological investigations is an important part of the NRA ethos as a publicly funded body. To date the NRA have published ten road scheme monographs, nine monographs on the annual proceedings of national archaeological seminars, seven issues of the annual NRA Archaeology Magazine and contributed to numerous national and international journals and conferences. However, due to the time required for post-excavation analysis, there is often a significant time-lag between a geophysical assessment of a road scheme and direct feedback (Table 2). In terms of meaningful feedback, earlier studies of ground-truthed geophysical data have demonstrated that comparisons are effective for a reasonably large area rather than test trenches (*Gaffney 1997; Hey - Lacey 2001; Jordan 2007; 2009; Knight et al. 2007*). Test trenching investigations offer an insight into the potential archaeological resource, however they are limited in area coverage and can be dependent upon weathering in order to successfully identify a cultural deposit. In these cases, a grey literature final excavation report is generally available three to six years or more after the geophysical survey, and a final publication may often be several years onward again.

The Geology and Soils of Ireland

Ireland is dominated by sedimentary rock across most of the country, with exceptions in the NW and SE (Fig. 2). The remainder of the country contains almost equal amounts of igneous and metamorphic rock. The most widely distributed rocks on the island of Ireland are 1) carboniferous limestone, 2) shales and sandstone, 3) sandstone, 4) slates and shales, 5) gneiss, schist and quartzite, 6) granite and 7) basalt which is confined to Northern Ireland only (*Gillmor 1971*).

Sedimentary rocks are formed from layered and compressed sediments of sand, shells, pebbles and other fragments of

Fig. 2. Distribution of geology in the Republic of Ireland (After Bonsall et al. 2013a). Geological formations from Northern Ireland are excluded.

material. Types of sedimentary rock in Ireland include carboniferous limestone, shale, siltstone, sandstone (including greywacke sandstone), mudstone and grit. Deposits of chalk ('Ulster White Limestone') are limited to the NE coast of Northern Ireland and to isolated pockets (<9 hectares in size) in Co. Kerry, in the SW of the country. There are no other chalk deposits in the Republic of Ireland, which contrasts with the UK and Europe where chalk deposits are frequently encountered. Metamorphic rocks are formed by intense heat and pressure causing major alterations to pre-existing rocks. These rocks are found in isolated regions in the SE and parts of the NW. Types of metamorphic rock in Ireland include slate, graphitic, marble, quartzite, phyllite and schist. Igneous rocks are formed from the cooling and hardening of magma. These are mostly found near areas of metamorphic rocks, principally in Northern Ireland (which contains the most frequent igneous deposits for the island of Ireland), the SE, parts of the west and the NW. The Munsterian glaciation deposited erratic igneous rocks across the country. Intrusions of igneous dykes are also common occurrences within sedimentary geology. Types of igneous rock in Ireland include volcanic, granite, dolerite, gabbro, basalt, diorite and felsite.

The majority of surface geology is till (boulder clay), which has a high calcium carbonate content. Other surface geologies include alluvium, colluvium and deposits dating from the Munsterian and Midlandian glaciation. Drumlins and eskers are international geological terms that originate from the distinctive Irish landforms that describe them (*droimnín* and *eiscir*). Drumlins are thick covers of till (boulder clay) deposited in the form of small hills that cover about 11 % of Ireland in one of the most extensive drumlin fields in the world (*Gardiner - Radford 1980*), and can be in excess of 7.7 drumlins per sq km. They are oval in plan and can be up to 800 m in length and 90 m in height. Formed beneath moving ice, drumlins stand out as islands surrounded by marshy flats or lakes. Eskers are widespread in areas affected by the Midlandian glaciation and can be found running across the middle of the country, aligned mostly east-west and are considered archaeologically prospective as many eskers, such as the Esker Riada (*Geissel 2006*), were exploited as natural dryland routeways to navigate through low lying bog, marsh or peatland.

The topography is determined by bedrock and surface soils which were particularly shaped by glacial action. *Gardiner -*

Radford (*1980*) describe five major physiographic divisions for Ireland that have influenced the development of soil properties. 49.6 % of the land was described as very poor or limited in its range of potential uses due to poor drainage. 36 % of the country is comprised of flat to undulating lowland with mostly well-drained limestone soils. Rolling lowland (excluding low level blanket peat) covers 31 % of the country and is formed from shales, sandstone, granite or mica schist, it consists mainly of acid brown earths and brown podzolics, with extensive areas of gley soils formed over both Carboniferous shale and Old Red Sandstone. 16 % of Ireland is represented by mountain and hill soils that consist mainly of peaty podzols, peaty gleys, blanket peat, lithosols and common occurrences of rock outcropping. Lower hill soils cover 6 % of the land and are mainly acidic, being formed from shale, sandstone or granite, with brown podzolics as the principal soils, and rendzinas, gleys and outcropping rocks.

The most widely distributed soils in the country are podzols (>25 %), followed by poorly drained gley soils and peats (mostly in the NW) and free-draining brown soils mostly in the south and east (*Woodcock 1994*). This contrasts quite strongly with English soils where podzols account for <12.5 % of soils. Extensive rock-outcrops of karstic carboniferous limestone landscapes account for some of the <10 % of thin lithomorphic soils, in some cases soils are absent, e.g. at the Burren, in County Clare, one of the largest karst landscapes in Europe.

Ireland has the third highest peat coverage (16.5 %) in Europe, after Finland and Estonia (*Montanarella et al. 2006*), a strong contrast with the 3 % found in England/ Wales and 10 % in Scotland (*Avery 1990*). Many archaeological sites in Ireland that date to the Neolithic and later periods were buried beneath peat, including extensive field systems, megalithic monuments and wooden trackway sites (*Avery 1990; Raftery 1996; Warren 2008; Warren et al. 2009; Verrill - Tipping 2010*). A classification of Irish mires (accumulations of organic material from the last 8,000 years) indicates that the non-industrial mires include 263,840 hectares of raised bogs with an average depth of 2.5-7.0 m; 101,810 hectares of fens averaging at 1.2 m depth and 896,540 hectares of blanket bog with an average depth of 1.2-3.0 m (*Avery 1990*). Industrial mires, account for an additional 820,800 hectares of unreported depth.

The Influence of Irish Geology and Soil Types on geophysical surveys

The influence of geology is a major consideration for geophysical surveys, particularly on areas of igneous bedrock or surface deposits (*Allsop 1992*). Geology commonly determines which technique(s) should or should not be used. *Tite - Mullins* (*1971*) were the first to examine the mass specific magnetic susceptibility (MS) responses of archaeological features with reference to geology in the UK. They demonstrated that contrasts existed between the subsoil, topsoil and archaeological pits and ditches on sites

dating between the Bronze Age and Saxon periods, mostly located in the SE of England, mostly on sand and gravel, or limestone. Chalk was found to give some of the best responses, however chalk is predominantly absent from Ireland. The reliance on magnetometry in some parts of the world, including Ireland, is explained by specific advice from English Heritage (*David et al. 2008*) "providing no overriding geophysical contra-indications exist (e.g. unfavourable geology or soils, preponderance of modern ferrous interference, etc.), then magnetometer survey should provide the most cost-effective method of evaluation. A sample density of at least 0.25 m x 1 m should be used." The response of magnetometry (presumably at a 1 m x 0.25 m spatial resolution) to geology for common English soils was examined by *David et al.* (*2008*). Although some discussions of specific soils and formations may not be applicable to Irish geology, much of the information is relevant.

Sedimentary rocks were found to be generally suitable for magnetometry (depending on the overlying surface soils), although carboniferous limestones (the only substantial limestone deposits in Ireland) respond less well compared to the Cretaceous, Jurassic and Magnesian limestones that are absent in Ireland but found in the UK and elsewhere. Similar results were confirmed by a study of legacy data and subsequent ground truthing in the Trent Valley, UK (*Knight et al. 2007*), which found that magnetometry on carboniferous limestone soils were approximately 70 % less successful than those on chalk. The prevailing carboniferous limestone geology may be expected to have a less successful response for magnetometry (compared to other limestone soils in the UK) due to a low MS contrast between earth-cut archaeological features and the background soils. A low contrast background is not necessarily suited to the detection of thermoremanent features. Surveys at Pessinus, Turkey, encountered magnetically low contrast metamorphic marbles that had low magnetic susceptibilities on marble blocks, soils and burnt soils, resulting in magnetometer data ranging below ±1nT (*Schmidt et al. 2011*). *Gaffney* (*1997*) found good responses to sites in the UK underlain by Oolitic limestone (a calcite mineral, also present in Ireland), although those sites were Roman settlements which tend to respond well to magnetometry and differ substantially from the isolated and nucleated settlement tradition in Ireland, one of the few European countries that lacks Roman settlement activity. The response of magnetometry to other sedimentary soils relevant for Ireland are also less than ideal with poor responses being recorded for both sandstone and mudstone (*David et al. 2008*). Ireland also suffers from naturally occurring geological features that appear similar to commonly identified archaeological sites. Circular and ovoid structures (commonly found in sedimentary rocks) such as dolines (or sinkholes) mimic the regular circular shape and low-contrast magnetometer response of ringfort enclosures and other ring-ditch features.

Igneous rocks have been described as 'problematic' (*Gaffney - Gater 2003*) although successful surveys have been carried out. Soils from iron-rich parent materials exhibit a greater mass specific MS enhancement than iron-poor materials, which could allow for the detection of archaeological deposits on igneous rocks (*Singer - Fine 1989*). However, the thermoremanent and induced magnetisation properties of igneous geology limit and challenge magnetic prospection techniques. Early experiments with magnetometry on basalts in Northern Ireland found that the natural thermoremanent magnetism of the igneous rocks was so great that it ruled out the detection and location of archaeological features, including strongly magnetic kilns (*Aitken 1961*). Research in Ireland and Iceland found that ditches on igneous deposits could be identified from a negative magnetometer anomaly (*Doggart 1983; Horsley et al. 2003; Horsley 2004*). *Horsley* commonly found that the expected polarity of a positive response was inverted and negative anomalies were encountered for earth-/rock-cut ditches as the in-filled material had a lower MS contrast than the surrounding thermoremanent rock. Similarly clear negative anomalies were reported by *Clark* (*1996*) for the Vallum ditch at Staffa, also on basalt geology. *Horsley* (*2004*) found that basalts <0.5 m below the surface returned very little archaeological information; for deposits 0.5-1 m below the surface it was generally only possible to identify discrete positive and bipolar anomalies produced by the combined remanent and induced magnetisations of shallower igneous rocks. The influence of igneous rocks lessened as their depth increased (as the thickness of the surface geology increased). Deeply buried (>1 m) igneous rocks allowed for the detection of subtle magnetic anomalies due to normalised magnetic susceptibility contrasts between soils and sediments, thus a thick overlying surface geology masks the thermoremanent influence of igneous bedrocks – if the depth to bedrock can be gauged in advance of prospection then a realistic estimation of magnetometry success (or effectiveness) can be made. *Horsley* demonstrated that whilst some good magnetometry results were achievable on igneous rocks in Iceland, they should be carried out in conjunction with other geophysical techniques. In Ireland, igneous dykes (and granite erratics) encountered on sedimentary geology create strongly magnetic anomalies similar to those reported in the Orkney Isles (*Clark 1996*). The experience of commercial prospection surveys on igneous dykes in the NE of Ireland found that they produce an anomaly which varies between 5-10 m in width, up to 200 m in length and up to 88nT in magnitude, often accompanied by negative halos as low as -24nT (*Bonsall - Gimson 2004; 2005a; 2005b; 2007*).

Gaffney (*1997*) examined the influence of surface geology on fluxgate gradiometer data by comparing them to ground-truthed data. Surveys over 'sand' or 'sand without gravel' were more successful than geologies that contained 'gravel' deposits (including 'mixed sands and gravels'), however *Gaffney* demonstrated that there was no statistically significant relationship between the presence/absence of gravel and the technical accuracy of the gradiometer results. Tills (boulder clays) are impermeable materials that can be associated with waterlogged soils in areas of

reasonably flat topography. Surveys on tills in the UK report mixed experiences; some were likely to have a "successful outcome" with a true positive result of 90.9 % for 11 survey areas (*Gaffney 1997*); some had enhanced mass specific MS responses (*Clark 1996*), others were "variable" (*Gaffney - Gater 2003*) or were found to be "generally poor" (*David et al. 2008*). There have been no attempts to assess the varying parent materials or the archaeological features encountered for these studies, which are likely to strongly influence these different outcomes on tills.

Podzols – the most common soil type in Ireland – are depleted of nutrients through leaching; these become acidic via the removal of iron and aluminium from the surface horizons. The average rate of precipitation in Ireland exceeds evapotranspiration by over 500 mm with an annual average of approximately 1,230 mm (*Walsh 2012; Met Éirrean 2013*). The level of precipitation is responsible for higher rates of podzols in Ireland compared to other European countries, and a correspondingly lower iron mineral content which has contributed to low magnetic contrasts between archaeological features and host soils. Podzolisation is further influenced by the formation of concentrated layers of iron pan that can lead to widespread increases in MS; these influence magnetometer data and may cause anomalies that mimic or obscure archaeological deposits. In contrast, the brown soils (or brown earths) are relatively mature and well drained, with little leaching or degradation and no obvious signs of removal or deposition of iron oxides, humus or clay. As such, these soils are particularly suited to the use of magnetometry and appropriate increases in MS may be expected for anthropogenically-altered soils. Unfortunately, with the exception of lithosols, brown soils are the least common soil type in Ireland.

Peats and alluviated soils are particularly problematic as peats cover 1/6 of the country. The physical and chemical properties of peat and alluvium strongly influence geophysical assessments even in the short term, when such properties may vary; some anomalies representing archaeological deposits may appear or disappear from year to year. A large proportion of Irish ringfort enclosures would have had waterlogged ditches since many were cut into heavy boulder clay (tills) and exposed to a generally wet climate, promoting the growth of peat and the eventual depletion of iron-oxides (*Doggart 1983*). This would lead to low- or non-contrasting anomalies for enclosures that occur in similarly waterlogged or peat environments. *Weston* (*2004*) thoroughly examined why floodplains and alluviated soils respond so poorly to conventional magnetic surveys and found that waterlogging impeded and/or prevented MS enhancement – soils that are *heated* rather than *burnt* in waterlogged environments actually suppress the MS of a soil, hence heating need not always lead to enhancement, or as much enhancement as one might expect. Magnetometry and MS surveys were of limited use on peatland, gleys and waterlogged sediments (*Singer - Fine 1989; Weston 2004; Armstrong 2010*) which are found extensively in Ireland. Research from Northern California (*Singer - Fine 1989*) showed that moisture ingress via high annual precipitation increases mass specific MS, however excessive waterlogging and poor drainage can reduce the same property compared to well-drained soils. *Clark* (*1993*) noted that on alluvium, the spatial definition of archaeological features declines with depth. *Linford* (*1994*) found that archaeological features exhibiting a distinguishable mass specific MS profile in areas of floodplain did not reflect an identifiable magnetometer anomaly or a (consistent) contrast in topsoil MS, nor did it correspond to earth resistance anomalies for sites where extensive archaeological remains were missed by those techniques.

The general response of magnetometry to alluvium/colluviums is reported as "average to poor" (*David et al. 2008*). *Weston* (*2001*) found that alluvial soils can misrepresent the extent of archaeological features and create anomalies or trends that are often misinterpreted as archaeological. Alluvium can also mask responses from – potentially – all geophysical techniques. Additionally, alluvial cover can also create a low and often uniform magnetic background for magnetometry that is not necessarily advantageous – the deposits increase the distance between the archaeological target and the sensor, reducing the magnitude of an archaeological deposit. *Linford et al.* (*2007*) used high sensitivity cart-mounted caesium magnetometers to identify features buried beneath alluvium, however this research was limited to very favourable examples with good magnetic targets on English chalkland, over thin soils and good ground conditions that may not be easily replicated for other archaeological deposits or soils elsewhere. Gravel river terraces can also be affected by iron concretions that reduce the MS contrast within the topsoil (*Clark 1996*).

To conclude our review of geological influences, magnetometry surveys rely on the presence of iron oxides in the topsoil which are dictated by the geology for a given survey area and may change through time via weathering and other natural processes. Providing that the soils and geology are iron-rich, archaeological features have great potential to become magnetically enhanced which can facilitate the successful use of magnetometry. Ireland contains a substantial amount of challenging bedrock geologies, surface geologies and soils that offer low magnetic contrasts (and occasionally no contrast) due to often iron-poor parent materials, heavy precipitation (and waterlogging) and acidic soils.

Comparison of Magnetometry Data and Ground-Truthed Evidence

Magnetometry data acquired from 68 sites from eight road schemes were directly compared to plans generated by subsequent open-stripped archaeological excavations, using GIS to assess the level of success at each site. The method is based on that used by *Hey - Lacey* (*2001*) carried out

by *Linford - David* (*2001*). This method used a 2 m buffer around each anomaly that was binned into five sub-sets at 0.5 m intervals, to indicate how accurate the location of each true positive anomaly was compared to the excavated deposits. The terminology used by the research to assess success was:

Common Area: A defined area containing co-registered magnetometry survey data and excavation data.

True Positive: An anomaly identified by the geophysical interpretation plan and subsequently excavated feature (within a 2 m buffer);

False Positive: An anomaly identified by the geophysical interpretation plan that failed to correlate with a subsequently recorded archaeological feature within the same 2 m buffer;

True Negative: An area of the geophysical interpretation plan that indicates the absence of anomalies, subsequently confirmed to contain no archaeological activity;

False Negative: An area of the geophysical interpretation plan that indicates the absence of anomalies, subsequently found to contain archaeological activity.

Magnetometry interpretations that identified anomalies in areas that were *not* excavated have not been assessed; it is assumed, on the basis of test trenching and monitoring, that those results were false positives and did not lead to the identification of an archaeological site.

Each of the magnetometry surveys were carried out using fluxgate gradiometers at a sample resolution of 1 x 0.25 m or better. The archaeological features, bedrock and surface geology of each site varied substantially although the predominance of sedimentary rocks in Ireland has led to a high occurrence of these in the sample (Table 3). The archaeological sites represent earth-cut and thermoremanent features that are suitable for detection by magnetometry.

The results from Dowdstown 2, one of 14 archaeological sites examined on the M3 Clonee-Kells Motorway, are examined in detail, to illustrate the process (Fig. 3.). The excavation at Dowdstown 2 revealed extensive evidence for an early medieval settlement, contemporary field system around the settlement and a number of cereal-drying kilns; the site dated to the late 5th to 12th centuries AD. The GIS analysis of detailed magnetometry at Dowdstown 2 (and the M3 Motorway, generally) reveals a very strong correlation with archaeological features (Table 4). The M3 Motorway scheme was initially subjected to magnetometry scanning – the validity of the interpretation, using the GIS analysis described above, occurred on 14 sites that were subsequently assessed with detailed magnetometry in areas felt to be of archaeological potential, based on the scanning. The scanning survey encountered a wider variety of surface geology than the detailed surveys and it is significant to note

Table 3. Archaeological sites or road schemes analysed, with reference to geology.

Archaeological Site or Scheme	No. of Sites	Common Area (Hectares)	Bedrock Geology	Surface Geology
Dowdstown 2, M3 Motorway Scheme	1	1.31	Shale	Limestone Sand and Gravel
M3 Motorway Scheme	14	5.47	Limestone; Shale; Sandstone	Limestone Till; Limestone Sand and Gravel
Churchtown, N15 Lifford-Stranorlar	1	0.08	Marble; Quartzite; Psammite; Graphitic	Colluvium
M1 Dundalk Western Bypass	3	1.54	Greywacke (Sandstone); Limestone (+igneous dykes)	Unknown
Davidstown, N25 Waterford-Glenmore	1	0.06	Conglomerate; Sandstone	Bedrock near surface
N8 Fermoy-Mitchelstown	30	1.63	Sandstone; Mudstone; Limestone	Till
N11 Arklow-Rathnew	5	0.89	Sandstone; Siltstone; Diorite	Sandstone Till; Sand and Gravel
N25 Waterford Bypass	12	0.84	Slate; Siltstone	Unknown
Cuffsborough, M7/M8 Motorway	1	0.35	Limestone	Sand and Gravel
Total	*68*	*12.17*		

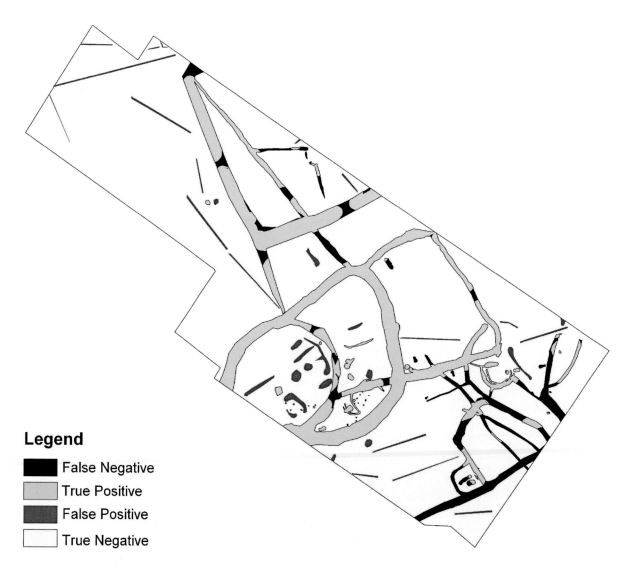

Legend

■ False Negative

▨ True Positive

▨ False Positive

☐ True Negative

Fig. 3. Analysis of magnetometry success at the archaeological site of Dowdstown 2.

Table 4. Results of archaeological site or road scheme analysis using ground truthed data.

Archaeological Site(s)/ Method	True (False) Positive			True Negative	False Negative
Dowdstown 2, M3 Motorway Scheme Fluxgate Gradiometer, 1m x 0.25m	75% (25%)	0.0m 0.5m 1.0m 1.5m 2.0m	17% 15% 15% 15% 13%	81%	0.12%
M3 Motorway Scheme Fluxgate Gradiometer, 1m x 0.25m	74% (26%)	0.0m 0.5m 1.0m 1.5m 2.0m	15% 14% 15% 16% 15%	83%	0.82%
Churchtown, N15 Lifford-Stranorlar Fluxgate Gradiometer, 1m x 0.25m	12% (88%)	0.0m 0.5m 1.0m 1.5m 2.0m	<1% 5% 4% 3% <1%	94%	1.55%
M1 Dundalk Western Bypass Fluxgate Gradiometer, 1m x 0.25m	25% (75%)	0.0m 0.5m 1.0m 1.5m 2.0m	6% 5% 5% 5% 4%	91%	12.8%
Davidstown, N25 Waterford-Glenmore Fluxgate Gradiometer, 1m x 0.25m	15% (85%)	0.0m 0.5m 1.0m 1.5m 2.0m	8% 3% 2% 1% 1%	76%	0.61%
N8 Fermoy-Mitchelstown Fluxgate Gradiometer, 1m x 0.125m	95% (5%)	0.0m 0.5m 1.0m 1.5m 2.0m	68% 8% 6% 7% 6%	92%	18.3%
N11 Arklow-Rathnew Fluxgate Gradiometer, 1m x 0.125m	76% (24%)	0.0m 0.5m 1.0m 1.5m 2.0m	63% 5% 4% 2% 2%	73%	1.03%
N25 Waterford Bypass Fluxgate Gradiometer, 1m x 0.25m	76% (24%)	0.0m 0.5m 1.0m 1.5m 2.0m	28% 14% 13% 12% 9%	78%	0.79%
Cuffsborough, M7/M8 Motorway Fluxgate Gradiometer, 1m x 0.25m	95% (5%)	0.0m 0.5m 1.0m 1.5m 2.0m	22% 20% 19% 18% 16%	86%	0.16%
Totals	*60% (40%)*	*0.0m 0.5m 1.0m 1.5m 2.0m*	*25% 10% 10% 9% 7%*	*84%*	*4.02%*

that no (subsequently identified) archaeological sites on alluvium were chosen as areas of archaeological potential; which suggests that scanning surveys are of limited use on alluvial deposits.

The survey at Dowdstown 2 was enough to substantially identify and map a significant series of enclosures and a comparison with the excavation data reveals that 75 % of the interpreted anomalies were true positives. True negatives (correctly identified areas of empty space) were correct for

81 % of the survey area, which gives further confidence in the ability of magnetometry to correctly identify areas where archaeological features are absent. False negatives (archaeological features that were missed) occurred at a rate of 0.12 %. The false negatives were mostly ditches, the majority of which occurred in one region of the survey area which may indicate a change in soil type and depth in that area. The false negative ditches were partly identified as true positives along small sections of the ditches, suggesting non-uniform magnetic responses for different fills within

the same feature. Only one significant ditch was missed in its entirety. All five hearths in the common area were correctly interpreted as archaeological features, however only three of the nine kilns excavated were identified by the geophysical survey, which could suggest potential problems in the recognition of these anomaly types, particularly amongst background noise or in areas of complex and dense archaeology. The false positives were at 25 % and are mostly accounted for by ill-defined weak magnetic trends that could have represented archaeological or natural features.

The presence of false positives is especially significant at Dowdstown 2, as they hint at the limitations of the GIS method which relies on accepting the excavation evidence as the most reliable account of the archaeological deposits. In Dowdstown 2, nine separate false positive anomalies can be seen as 'internal features' within an enclosure. The excavation (*Cagney et al. 2009*) report notes that Dowdstown 2 had been extensively damaged by reclamation and landscape work in the 20th century that may perhaps explain the lack of associated features within the interior of the main settlement enclosures. Thus, whilst internal features were mostly absent from the excavation data, a strong possibility exists that they were removed or destroyed and the only evidence of their existence is recorded in the magnetometry survey, probably as disturbed remains in the subsoil or topsoil. In this case the excavation may be incapable of recording all of the archaeological features, which in turn limits the GIS method of assessing ground-truthed data which cannot take account of 'ghost features' – archaeological deposits that are invisible to the naked eye. The same inaccuracy could be applied to other sites as well, particularly in those instances where magnetometry records the presence of 'anthropogenic' features (e.g. late 19th century ditches, drainage ditches or modern bonfires), which may be excluded from an 'archaeological' site plan. Thus high instances of false positives should be treated with caution and true positive rates might be regarded as an indicative 'minimum number' that could be revised upwardly.

Despite the potential limitations of the method for false positive responses, the GIS analysis does give an indication of high rates for true positives for a number of schemes. It is clear that the limestone, sandstone, mudstone, siltstone, slate and shale were suitable for the identification of archaeological sites on the M3 Motorway, N8 Fermoy-Mitchelstown Scheme, N25 Waterford Bypass, and one isolated site at Cuffsborough on the M7/M8 Motorway.

The N8 Fermoy-Mitchelstown scheme recorded the highest true positive (95 %) rates, and the highest rate of false negatives (18.3 %). The magnetometry survey on this scheme was the narrowest of all those examined, and was limited to a 15 m wide sample strip on the centre of the road. When a ditch passes across the magnetometry strip it can be clearly identified (hence the high rate of true positives), however smaller scale archaeological sites

within the strip appear as small anomalies that were not conducive to the sampling strategy and account for the large number of archaeological sites that were missed as a result.

The N11 Arklow-Rathnew scheme appears to have a high level of success (76 % true positive), however this is limited to the five archaeological sites that occurred on sandstone, siltstone and diorite. A further 24 archaeological sites on the same scheme were also covered by detailed magnetometry that failed to identify them at all – they occurred on volcanic, slate, phyllite and schist geologies that were not suitable for magnetometry. By examining the data beyond the GIS analysis, we can see that the N11 road scheme, which passed though igneous, metamorphic and sedimentary rocks, had a limited true positive success of 17.2 % in the identification of archaeological sites.

The M1 Dundalk Western Bypass scheme was carried out on carboniferous limestone that encountered frequent igneous dykes. The strong thermoremanence of the dykes strongly disturbed the magnetometer data and returned very poor results for true positives (25 %) and very high rates of false negatives that were the result of archaeological features being masked or obscured by stronger thermoremanent anomalies.

For all the sites examined, the average true positives were 60 % (40 % false positives), which is encouraging given the expected rate of failure for igneous deposits. The accuracy of true positive responses is generally very high, with most being found in the 0.0-0.5 m bracket and very few found more than 1.5 m away from the source of the anomaly. This is particularly encouraging given the potential for discrepancies between the methods (and accuracy) of geophysical and excavation grid set outs, as well as a slight lateral movement (0.17-0.18 m) of the anomaly source for fluxgate gradiometers (*Aspinall et al. 2008*).

Schemes that occurred on exclusively sedimentary deposits (Table 5) had true positive rates of 88 % (12 % false positive). No exclusively igneous or metamorphic geologies were assessed by the road schemes examined, in those schemes that passed through mixtures of sedimentary, metamorphic and/or igneous deposits the rates vary considerably. The worst results were for sedimentary and igneous which represents the M1 Dundalk Western Bypass that occurred on limestone and igneous dykes. True negatives are consistently high (≥73 %) across all the geological types, which adds further confidence in the ability of magnetometry to distinguish between areas of activity and empty spaces.

Other forms of comparison

The limited availability of georectified excavation plans has impacted upon the number of sites/schemes that can be assessed with the GIS method. There are a number of road schemes in the NRA archive that have excavation data only available as non-georectified diagrams – other studies have

Table 5. Results by geological types.

Basic Geology (number of sites assessed)	True Positive	False Positive	True Negative	False Negative
Sedimentary (46)	88%	12%	87%	6.4%
Sedimentary & Igneous (3)	25%	75%	91%	12.8%
Sedimentary & Metamorphic (14)	34.3%	65.6%	82.6%	0.93%
Sedimentary, Metamorphic & Igneous (5)	76%	24%	73%	1%

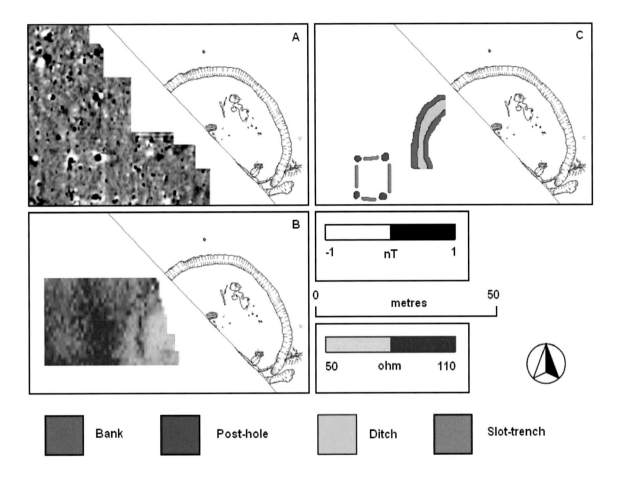

Fig. 4. Geophysical survey of a ringfort enclosure and timber structure. A: High resolution magnetometry. B: Earth resistance. C: Interpretation.

demonstrated that these plans can still be useful for a basic visual comparison with geophysical data (*Gaffney 1997; Jordan 2007, 2009*) rather than the GIS method of analysis. Seven such road schemes from the west of Ireland were carried out on carboniferous limestone bedrock covered by frequent peats or waterlogged soils. As discussed above, the combination of low contrast geology and peats, which can impede the MS of archaeological deposits, can lead to poor quality results. On those road schemes, 51 % of ring-ditches (including occupation enclosures and barrows) could not be identified in detailed magnetometry (i.e. 51 % false negative). This is a significant drop in success compared to the GIS analysis of similar archaeology on limestone deposits and suggests that the prevalence of peat on west of Ireland limestones is a significant factor. The responses were also affected by the presence of strongly magnetic 18th/19th century cultivation furrows that frequently obscured lower contrast features.

A typical example is that of an early medieval circular ringfort enclosure, half of which was excavated on the N4 Sligo Inner Relief Road. The excavation (*Danaher 2007*) suggested that the remains of the ringfort continued beyond the road scheme, however a 1 x 0.25 m magnetometry survey failed to identify any anomaly associated with the enclosure. This is a commonly applied spatial resolution for magnetometry that may be inappropriate for some Irish soils. There is significant potential to further investigate the use of 0.5 m traverse separations for magnetometry to determine if meaningful returns are made for an investment in intensive data collection. The same area was resurveyed with high resolution (0.5 x 0.1 m) magnetometry which also failed to identify any anomaly associated with the enclosure (Fig. 4.). An earth resistance survey did successfully image the enclosure ditch. Despite the absence of an earth-cut enclosure feature, the high resolution magnetometry data did suggest the presence of discrete burnt deposits that arc believed to mark the four corners of a timber structure, which was an unexpected yet successful indicator of the benefits offered by high resolution surveys. It is clear however that magnetometry has particular problems identifying earth-cut features on low-contrast soils, although thermoremanent anomalies can be clearly identified.

Multi-depth electromagnetic (EM) surveys offer the chance to examine archaeological features at various depths. *Simpson et al. (2009)* have shown promise for the study of archaeological features buried beneath alluvium using instruments with a large coil spacing to obtain greater depth penetration. There are also promising apparent magnetic susceptibility results comparable to magnetometer data and apparent conductivity results comparable to earth resistance data (*De Smedt et al. 2011; De Smedt et al. 2013; Bonsall et al. in press*). There are suggestions that rapid multi-frequency EM instruments might be suitable for archaeological prospection on the challenging soils that are frequently encountered in Ireland, including extensive peats, tills and other low contrast soils.

Conclusion

Ireland presents a series of challenging geological conditions for magnetometry surveys. A reappraisal of 10 years of magnetometer data following ground truthing found that generally, for the 68 sites assessed, there are significant trends for the success of magnetometry, particularly on sedimentary geology where a number of examples have shown consistently positive results. Statistical analyses of ground-truthed data suggest that magnetometer surveys upon shale, siltstone, sandstone, slate and limestone have been particularly good, however when igneous dykes are encountered on limestone the results are very poor. Very poor results are also achieved over any geology overlain by peat deposits >0.3 m thick. Consistently high rates of true negative results increase the confidence levels in magnetometry survey for curators and end-users.

Small-scale earth-cut features (post-pits, post-holes, inhumations) are unlikely to be identified using a standard spatial resolution (1 x 0.25 m), even upon favourable geologies and high resolution methods should be considered for these features and larger features on low-contrast geologies. Road schemes are narrow corridors typically 40-60 m in width that cross widely varying landscapes, soils and geologies. By sampling these corridors with very narrow strips of magnetometry survey of 15-20 m in width, the 'wider appreciation' of anomalies within a larger context is limited and such narrow survey areas should be avoided where possible. The assessment of non-magnetic or low-contrast archaeological features or sites on unfavourable geologies, will require alternative – and in some cases, more labour intensive – techniques to suitably appreciate the underlying archaeology. Traditionally these have included the use of earth resistance surveys, however modern electromagnetic surveys may offer a suitable and rapid alternative.

References

AIP 2012: Archaeological Investigations Project. Bournemouth University. Available from http://csweb.bournemouth.ac.uk/aip/aipintro.htm: Accessed 14/03/2013.

Aitken, M.J. 1961: Magnetic Location in Britain. Archaeometry 4(1): 83-84.

Allsop, J. 1992: The British Geological Survey: Geoprospection Techniques Applied to the Archaeological Landscape. In: Geoprospection in the Archaeological Landscape (Oxbow Monograph, No 18): 121-140. Oxbow Books.

Armstrong, K. 2010: Archaeological geophysical prospection in peatland environments. PhD Thesis. Archaeology. Bournemouth University.

Aspinall, A. - Gaffney, C. - Schmidt, S. 2008: Magnetometry for Archaeologists. Geophysical Methods for Archaeology.

Avery, B.W. 1990: Soils of the British Isles. Wallingford, Oxon: CAB International.

Bonsall, J. – Gimson, H. 2004: Proposed Extension to IDA Park, 110 and 40 acre sites, Mullagharlin, Dundalk, County Louth. Earthsound Archaeological Geophysics, Unpublished Report No. EAG 26.

Bonsall, J. – Gimson, H. 2005a: Area 2, Land Adjacent to the R132, Haynestown and Haggardstown, Dundalk, County Louth. Earthsound Archaeological Geophysics, Unpublished Report No. EAG 61.

Bonsall, J. – Gimson, H. 2005b: Housing Development adjacent to Carrick Road (R178), Lisnawully, Dundalk, County Louth. Earthsound Archaeological Geophysics, Unpublished Report No. EAG 65.

Bonsall, J. – Gimson, H. 2007: Proposed Development, Fairhill Townland, Dundalk, County Louth. Earthsound Archaeological Geophysics, Unpublished Report No. EAG 114.

Bonsall, J. - Gaffney, C. - Armit, I. 2013a: Preparing for the future: A reappraisal of archaeo-geophysical surveying on National Road Schemes 2001-2010. University of Bradford report for the National Roads Authority of Ireland.

Bonsall, J. - Sparrow, T. - Gaffney, C. - Armit, I. 2013b: The NRA Archaeological Geophysical Survey Database. University of Bradford. Available from http://www.field2archive.org/nra/

Bonsall, J. - Fry, R. - Gaffney, C. - Armit, I. - Beck, A. - Gaffney, V. In Press: Assessment of Multi Depth Prospection Capabilities using a new Low Frequency Electromagnetic Device. Archaeological Prospection Submitted for Peer Review 08/04/2013.

Cagney, L. - O'Hara, R. - Kelleher, G. - Morkan, R. 2009: M3 Clonee–Kells Motorway, Contract 2 Dunshaughlin-Navan: Report on the Archaeological Excavation of Dowdstown 2. Archaeological Consultancy Services Limited, Unpublished Report.

Campana, S. 2011: 'Total Archaeology' to reduce the need for Rescue Archaeology: The BREBEMI Project (Italy). In: D.C. Cowley ed., EAC Occasional

Paper No. 5. Occasional Publication of the Aerial Archaeology Research Group No. 3. Remote Sensing for Archaeological Heritage Management. Proceedings of the 11th EAC Heritage Management Symposium, Reykjavík, Iceland, 25-27 March 2010. Brussels: Europae Archaeologia Consilium.

Campana, S. - Dabas, M. 2011: Archaeological Impact Assessment: The BREBEMI Project (Italy). Archaeological Prospection 18, 139-148.

Catherall, P.D. - Barnett, M. - McClean, H. 1984: The Southern Feeder. The Archaeology of a Gas Pipeline. London: The British Gas Corporation.

Clark, A.J. 1993: Archaeogeophysical prospecting on alluvium. In: M.G. Macklin – S.P. Needham eds, Alluvial Archaeology in Britain. Oxford: Oxbow Books.

Clark, A.J. 1996: Seeing beneath the soil : prospecting methods in archaeology (rev. ed). London: Batsford.

Cleary, R.M. - Hurley, M.F. - Twohig, E.A. 1987: Archaeological Excavations on the Cork-Dublin Gas Pipeline (1981-1982). Cork Archaeological Studies No. 1. Department of Archaeology, University College Cork.

Council of Europe 1992: European Convention on the Protection of the Archaeological Heritage (Revised). Valletta, 16th January 1992.

DAHGI 1999: Policy and Guidelines on Archaeological Excavation. Dublin: Government Publications Sales Office.

DAHGI - NRA 2000: Code of Practice between the National Roads Authority and the Minister for Arts, Heritage, Gaeltacht and the Islands. Dublin: Government of Ireland.

Danaher, E. 2007: Monumental Beginnings: The Archaeology of the N4 Sligo Inner Relief Road. NRA Scheme Monographs 1. Dublin: National Roads Authority.

David, A. - Linford, N. - Linford, P. 2008: Geophysical Survey in Archaeological Field Evaluation (Second Edition ed). English Heritage.

Dawson, M. - Gaffney, C.F. 1995: The application of geophysical techniques within a planning application at Norse Road, Bedfordshire (England). Archaeological Prospection 2(2), 103-115.

De Smedt, P. - Van Meirvenne, M. - Simpson, D. 2011: Multi-signal EMI and geoarchaeology - Evaluating integrated magnetic susceptibility measurements for archaeological prospection. In: M.G. Drahor – M.A. Berge eds, 9th International Conference on Archaeological Prospection: 54-57. Izmir, Turkey.

De Smedt, P. - Van Meirvenne, M. - Herremans, D. - De Reu, J. - Saey, T. - Meerschman, E. - Crombe, P. - De Clercq, W. 2013: The 3-D reconstruction of medieval wetland reclamation through electromagnetic induction survey. Scientific Reports 3: 1517-1522.

Doggart, R. 1983: The use of magnetic prospecting equipment in Northern Ireland. In: T. Reeves-Smyth – F. Hamond eds, Landscape Archaeology in Ireland. British Archaeological Reports 116, 35-46. Oxford.

Gaffney, C. - Gater, J. 2003: Revealing the Buried Past: Geophysics for Archaeologists. Stroud: Tempus Publishing.

Gaffney, S. 1997: The use of fluxgate gradiometry in archaeological investigations : an investigation into the most appropriate use.....with particular reference to geology. PhD Thesis. Bradford.

Gardiner, M.J. - Radford, T. 1980: Soil Associations of Ireland and Their Land Use Potential. Explanatory Bulletin to Soil Map of Ireland. Dublin: An Foras Talúntais.

Geissel, H. 2006: A Road on the Long Ridge. Newbridge: CRS Publications.

Gillmor, D. 1971: A systematic geography of Ireland. Dublin: Gill and Macmillan.

Hey, G. - Lacey, M. 2001: Evaluation of Archaeological Decision-making Processes and Sampling Strategies. European Regional Development Fund Interreg IIC - Planarch Project. Oxford: Oxford Archaeological Unit.

Horsley, T.J. 2004: The potential of geophysical prospection techniques for archaeological field evaluation in Iceland: an exploration of the methodology, environmental conditions and archaeological factors affecting the use of archaeological prospection in Iceland. PhD Thesis. Department of Archaeological Sciences. University of Bradford.

Horsley, T. - Schmidt, A. - Dockrill, S. 2003: The potential of archaeological prospection techniques in Iceland. Archaeologia Polona 41, 205-207.

Jordan, D. 2007: Evaluating Aggregate in North West England. Report on English Heritage ALSF project number 3835. http://ads.ahds.ac.uk/catalogue/resources.html?nwgeophysics_eh_2007.

Jordan, D. 2009: How Effective is Geophysical Survey? A Regional Review. Archaeological Prospection 16, 77-90.

Kirwan, S. 2003: Legislation and policy on the protection of the archaeological heritage during road construction. In: J. O'Sullivan ed., Archaeology and the National Roads Authority Monograph Series No. 1. Proceedings of two seminars in 2002 on provisions for archaeological work within the National Roads Programme, 1-12. Dublin: Wordwell.

Knight, D. - Pearce, M. - Wilson, A. 2007: Beneath the Soil from Trent to Nene: Assessment of the Performance of Geophysical Survey in the East Midlands. Archive Report. York: University of Nottingham.

Linford, N. 1994: Mineral magnetic profiling of archaeological sediments. Archaeological Prospection 1, 37-52.

Linford, N. - David, A. 2001: Appendix 2: Study of Geophysical Surveys. In: G. Hey – M. Lacey eds, Evaluation of Archaeological Decision-making Processes and Sampling Strategies. European Regional Development Fund Interreg IIC - Planarch Project. Oxford: Oxford Archaeological Unit.

Linford, N. - Linford, P. - Martin, L. - Payne, A. 2007: Recent results from the English Heritage caesium magnetometer system in comparison with recent fluxgate gradiometers. Archaeological Prospection 14, 151-166.

Met Éirrean 2013: Climate of Ireland. Available from http://www.met.ie/climate/climate-of-ireland.asp: Accessed 19/04/2013.

Montanarella, L. - Jones, R.J.A. - Hiederer, R. 2006: The distribution of peatland in Europe. Mires and Peat 1, 1-10.

NMS 2008: Detection Licence Spreadsheet 1997-2006. Unpublished Database, National Monuments Service.

NMS 2012: Detection Licence Spreadsheet 2007-May 2012. Unpublished Database, National Monuments Service.

NRA 2005: Guidelines for the Assessment of Archaeological Heritage Impacts of National Road Schemes. Dublin: National Roads Authority.

O'Rourke, D. 2003: Archaeology and the National Roads Authority. In: D. O'Rourke ed., Archaeology and the National Roads Authority Monograph Series No. 1. Proceedings of two seminars in 2002 on provisions for archaeological work within the National Roads Programme, 19-24. Dublin: Wordwell.

Raftery, B. 1996: Trackway Excavations in the Mountdillon Bogs, Co. Longford, 1985-1991. Transactions of the Irish Archaeological Wetland Unit 3. Dublin: Crannóg Publication, University College Dublin.

Sarris, A. - Jones, R.E. 2000: Geophysical and Related Techniques Applied to Archaeological Survey in the Mediterranean: A Review. Journal of Mediterranean Archaeology 13(1), 3-75.

Schmidt, A. - Parkyn, A. - Tsetskhladze, G. 2011: Pessinus: A City without Contrasts? In: M.G. Drahor – M.A. Berge eds, 9th International Conference on Archaeological Prospection, 78-80. Izmir, Turkey.

Simpson, D. - Van Meirvenne, M. - Saey, T. - Vermeersch, H. - Bourgeois, J. - Lehouck, A.- Cockx, L. - Vitharana, U.W.A. 2009: Evaluating the Multiple Coil Configurations of the EM38DD and DUALEM-21S Sensors to Detect Archaeological Anomalies. Archaeological Prospection 16, 91-102.

Singer, M.J. - Fine, P. 1989: Pedogenic Factors Affecting Magnetic Susceptibility of Northern California Soils. Soil Science Society of America Journal 53, 1119-1127.

Stamnes, A.A. – Gustavsen, L. this volume: Archaeological Usage of Geophysical Methods in Norwegian Cultural Heritage Management – a Review. In: H. Kamermans – M. Gojda – A. G. Posluschny eds, A Sense Of The Past. Studies in current archaeological applications of remote sensing and non-invasive prospection methods.

Stäuble, H. 2012: Why Never Play Off (Bad) Destructive Against (Good) Non-invasive Methods in Cultural Heritage Management as They Are Not Alternatives! In: A.G. Posluschny – M. Gojda eds, European Association of Archaeologists. Session on Advanced Prospection Methods for Cultural Heritage Management - Experiences and Challenges.

Tite, M.S. - Mullins, C. 1971: Enhancement of the magnetic susceptibility of soils on archaeological sites. Archaeometry 13(2), 209-219.

Verrill, L. - Tipping, R. 2010: Use and abandonment of a Neolithic field system at Belderrig, Co. Mayo, Ireland: Evidence for economic marginality. The Holocene 20, 1011–1021.

Viberg, A., Trinks, I. - Lide, K. 2011: A Review of the Use of Geophysical Archaeological Prospection in Sweden. Archaeological Prospection 18, 43-56.

Visser, C.A. - Gaffney, C. - Hessing, W.A.M. 2011: Het gebruik van geofysische prospectietechnieken in de Nederlandse archeologie: Inventarisatie, analyse en evaluatie van uitgevoerde onderzoeken tussen 1996 en 2010. Vestigia BV Archeologie & Cultuurhistorie, Report number V887; Project number V10-1968; 30 June 2011.

Walsh, S. 2012: Climatological Note No.14: A Summary of Climate Averages for Ireland 1981-2010. Dublin: Met Éireann.

Warren, G. 2008: Fieldwork in Belderring, Co. Mayo, 2004-2008 (04E0893). School of Archaeology, University College Dublin, unpublished report.

Warren, G. - McIlreavy, D. - Rathbone, S. - Walsh, P. 2009: Archaeological Excavations at Behy (E747) Stratigraphic Report. Neolithic and Bronze Age Landscapes of North Mayo. Dublin: UCD School of Archaeology, Irish National Strategic Archaeological Research Fund 2009.

Weston, D.G. 2001: Alluvium and Geophysical Prospection. Archaeological Prospection 8, 265-272.

Weston, D.G. 2004: The Influence of Waterlogging and Variations in Pedology and Ignition upon Resultant Susceptibilities: a Series of Laboratory Reconstructions. Archaeological Prospection 11(2), 107-120.

Woodcock, N.H. 1994: Geology and environment in Britain and Ireland. London: University College London Press.

ARCHAEOLOGICAL USE OF GEOPHYSICAL METHODS IN NORWEGIAN CULTURAL HERITAGE MANAGEMENT – A REVIEW

Arne Anderson Stamnes and Lars Gustavsen

Abstract: *The aim of this paper is to review the way geophysical prospection methods have been used in Norway, and gain a better understanding of the role and status of geophysical methods within Norwegian cultural heritage management. This is done by reviewing and analysing the content of a database on all known geophysical surveys conducted in Norway over the last 40 year - 197 surveys in all. The results show that the number of surveys in Norway has increased since the beginning of this millennium, but geophysical surveys are nothing new. 64 % of all surveys were initiated for research purposes and 36 % for management purposes - a number much lower than in England and Ireland. Only 29 % of all surveys involved more than one geophysical method. While strategic documents and signed treaties justify the use of geophysical methods, the analysis shows that the application of such methods has yet to be generally accepted within the existing cultural heritage management in Norway. The reasons for this is a combination of lack of resolution and technical limitations of earlier surveys, challenging natural conditions and ephemeral archaeology, combined with a lack of trained personnel and competence. Recent research initiative by domestic institutions related to the application of and research on geophysical methods is considered to be a step toward building up domestic experience and knowledge.*

Keywords: *Archaeology – Cultural Heritage management – Geophysical Survey Methods – Norway*

Introduction

Geophysical methods of prospection, defined as *"The examination of the Earth's physical properties using non-intrusive ground surveys techniques to reveal buried archaeological features, sites and landscapes"* (*Gaffney - Gater 2003*, 12), have been used with success for some time in countries such as Great Britain, Italy, Austria, Germany and elsewhere *(Doneus et al. 2001; Gaffney - Gater 2003; David 2008; Piro 2009)*.

This is often done by applying a range of geophysical methods based on different physical principles. The most widely used methods are electric, magnetic or electromagnetic methods, employing a variety of instrumentation and field procedures. There are also instances in which seismic or microgravity methods have been applied *(Clark 1996; Gaffney - Gater 2003)*. The following benefits of geophysical surveys have been highlighted: the non-intrusive nature of the methods and the potential for acquiring more information about archaeological sites without destroying them, the fast speed at which surveys can be conducted, yielding a large amount of information in a short amount of time, and a level of accuracy and detail providing a useful means for pinpointing the location of interesting anomalies and activity zones (*Clark 1996; Gaffney - Gater 2003; Lockhart - Green 2006; Gaffney 2008; Ernenwein - Hargrave 2009, 9-13; Viberg et al. 2011*).

While all of these aspects appear beneficial to a proper management of archaeological heritage, widespread use and acceptance of remote sensing methods has not been forthcoming in Norway, and the impact of geophysical prospection methods on the archaeological community might be claimed to be less than elsewhere in Europe. It is therefore interesting to note a change in the application of these methods within the last decade, when several well-performed surveys have produced interesting results *(Gustavsen - Stamnes 2012)*.

The aim of this paper is therefore to review the way in which geophysical prospection methods have been used in Norway, in order to gain a better understanding of the reasons behind the delay in their use. This will increase our understanding of the role and status of geophysical methods within Norwegian cultural heritage management. It involves analysing who commissioned such surveys, why they were undertaken, where and when, as well as how – i.e. the choice of methods applied. This will be combined with an analysis of the content of official documents from central government agencies concerning the application of or research on geophysical methods within the Norwegian heritage management system. Such an investigation will give some clues to important topics and objectives that should be addressed for further research in the future.

Method

A database containing information on geophysical surveys undertaken for archaeological purposes has been compiled by the authors of this article. This is a joint project of The Norwegian Institute for Cultural Heritage Research and The NTNU Museum of Natural History – Section for

Archaeology and Cultural History. The database covers all known geophysical surveys which have been identified in published literature, technical survey reports, media coverage, archival sources and other grey literature. The following information has been included in the database:

- Location (county, municipality, farm name and number)
- Time and date
- Survey type
- Archaeological site type
- Commissioning authority
- Survey company and personnel (representing either public archaeological institutions or private companies)
- Methods used (including instrument manufacturer and model details if known)
- Geological information and soil conditions (if known)
- The total number of survey schemes, and the number of projects they can be related to (sometimes several surveys were undertaken at different times within the same project)
- References

This database is a good source for investigating the aims of this paper. It provides an overview of the development over time, the geographical distribution of surveys, methodological choices and combination of methods. It is also a good source of information for further analysis of the reasons for performing geophysical surveys – be it for archaeological research purposes or heritage management. As the main aim of this article is to review how the methods have been used, a short historical overview will be presented, in which the main focus will be on general trends rather than on separate survey details. A general discussion on the results obtained and the identification of important challenges and experiences extracted from this overview will also be raised.

The second aim is to evaluate the current status of geophysical methods within Norwegian cultural heritage management. By investigating strategic documents and other documents from participants within cultural heritage management, their impressions of the applicability of geophysical methods and intentions for future use of such methods can be indicated. The combined results of such an analysis with information from the geophysical survey database will reveal important information on topics and objectives that can be addressed in the future. To make it easier for the reader to relate to this information, a short general description of the Norwegian heritage management system will also be provided.

A Short History of Archaeological Geophysics in Norway

The first documented use of geophysical prospection methods in Norway is a magnetometer survey at Stødleterrassen in the municipality of Etne in the county of Hordaland in 1968. This experimental work was directed by Norwegian archaeologist Bjørn Myhre, and led to the successful discovery of two Iron Age cooking pits (*Myhre 1968*). Another early survey was carried out for the "Hoset Project" in the municipality of Stjørdal in the county of Nord-Trøndelag, where an iron production site from the early Iron Age was mapped with a proton magnetometer. The results successfully delimited a slag heap and indicated the location of the furnace associated with the site (*Farbregd 1973; 1977*). The methods and technologies, however, were not generally accessible and not much further work was undertaken until the mid-1980s.

From these initial surveys and until the end of the 1990s, an increase in the number of surveys undertaken on a range of different archaeological sites can be observed (Fig. 1). This includes several georadar and magnetometer surveys at the mound cemetery at Borre in Vestfold county (*Myhre 2004*), as well as various magnetometer investigations carried out by the geologist Richard Binns. Binns' work includes an Iron Age courtyard site and activity areas associated with the Frosta *thing* site in Nord-Trøndelag county, where an early medieval farmstead and a ploughed-out burial mound were detected (*Binns 1994; 1996; 1997*). From the late 1980s software and hardware became more accessible, and it was increasingly possible for private companies and consultants to offer their services. The survey procedures chosen could be seen as normal for their time, but some of the results would today be deemed of limited value due to the lack of resolution and underdeveloped processing- and visualisation-techniques. Matrix plots of magnetometer data and the presentation of single georadar profiles printed on paper made it hard to relate the data to their physical position and therefore clearly limited good archaeological interpretations. This also gave the general impression of geophysical methods to be of limited value, either due to a lack of correlation between the geophysical results and the excavated archaeological features, poor quality of the archaeological interpretation of the geophysical data, or a limited understanding of the methods and their underlying geophysical principles – including the potentials and limitations associated with each method (*Gustavsen - Stamnes 2012*, 85-86).

With the introduction of more powerful computers, as well as the increased application of GIS-systems and accurate GPS-systems within the archaeological community, came new possibilities for accurately plotting the geophysical data geographically. It became easier to associate different data sources with archaeological findings (*Chapman 2006*). Increased amounts of data covering larger areas could be gathered and processed, and the quality of the known surveys increased from the turn of the millennium onwards (*Gustavsen - Stamnes 2012*). In this period we find several successful magnetometer investigations of iron production sites with associated activity, especially related to the "Gråfjell Project" in Hedmark county (*Risbøl - Smekalova 2001; Risbøl et al. 2002*), as well various surveys undertaken over ploughed-out burial mounds in cultivated fields throughout the country (*Lorra 2003; Binns 2004; Gjerpe 2005*). Generally, it could be argued

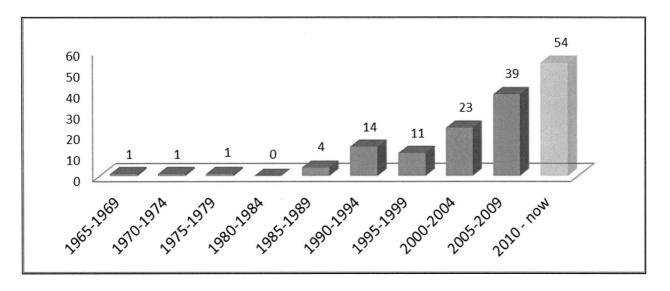

Fig. 1. Graph showing the incremental use of archaeological geophysics in Norway from 1968 until February 2013. The light blue bar indicates the current non-complete five-year period.

that surveys were often undertaken by professionals or companies not based in Norway. These were of a high technical quality, although a lack of focus on the reasons for undertaking such surveys as well as on the survey methodologies in general can sometimes be noticed. If the results were disappointing from an archaeological point of view, i.e. where archaeological features were not positively identified by geophysical methods, but were later found when excavating the site, there was often not an opportunity to investigate this further as part of the project. This limited the value of some of the surveys undertaken from a geophysical point of view. A lack of nationally based professionals and methodological research projects also led to a limited long-term gain and availability of skilled personnel and experience (*Gustavsen - Stamnes 2012*).

This changed in 2006 when the *Directorate for Cultural Heritage* chose the *Vestfold County Council* as collaborators in a national project concerning the use of geophysical methods. The goal of this methodological project was to investigate the potential and possibilities of geophysical methods on a range of sites, and the project was carried out in collaboration between the *Directorate*, the county archaeologists in Vestfold, as well as professionals and geophysicists from the *Swedish National Heritage Board*. From 2010 this county council proceeded with a collaboration with the *Norwegian Institute of Cultural Heritage Research* (NIKU) as partners in a multinational research led by the *Ludwig Boltzmann Institute for Archaeological Prospection and Virtual Archaeology* (LBI ArchPro) in Vienna, which is an on-going project for developing new technological and non-destructive methods for documenting and identifying archaeological sites, monuments and landscapes. This involves geophysical prospection methods as well as other remote sensing techniques such as aerial LiDAR scanning, hyper spectral scanning and satellite imagery. NIKU later invested in their own geophysical equipment. NIKU, in collaboration with

the LBI-project, has investigated substantial areas using several methods, and can demonstrate a range of positively identified archaeological features, and considerable experience in the applicability of such methods to a variety of natural conditions and archaeological monuments. Another archaeological institution that carried out methodological research is the *NTNU Museum of Natural History and Archaeology* in Trondheim, which have had a research interest in the application of geophysical methods since the beginning of the millennium. In 2007 the NTNU initiated a collaboration with the Irish company *Earthsound Associates*, and undertook several geophysical investigations in central Norway, as well as at the Iron Age centre of power and wealth at Avaldsnes in Hordaland county (*Barton et al. 2009*). NTNU was the first (and to this day – only) regional museum in Norway to invest in their own geophysical survey equipment and personnel, and was the first university body to engage a PhD-candidate on the subject of archaeological geophysics as from the autumn of 2011. The county of Vest-Agder has also commissioned several surveys on their own initiative, in collaboration with the *Moesgaard museum* in Denmark and geophysicist Tatjana Smekalova. These three initiatives in particular have led to the increase in the number of geophysical surveys from 2007 onwards, as noticed in (Figs. 1 and 2).

The Norwegian Cultural Heritage Management System

The cultural heritage management system in Norway is designed to preserve a representative selection of monuments and sites from all periods, and its aim is to provide an overview of the arts and crafts and the general way of life throughout Norwegian history. Through the Cultural Heritage Act of 1978, all monuments predating 1537 AD and standing buildings predating 1650 AD are automatically protected by law, while monuments more recent than 1537 or standing buildings built after 1650

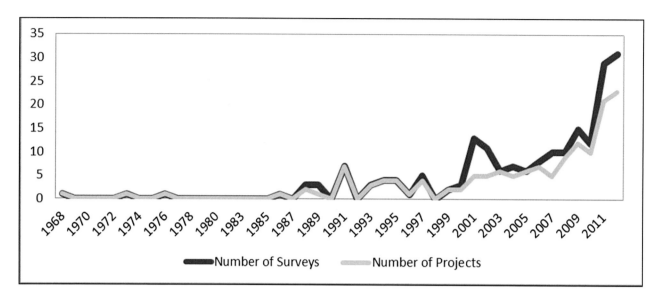

Fig. 2. Graph showing the development in the number of archaeological projects involving individual geophysical surveys (red) and the number of projects involving geophysical surveys (blue).

can be protected through a protection order granted on a case-by-case basis. All archaeological monuments predating 1537 are protected automatically whether or not they have been positively identified (*Kulturminneloven 1978*). A range of new monuments are being rediscovered or identified every year, either through archaeological excavations, by outfield visual surveys, through LiDAR image analyses or other mapping schemes. The Cultural Heritage Act can also justify the protection of cultural landscapes and environments.

As for managing, preserving, locating and documenting the archaeological heritage older than 1537, the responsibility is shared by a range of governmental or public institutions. Rescue archaeology is not privatised. The main bodies within the Norwegian Cultural Heritage Act are as follows:

The Ministry of Environment (MOE) (Miljøvern-departementet) – The MOE has the overall responsibility for ensuring that the policies of the government are being followed, and shapes the aims, objectives and management instruments according to the relevant political guidelines.

The Directorate for Cultural Heritage (Riksantikvaren) – The Directorate is responsible for the practical implementation of the Norwegian Cultural Heritage Act and the aims and objectives instituted by the MOE. It serves as counselling body to the MOE, and provides and disseminates relevant knowledge pertaining to cultural landscapes, monuments and buildings.

The County Administrations – Norway is divided into 19 counties, where each county has a duty to employ officers responsible for cultural heritage conservation, including planning permissions, and to advise the county administration and the public on questions regarding cultural conservation and dissemination. Archaeologists

employed by the county conduct initial archaeological investigations to decide whether or not a planned development might impose a threat to any archaeological monuments or remains.

The Regional Archaeological Museums – Norway is divided into five museum districts, where each regional archaeological museum is responsible for undertaking archaeological excavations needed when an exemption to the Cultural Heritage Act has been granted on the condition that the archaeology will be documented by record. They manage the archaeological collections, and are responsible for the preservation of cultural historical objects, as well as research and dissemination. The Regional Archaeological Museums are defined as university museums in their region. This means that they are often involved in higher education and the training of archaeologists, and that there is a close link between the relevant university in the region and the archaeological museum, which again leads to some opportunities for academic collaboration.

The Sámi Parliament – The Sámi parliament has the same responsibility as the county administrations for cultural heritage monuments, sites and landscapes defined as Sámi and older than 100 years. The Sámi, as an indigenous people of Norway, employ their own cultural heritage officers, based in four regional offices.

The Norwegian Institute for Cultural Heritage Research (NIKU) – This is an independent institute for research and development, and has a status as a national centre of competence in issues regarding cultural heritage management, including conservation, technology and methodology. It acts as a consultancy to any cultural heritage management body. It is by definition not a public institution but has, through licence, a responsibility for managing medieval monuments in the major medieval

Table 1. Summarising statistics on who commissioned surveys, as well as the number of surveys categorised as either "research" or "management". "Others" can involve local museums, local historical groups, private companies or other institutions.

Institution	# of surveys		Total	Total %
	Research	Management		
Regional Archaeological Museums	**49 (72%)**	**19 (28%)**	**68**	**34,5 %**
NIKU	**30 (57%)**	**23 (43%)**	**53**	**26,9 %**
Counties	**17 (44%)**	**22 (56%)**	**39**	**19,8 %**
Local Municipalities	**2 (50%)**	**2 (50%)**	**4**	**2,0 %**
Others*	**28 (85%)**	**5 (15%)**	**33**	**16,8 %**
Total Number of Surveys	**126 (64%)**	**71 (36%)**	**197**	

towns, as well as clerical buildings and monuments from this period.

(Sources for the list above: *Gaukstad - Holme 2000; Riksantikvaren 2012*).

Results

Statistics

As of February 2013, the geophysical database consists of 197 separate surveys conducted as part of 148 different projects. The reason for the separation between survey and project is that sometimes an area might be revisited, for instance in order to supplement an earlier survey or archaeological investigation with greater area coverage or by using an alternative geophysical method. (Figs. 1 and 2) show the development in the use of geophysical methods since the first known survey from Stødleterassen in 1968.

As our main aim is to review how the methods have been used, it is possible to shed further light on this by summarising some statistics from the compiled database by investigating who commissioned surveys, why they were undertaken, as well as where and how.

Who and why

It is of interest to investigate who commissioned geophysical surveys and why. The question of why can be multifaceted, and we have therefore chosen to separate the surveys into two categories: "research" and "management". While a survey initially conducted for research purposes might yield results that are interesting from a cultural heritage management point of view, it might not be why the survey initially was conducted. Surveys labelled "management" are either surveys conducted as part of a developer-led planning application and excavation, or they were conducted for specific dissemination purposes or to answer specific questions relating to the proper management of an archaeological site. The latter could for instance be the delineation of sites or providing further information on preservation conditions or additional archaeological features. While it is possible that some surveys have been conducted for several purposes, as well as being a collaboration between different institutions, we have to the

best of our ability separated them based on main purpose or contributor.

By separating surveys conducted for research purposes from surveys conducted in management contexts (dissemination and development), these results can shed light on how geophysical methods are being utilised by the different institutions. The following summarisation can be presented (Table 1):

While these results will be discussed more in-depth later, it is interesting to note the percentage of the total number of surveys, where 64 % were initiated for research purposes, whereas 36 % were for management purposes.

Where

The following map shows the distribution of known geophysical surveys in Norway at county level (Fig. 3):

Vestfold clearly stands out with 56 surveys, and is within the highest quantile together with Nord-Trøndelag (27 surveys) and Hedmark (25 surveys). Sometimes a large variance can be noticed between neighbouring counties. There does not seem to be a direct link between county size and the number of surveys. As the number of archaeological site evaluations performed by the county archaeologists in relation to planning permissions is a reasonable indicator of the rate of development in each county, it is interesting to compare this with the number of geophysical surveys undertaken within that county. This might indicate if this uneven geographical distribution is related to the rate of regional development in the various counties. The data for the number of archaeological investigations related to planning applications is gathered from the *Statistics Norway*'s KOSTRA database for municipal and county municipal activities[1]. As only statistics for the years 2007-2011 are available, the geophysical investigations in the same period was separated, and the following graph could be made (Fig. 4):

As can be seen, there is a wide variation of archaeological activity in relation to planning applications between

---

[1] http://www.ssb.no/english/subjects/00/00/20/kostra_en/ (last accessed 25.01.2013)

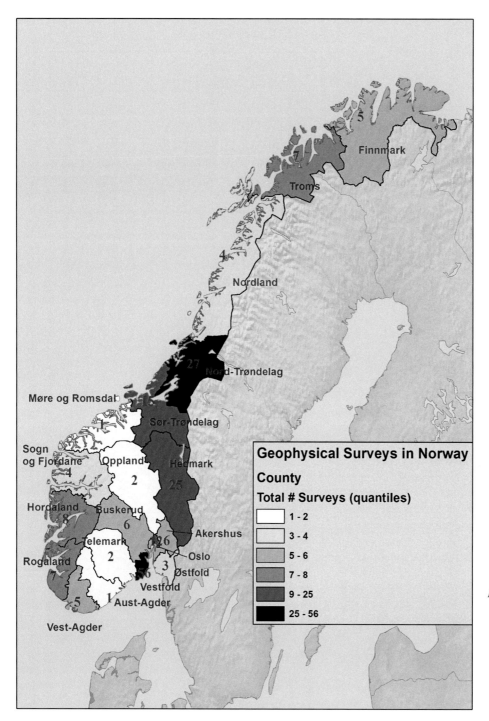

Fig. 3. Map of Norway showing the number of geophysical surveys undertaken for each county. Made with digital map data from Natural Earth and the Norwegian Mapping Authority.

the different county municipalities, and the number of geophysical surveys performed do not seem to be directly related to these. The Pearson r correlation coefficient for the correlation between these two variables was calculated to -0.19, where a number closer to ±1 is a perfect correlation (*Madsen 2011*, 114). This therefore means that there is no statistical linear relationship between the archaeological activity within each county and the use of geophysical methods at a national level.

How

Another way of evaluating the use of geophysical prospection methods to date is to evaluate how the

geophysical methods have been utilised. This involves both choices of methods, site selection and issues relating to resolution.

The choices of archaeological targets and geophysical methods, as well as the combination of several geophysical methods can be important in the success of a survey to positively identify archaeological remains. First of all the following figure can be presented (Figs. 5 and 6):

While (Fig. 7) also reflects the trend of the number of surveys performed (see Figs. 1 and 2), it is most relevant for noticing how the preferred method of choice has changed from magnetometers to ground penetrating radar.

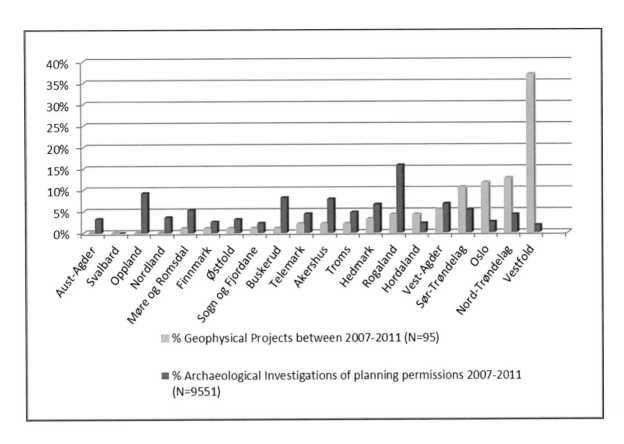

Fig. 4. The relationship between the number of geophysical surveys compared with archaeological investigations of planning permissions between 2007-2011. There is no data available on archaeological investigations for Svalbard in the KOSTRA database.

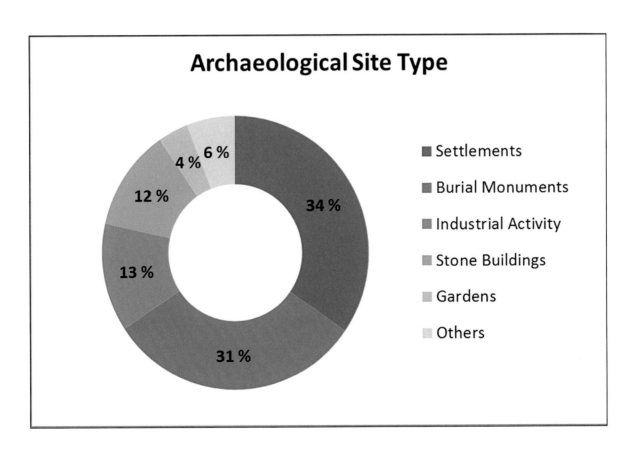

Fig. 5. The percentage distribution of different site types targeted by geophysical surveys in Norway as of 31.01.2013. Please note that separate surveys may have several objectives or cover different site types, and have therefore been classified as for instance both settlements and burial monuments. While the total number of surveys is 197, the total number of classified survey site types is 242.

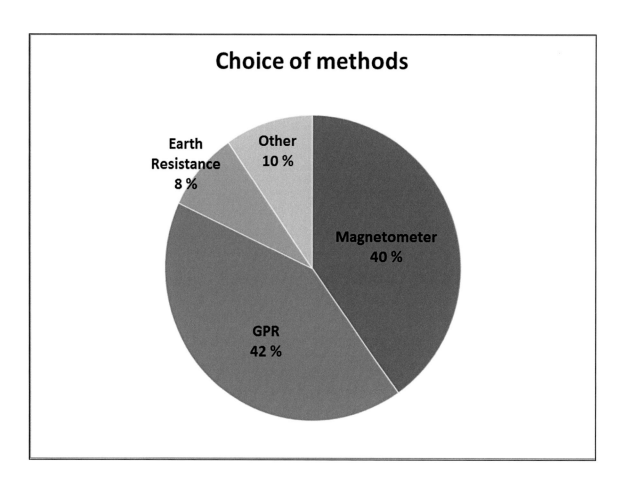

Fig. 6. Graph showing the degree of use of each main geophysical technique. This is based on 239 data inputs, where several methods may have been applied at one survey. This percentage is related to the number of surveys involving a technique, and not the size of the surveys.

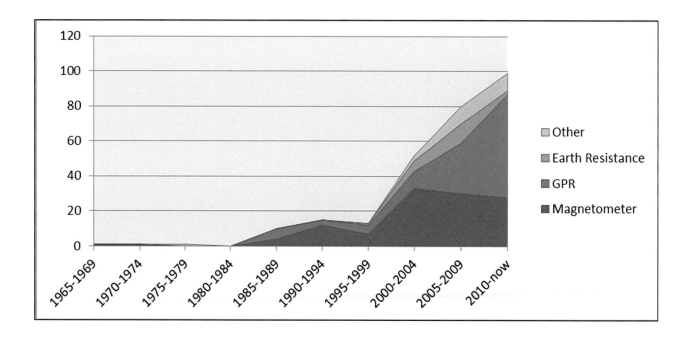

Fig. 7. This graph shows how the utilisation of different geophysical methods has developed over time. The category "Others" involve magnetic susceptibility mapping and different electromagnetic imaging techniques.

As a comparison, magnetometer surveys have long been considered as the main choice of methods in the UK (*Gaffney - Gater 2003; David 2008; Jordan 2009*), while in Norway it is one of the main methods together with georadar. Earth resistance surveys have never been used much in Norway, although good examples of successful application do exist (e.g. *Horsley 2003; Stamnes 2011*). Examples of electromagnetic imaging are known, as well as the use of topsoil magnetic susceptibility for delineating sites and activity areas (e.g. *Stamnes 2011*). Another way of investigating the application of geophysical methods is to look at the number of different techniques applied at each survey. This is relevant to understand the rate of success or scepticism related to the applicability of geophysical methods. An increase in the number of geophysical methods applied increases our understanding of the archaeological site, as each method can be used to characterise different physical properties of the subsoil. An archaeological feature can be seen in data from one technique, while being absent in data from another (*David 2008; Ernenwein - Hargrave 2009; Stamnes 2011; Gaffney - Gaffney 2011*).

Official documents

In the introduction, the following positive benefits of geophysical methods were highlighted:

- The non-intrusive and non-destructive nature of the methods
- The possibilities of acquiring more information about an archaeological site or cultural landscape without destructive interference
- The high speed of data gathering
- The high spatial precision, making it possible to pinpoint the location of interesting anomalies and zones of activity

(*Clark 1996; Gaffney - Gater 2003; Lockhart - Green 2006; Gaffney 2008; Ernenwein - Hargrave 2009, 9-13; Viberg et al. 2011*).

All of these points should be in the best interest of the cultural heritage management in Norway, as Norway has ratified several treaties and conventions such as the Valetta-convention and the ICOMOS-charter that both encourage the use of non-intrusive methods and the conservation of cultural heritage *in-situ* (*Valetta 1992; Icomos 1990; Gustavsen - Stamnes 2012, 87*).

A report commissioned by the *Research Council of Norway* on future research focus within cultural heritage management for the years 2004-2014 explicitly pointed out the need for development of and research on methods for locating and mapping sites, as well as tools to analyse and create prognoses for the potential for cultural heritage sites (*Norges Forskningsråd 2003*). The *Directorate for Cultural Heritage* have later indicated in a strategy plan for cultural heritage management valid for the years 2010-2020 that they wish to encourage the development of technological aids as a valuable supplement to the

methods generally used for identification and excavation of archaeology, with particular emphasis on non-intrusive methods (*Riksantikvaren 2010*, 11). The Cultural Heritage Act of 1978 does not specify how any archaeological investigation should be conducted in the different stages, but leaves it up to the county archaeologists or regional archaeological museum to decide how they choose to evaluate, investigate or excavate any area influenced by development (*Kulturminneloven 1978*). They need to get acceptance and support from the *Directorate for Cultural Heritage* for any decisions made, be it through acceptance of budgets or suggestions for field strategies and the inclusion of scientific methods in their budgets. As the Directorate is not directly involved in the actual field work, this is one way they might influence the strategic choices made for any field archaeological investigation. They have also released an advisory document for budgeting for excavations performed by the regional archaeological museums in instances where an exemption to the Cultural Heritage Act has been granted. Geophysical methods are not mentioned explicitly in this document, but it is possible to budget for scientific analyses. The use of scientific analyses should then be limited to the extent that is deemed necessary to "*decide, identify, date and interpret the site, cultural layers and finds*" (*Riksantivaren 2011*, authors' translation). This document is not valid for budgeting for the surveys performed by the county archaeologists in relation to the initial planning permission. It is then up to the county archaeologists to decide which method they find suitable. Another relevant document is an advisory document released by the Directorate in collaboration with the research institution *Sintef Byggforsk*, concerning archaeology and their collaboration with the construction engineering industry, where archaeology is explained to construction engineers and vice versa. This document explains the different methods, both intrusive and non-intrusive, that archaeologists use. The authors of this report note that the geophysical methods "*are still more at an experimental stage*" in Norway (*Karlberg - Jerkø 2009*, 121, authors' translation).

This short presentation of the main official documents regarding the use of geophysical methods in relation to practical cultural heritage management shows that an awareness of the methods does indeed exist, but that they have not necessarily been given much focus. While treaties and charters justifying the use of non-intrusive methods have been ratified, it is still left up to the responsible governmental institution or official to decide which methods to utilise. This will be discussed further in the next section.

Discussion

As seen in (Figs. 1 and 2), the use of geophysical techniques in archaeology in Norway has increased significantly within the last decade. It is also apparent that the application of such methods is not connected to the level of archaeological activity related to planning permissions in the different counties (Fig. 4). In total 36 % of all geophysical surveys have been conducted within a management context. This number becomes more informative when you compare it with data from Ireland and England.

In Ireland about 80.4 % out of 514 licensed geophysical surveys between 1999 and 2007 were conducted within a commercial management context, while the remaining 19.6 % were research surveys (*Bonsall et al. 2013*). Bournemouth University in England has made a database of so-called "grey" literature from different regional archives, registries and different contractors in England covering the years 1990-2010, as part of their "Archaeological Investigations Project"[2]. This "grey" literature consists typically of unpublished survey and excavation reports, as well as work related to research projects. The database is searchable online, and its content can be exported and analysed. By looking at the geophysical surveys only, it was possible to separate them into "planning" and "non-planning" surveys. Out of 3656 entries, 64 % was planning-related, 30 % was non-planning and 6 % was "other". The separation between these categories is somewhat ambiguous, and it is unclear which type of surveys the 6 % in the "other" group represent. It is possible that these involve mostly research or rescue surveys. While it is difficult to test the accuracy and quality of this information, the number of surveys categorised is generally quite high, improving the possible statistical significance. At the same time *Bonsall et al.* 2013 (this volume) has questioned the accuracy of the AIP Database due to the large number of duplicate records. The important aspect is that while 36 % of all surveys in Norway were within a management context, it was 80.4% in Ireland and 64 % in England. Some error may be introduced due to the timescale these compilations of surveys represent as well as possible duplicate records, but most importantly, the comparison demonstrates that geophysical methods do not seem to be an integrated part of Norwegian everyday archaeological practice to the same extent as in England and Ireland. (Table 1 and Fig. 4) support this conclusion.

The important question that arises from this result is why such methods are not applied to the same extent. This is probably related to two aspects: 1. How the methods have been used, and 2. The lack of domestic competence. These will be discussed in turn.

The interplay between expected archaeological site type, methodological choices and combination of geophysical methods is important. If archaeological features of a certain type are to be identified by a geophysical method, they need to have a sufficient geophysical contrast and a shape, form or pattern that can be recognised as archaeological by the interpreter. It is therefore important that the end user and field technician is able to properly understand the effect of different methodological choices, such as resolution, possibilities and limitations of each method. If the expected targets are small postholes and pits with a diameter of 50 cm or less, which is typical of Norwegian Iron Age settlement

sites (*Løken 1999, Myhre 2002*), the choice of resolution and method that can potentially identify such small features will be important. We see in (Fig. 5) that 34 % of all surveys performed in Norway targeted settlement sites. Unless these consisted of larger ditches, stone buildings or highly contrasting material from burnt material or stone-lined post holes, then surveying such a site with can be difficult. It is likely that several of the surveys were taken with an expectation of a better performance rate, due to a lack of understanding of the limitations present. Even so, we still have examples where buildings of postholes and pits have been located (*Trinks et al. 2007*). When the surveys targeted ploughed-out burial mounds, there are examples in which the ring-ditch was not visible in magnetic datasets, while they could be seen clearly in the GPR or electric resistivity data (*Stamnes 2011*). There is also an example from Gulli in Vestfold, in which ploughed-out burial mounds were not visible at all. The reasons for this last example were not investigated further from a geophysical point of view (*Gjerpe 2005*). We also notice in (Fig. 8) that a majority of all surveys, 71 %, involved just one method. The general consensus is that the more methods are applied, the better is the information gain concerning a site or feature and the higher are the chances of positively identifying a feature (*Clark 1996; Gaffney - Gater 2003; David 2008; Ernenwein - Hargrave 2009; Gaffney - Gaffney 2011*). Several case studies from Norway demonstrate this (i.e. *Trinks et al. 2007; 2010; Stamnes 2011*). Magnetometers had been the preferred method of choice until around the turn of the millennium, when the number of GPR surveys appears to increase. Magnetometers were involved in 40 % of all surveys, and we know that the earlier surveys were often conducted with a relatively low spatial resolution using limited software options for data processing and presentation. We consider it likely that earlier surveys sometimes created an impression of archaeological geophysics as being unreliable and inefficient, since the surveys failed to positively identify archaeological features which were found during subsequent excavations, or that over-interpretation or high expectations led to a false impression of the applicability of the methods. This does not necessarily imply that the actual geophysical mapping was poorly performed, but rather that technical restrictions reduced the actual applicability under the conditions present. An understanding of the geophysical principles, possibilities and limitations is therefore necessary to provide a proper archaeological interpretation of the geophysical data as well. The quality of such interpretations will increase with experience.

Today there are two domestic institutions that execute geophysical surveys for archaeological purposes: The *NTNU Museum of Natural History and Archaeology*, which is connected to the *Norwegian University of Science and Technology*, and the *Norwegian Institute for Cultural Heritage Research* (NIKU). Their venture into archaeological geophysics is something relatively new within Norwegian archaeology, starting in the second half of the last decade. Other practitioners are rare, and are often

---

[2] http://csweb.bournemouth.ac.uk/aip/aipintro.htm (last accessed 24.05.2013)

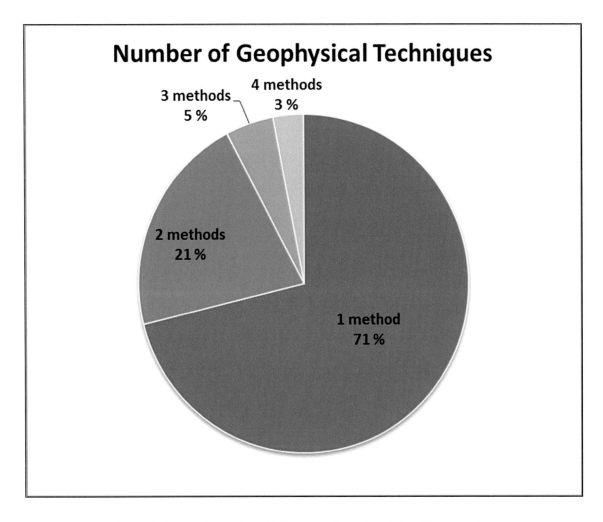

Fig. 8. Graph showing the number of different geophysical methods utilised at each survey.

either smaller private companies or professional competence from abroad, often delivering work of high technical quality. This might create a problem, as competence is not being embedded into institutions involved with archaeological geophysics on a regular basis, and thus specialist knowledge is lacking. The possibilities of acquiring domestic experience-based knowledge have therefore not been ideal. The fact that NTNU and NIKU have started building competence and gaining experience in the field is therefore a positive development of archaeological geophysics in Norway. This creates new possibilities in identifying relevant research questions and developing geophysical field methodologies to tackle the prevailing natural conditions and to better investigate cultural historical sites and features. Archaeological geophysics has not been part of archaeological academic education in Norway, which might have restricted the knowledge about the possibilities and limitations of such methods within the different decision-making bodies responsible for various stages within the Norwegian cultural heritage management. While there is a large expertise in geophysics for marine oil exploration and geological application in Norway both professionally and academically, the possibilities of collaboration and cross-disciplinary knowledge exchange have yet to be exploited.

It is the county archaeologists who are given the main responsibility for the daily management and initial responses to various planning applications. It is here that sites and monuments are being discovered, in addition to some responsibility regarding dissemination and questions from the public. It is therefore interesting to note that only 20 % of the total number of surveys undertaken were commissioned by various county units. Of these, only 22 out of 39 surveys initiated by the counties (out of a total of 197) were for management purposes. This leaves only a total of 11 % of all surveys that were performed in relation to archaeological field evaluation prior to all other archaeological stages. It is also clear that the use does not correlate with the amount of archaeological fieldwork they undertake (Fig. 4). Presently, the Cultural Heritage Act leaves it up to the county archaeologists to choose which method they find suitable to investigate whether or not an area may contain any archaeology protected by law. The uneven distribution of surveys, both geographically (Fig. 3) and compared to the number of archaeological investigations initiated by the county officials due to planning applications (Fig. 4), indicates that there is something else that governs this distribution. The geographic location of available technical personnel, or institutions able to perform a geophysical survey probably influence this distribution. Another factor is the personal interest and knowledge of the official responsible for archaeological field projects related to planning applications or excavations. A notion that the methods are not properly developed, or that their applicability has not been proven, makes it difficult to argue for the additional costs.

The Directorate is currently working on guidelines for counties budgeting for archaeological investigations, i.e. what the developer will have to pay for, but these guidelines were not yet implemented as of March 2013. At present, it is up to the Directorate to approve the budgets, including field methodologies and strategies concerning final excavations performed by the regional archaeological museums, ensuring a fair management practice nationwide. It is likely that the new budget guidelines for the county officials may have implications for or impose restrictions on the approval of choices made by the county archaeologists. Even today the use of geophysical methods is limited, so it will be more important than ever that the personnel involved at county level and in the Directorate have a reasonable knowledge of geophysical methods, if they are to be generally accepted and integrated further so that an optimal gain can be made. It is still difficult to guarantee that any archaeological features will be safely identified by applying geophysical methods, and this creates problems for justifying the application of such methods within a heritage management framework. While the Directorate is positive about the use of non-intrusive methods, they cannot impose costs for research or methodological development on the developer. From a developer's perspective, experience has shown that a good investigation of a planned area early in the planning process could save time and money later in the development process by revealing hindrances, complications and problems early. If alterations are required to the initial planning permission, such costs will be increasingly higher the later on in the process they appear. An inadequate initial archaeological evaluation may lead to additional costs for the developer in later stages (*Karlberg - Jerkø 2009,* 79, 84 and 126). While investigations for the effectiveness of geophysical methods exist elsewhere (for instance *Horsley - Dockrill 2002; Lockhart - Green 2006; Jordan 2009; Viberg 2012; Bonsall et al. 2013*), a detailed study is not yet available in Norway. Studies of cost-benefit aspects of integrating geophysical methods within a cultural heritage management point of view are even scarcer, although a couple of examples from the United States do exist (i.e. *Johnson - Haley 2006; Monaghan et al. 2006*). It is therefore clear that more research on topics such as effectiveness, cost-benefit analysis, and general assessment of different geophysical techniques under varying natural and archaeological conditions is needed. It would also be very interesting to investigate the potential effect of performing geophysics as early in the planning stage as possible, and how the results might alter or impact on the decision-making process throughout the whole project. One potential situation may be that overall costs increase, but that the quality of the management and the degree of

protection without the destruction of monuments or features may improve as a result of such integration.

To achieve a general increase in knowledge of the applicability, possibilities and restrictions that exist for the use of geophysical methods, it is important to strengthen the domestic research on the application of such methods. Within Norway there is a vast range of natural conditions and archaeological site types, which can make it problematic to automatically transfer field methodological routines for geophysical surveys from elsewhere. That said, it is not unlikely that several applications could be more or less directly integrated into research and excavation projects, as good parallel examples exist elsewhere. Sometimes scepticism may exist to a proposed application because of a lack of domestic examples, or because the officials are not aware of either domestic or international examples. In such instances it is up to the practitioner and institutions performing geophysical surveys to provide information on the existence and applicability of such examples. An impression we gained when reviewing past geophysical work is that the geophysical reason for a site or feature not being seen in the geophysical data was not revisited and investigated. The archaeological result was in focus, and not the methodological development. This is quite surprising considering that 64 % of all geophysical surveys were performed within a research context. This does not necessarily mean within an archaeological-*geophysical* research context. If the initial integration of such methods in the research project had also included an element of research on the actual geophysical data, and not only expecting archaeologically important information, new lessons could have been learned. Comparisons of the geophysical data with archaeological excavation results is important, and ground-truthing and additional analysis of the geophysical data might provide information that improves our ability to process, analyse and interpret such data (i.e. as described by *Hargrave 2006*), which will in turn influence the way in which the geophysical methods are applied or integrated in future cultural heritage management. This new knowledge needs to be disseminated through published research, at conferences and seminars, as well as at the academic institutions teaching archaeology. It is also important to have targeted research questions to the use of geophysical methods that are connected to issues relevant for current archaeological research and heritage management.

Conclusion

The aim of this paper was to review the archaeological use of geophysical methods in Norwegian cultural heritage management. A database has been compiled with all identified geophysical surveys conducted for archaeological purposes in Norway, which has been used for further analysis. By investigating factors such as who commissioned geophysical surveys, why they were undertaken as well as where, when and how, a deeper understanding of the application of geophysical methods on archaeological sites in Norway could be presented. By combining this with an analysis of the content of official documents from central government agencies, the current status of geophysical methods within the Norwegian cultural heritage management system could be evaluated.

Analysis of the database showed that the use of geophysical has increased within the last decade, with several institutions being involved in the application of geophysical methods. A range of site types had been targeted, with settlement sites and burial monuments dominating. Of all surveys, GPR application has taken over as the most used method, while magnetometers used to dominate – though is still often applied. 71 % of all surveys utilised only one method. Several examples show us that a combination of methods measuring different geophysical properties increases the detectability and available knowledge of an archaeological site (i.e. (*David 2008; Ernenwein - Hargrave 2009; Stamnes 2011; Gaffney - Gaffney 2011*), so this may have restricted the level of success of the surveys. The geographical spread of surveys conducted was large, and there was no correlation between the archaeological activity frequency at county level and the application of geophysical methods within each county. 36 % of all surveys conducted were undertaken for management reasons, while the remaining 64 % were for research purposes. The resulting conclusion of this is that geophysical methods are not an integrated part of everyday cultural heritage management in Norway. While official documents encourage the use of geophysical methods, their application has yet to be generally accepted within the existing cultural heritage management Scheme.

The reason for this is multifaceted. Earlier examples were sometimes of limited value compared with the standards of today, due to poor resolution or technical limitations concerning speed of survey, processing options or visualisation, or methodological choices made. This may have created an impression that such methods "do not work". However, there are several good examples of interesting survey results in the prevailing natural and archaeological context. We believe that there is large unexplored potential for the successful use and integration of such methods within Norwegian cultural heritage management. Targeted research on field-methodological use of geophysical methods under various natural and archaeological conditions is vital to properly understand how these methods can be beneficial within Norwegian cultural heritage management. This should also involve ground truthing, as well as cost-benefit analysis of the added knowledge gain for proper management and legal protection of sites. Financial aspects of introducing geophysical methods should also be evaluated. The increased focus of such methods within the last decade is seen as positive, and the relatively recent initiative taken by institutions such as the Norwegian Institute of Cultural Heritage Research and the NTNU Museum of Cultural History and Archaeology related to geophysical methods is a step in the right direction for building up domestic experience and knowledge.

Acknowledgements

The authors want to express special thanks to Dr. Chris Gaffney, University of Bradford, and to Lars F. Stenvik at the Norwegian University of Science and Technology for commenting on initial drafts of this article. We also want to thank all who provided us with access to unpublished report, articles and other sources that made it possible to build up our geophysical survey database.

References

Barton, K. - Stenvik, L. - Birgisdottir, B. 2009: A Chieftain's Hall or a Grave; Ground Penetrating Radar in an Archaeological Geophysics Survey to Target the Excavation of a Cropmark near Stiklestad, Nord-Trøndelag, Norway. 5th International Workshop on Advanced Ground Penetrating Radar, IWAGPR2009. University of Granada.

Binns, R. 1994: Med røntgenblikk på fortiden. Spor 2, 12-15.

Binns, R. 1996: Undersøkelse med Fluxgate Gradiometer på Agdenes, Sør-Trøndelag: Rapport fra del 2 av arbeidet. Unpublished report, NTNU. Trondheim: NTNU Vitenskapsmuseet.

Binns, R. 1997: Undersøkelse med Fluxgate Gradiometer på et gravfelt og på en bygdeborg ved Gjævran (201/1), Steinkjer, Nord-Trøndelag, 5-10. oktober og 24. november 1997. Unpublished report, NTNU. Trondheim: NTNU Vitenskapsmuseet.

Binns, R. 2004: Gradiometer avdekker stor gravhaug på Stiklestad. Spor 19(1), 31.

Bonsall, J. - Gaffney, C. - Armit, I. 2013: A Decade of Ground Truthing: Reappraising Magnetometer Prospection Surveys on Linear Corridors in light of Excavation evidence 2001-2010. In: H. Kamermans – M. Gojda – A. G. Posluschny eds, A Sense Of The Past. Studies in current archaeological applications of remote sensing and non-invasive prospection methods.

Chapman, H. 2006: Landscape Archaeology and GIS. Stroud: Tempus Publishing.

Clark, A. 1996: Seeing beneath the soil: prospecting methods in archaeology. London: Routledge.

David, A. 2008: Geophysical survey in archaeological field evaluation. English Heritage.

Doneus, M. - Eder-Hinterleitner, A. - Neubauer, W. 2001: Archaeological Prospection: Fourth International Conference on Archaeological Prospection, Vienna, 19-23 September 2001, Austrian Academy of Sciences Press.

Ernenwein, E.G. - Hargrave, M.L. 2009: Archaeological Geophysics for DoD Field Use: a Guide for New and Novice Users. Guidance document submitted to the Environmental Security Technology Certification Program (ESTCP). U.S. Department of Defence.

Farbregd, O. 1973: Hosetprosjektet 1973. Arkeologisk utgravning. Unpublished archaeological report, digital document number 7550 in the topographical archives at the NTNU Museum of Natural History and Archaeology, Trondheim, Norway.

Farbregd, O. 1977: Archaeological Field Work and Evidence. Norwegian Archaeological Review 10, 119-127.

Gaffney, C. 2008: Detecting trends in the prediction of the buried past: a review of geophysical techniques in archaeology. Archaeometry 50, 313-336.

Gaffney, C. - Gater, J. 2003: Revealing the buried past : geophysics for archaeologists. Stroud: Tempus.

Gaffney, C. - Gaffney, V. 2011: Through an imperfect filter: geophysical techniques and the management of archaeological heritage. In: D. Cowley ed., Remote sensing for archaeological heritage management in the 21st century. Europae Archaeologiae Consilium, 117-128.

Gaukstad, E. - Home, J. 2005: Hovedaktørene i kulturminneforvaltningen. In: J. Holme eds, Kulturminnevern. Lov forvaltning, håndhevelse. Bind I. Økokrim, 2. edition. Chapter. 3.5., 136-145.

Gjerpe, L.E. ed. 2005: Gravfeltet på Gulli: E-18 prosjektet Vestfold : Bind 1, Oslo.

Gustavsen, L. - Stamnes, A.A. 2012: Arkeologisk geofysikk i Norge – En historisk oversikt og statusevaluering. Primitive Tider 14, 77-95.

Hargrave, M.L. 2006: Ground Truthing the Results of Geophysical Surveys. In: J. Johnson - M. Giradano - K. Kvamme eds, Remote Sensing in Archaeology: An Explicitly North American Perspective. Tuscaloosa: The University of Alabama Press, 269-304.

Horsley, T.J. 2003: Olav's Wall, Sarpsborg, Østfold, Norway. Report on Geophysical Surveys, November 2002 for Borgarsyssel Museum. Unpublished report, University of Bradford/Borgardsyssel Museum.

Horsley, T.J. - Dockrill, S.J. 2002: A Preliminary Assessment of the Use of Routine Geophysical Techniques for the Location, Characterisation and Interpretation of Buried Archaeology in Iceland. Archaeologia Islandica 2 (2002), 10-33.

Icomos 1990: Charter for the Protection and Management of the Archaeological Heritage (1990). International Council on Monuments and Sites (Icomos). Unesco. Available online: http://www.international.icomos.org/charters/arch_e.pdf. Last visited: 07.02.2013.

Johnson, J.K. - Haley, B.S. 2006: A Cost-Benefit Analysis of Remote Sensing Application in Cultural Resource Management Archaeology. In: J.K. Johnson ed., Remote Sensing in Archaeology. An Explicitly North American Perspective. Tuscaloosa: The University of Alabama Press.

Jordan, D. 2009: How effective is Geophysical Survey? A Regional Review. Archaeological Prospection, vol. 16- 2009, 77-90.

Karlberg, I. – Jerkø, S. 2009: Veileder i utbygging for arkeologer og i arkeologi for byggebransjen. ACES - Archaeology and Construction Engineering Skills guidance document. Riksantikvaren and Sintef Byggforsk, Oslo. Available online: http://www.

riksantikvaren.no/filestore/ACES-Veileder-skbar.pdf. Last visited: 07.02.2013.

Kulturminneloven 1978: Lov 9. juni 1978 nr. 50 om kulturminner (Kulturminneloven). English translation available online: The Cultural Heritage Act of 1978. http://www.regjeringen.no/en/doc/laws/Acts/cultural-heritage-act.html?id=173106. Last accessed: 07.02.2013.

Lockhart, J.J. - Green, T.J. 2006: The Current and Potential Role of Archaeogeophysics in Cultural Resource Management in the United States. In: J.K. Johnson ed., Remote Sensing in Archaeology. An Explicitly North American Perspective. Tuscaloosa: The University of Alabama Press, 17-32.

Løken,T. 1999:. The longhouse of Western Norway from the late Neolithic to the 10th Century AD: Representatives of a common Scandinavian building tradition or a local development? In: H. Schjelderup – O. Storsletten eds, Grindbygde hus i Vest-Norge. NIKU-seminar om grindbygde hus, Bryggens Museum 23-25.03.98. NIKU temahefte 030, 1-128.

Available online: http://www.niku.no/filestore/Publikasjoner/NIKUTemahefte30.pdf Last accessed: 13.09.2013

Lorra, S. 2003: Geophysical Exploration of the Sites Gulli and Rom Vestre Using Ground Penetrating Radar and Magnetics. Report on Field Survey and Results July 2003. Unpublished report. KHM, UIO. Oslo: Museum of Cultural Heritage.

Madsen, B. 2011: Statistics for Non-Statisticians. Berlin/Heidelberg: Springer-Verlag.

Monaghan, G.W. - Egan-Bruhy, K.C. - Hambacher, M.J. - Hayes, D.R. - Kolb, M.F. - Peterson, S. – Robertson, J.A. – Shaffer, N.R. 2006: The Minnesota Deep Test Protocol Project. Minnesota Department of Transportation. Available online: http://www.dot.state.mn.us/culturalresources/studies/deeptest.html. Last accessed: 12.02.2013.

Myhre, B. 1968: Innberetning om utgravning av områder hvor magnetometeret ga utslag. Sørheim, gnr. 36 bnr. 12.: Top. ark. Bergen museum.

Myhre, B. 2002: Landbruk, landskap og samfunn 4000 F.KR.-800 E.KR. In: B. Myhre - I. Øye eds, Norges Landbrukshistorie 1. 400 f.kr.-350 e.Kr. Jorda blir levevei. Det norske samlaget, 11-213.

Myhre, B. 2004: Undersøkelse av storhauger på Borre i Vestfold. In: J.H. Larsen – P. Rolfsen eds, Halvdanshaugen - arkeologi, historie og naturvitenskap. Oslo: University of Oslo.

Norges Forskningsråd 2003: Kulturminner og kulturmiljøer. Utredning av forskningsbehov 2004-2014. Oslo: Norges forskningsråd.

Piro, S. 2009: Introduction to geophysics for archaeology. In: S. Campana – S. Piro eds, Seeing the unseen: Geophysics and Landscape Archaeology. Leiden: CRC Press.

Riksantikvaren 2010. Strategisk plan for forvaltning av arkeologiske kulturminner og kulturmiljøer 2011-2020. Utvidet versjon. Available online: http://www.riksantikvaren.no/Norsk/Veiledning/For_forvaltningen/

Arkeologi/Arkeologi_mot_2020/. Last accessed 13.02.2013.

Riksantikvaren 2011: Utgifter til særskilt gransking av automatisk fredete arkeologiske kulturminner og skipsfunn, jf. Kulturminneloven §§8 og 14, jf. § |0. Retningslinjer for budsjettering og regnskap. Riksantikvaren, Oslo. Available online: http://www. riksantikvaren.no/filestore/Arkeologiske_kulturminner_ retningslinjer_budsjettering_2011.pdf. Last accessed 07.02.2013.

Riksantikvaren 2012: Veileder i saksbehandlingsrutiner. Available online: http://www.riksantikvaren.no/Norsk/ Veiledning/For_forvaltningen/Arkeologi/Veileder_-_ Arkeologi/. Last accessed 13.02.2013 .

Risbøl, O. - Smekalova, T. 2001: Archaeological survey and non-visible monuments - the use of magnetic prospecting in outfield archaeology. Nicolay 85, 32-45.

Risbøl, O. - Risan, T. - Bjørnstad, R. - Fretheim, S. - Eketuft Rygh, B.H. 2002: Kulturminner og kulturmiljø i Gråfjell, Regionfelt Østlandet, Åmot kommune i Hedmark: arkeologiske registreringer 2002, fase 4. NIKU publikasjoner 125, 1-201. Available online: http://www.

niku.no/filestore/Publikasjoner/NIKUPublikasjoner125. pdf. Last accessed 24.05.2013.

Stamnes, A.A. 2011: Georadar avdekker fortidsminner. Spor 1(11), 30-33.

Trinks, I. - Karlsson, P. - Westergaard, B. - Eder-Hinterleitner, A. - Larsson, L.I. 2007: Professional archaeological prospection - Borre Sites 1 & 2. Digital document.Vestfold Fylkeskommune.

Trinks, I. - Gansum, T. - Eder-Hinterleitner, A. 2010: Mapping iron-age graves in Norway using magnetic and GPR prospection. Antiquity (project gallery) 84.

Valetta 1992: European Convention on the Protection of the Archaeological Heritage. Valetta, 16.1.1992. Council of Europe. Available online: http://conventions.coe.int/ treaty/en/treaties/html/143.htm. Last visited: 17.02.2013.

Viberg, A. 2012: Remnant echoes of the past. Archaeological geophysical propection in Sweden. Doctoral Thesis in Archaeological Science at Stockholm University, Sweden.

Viberg, A. - Trinks, I. - Lidén, K. 2011: A review of the use of geophysical archaeological prospection in Sweden. Archaeological Prospection 18, 43-56.

Preservation Assessment of Ancient Theatres through Integrated Geophysical Technologies

A. Sarris, N. Papadopoulos, M.C. Salvi and S. Dederix

Abstract: *Recently, the restoration of ancient theatres has appealed to the local authorities and communities, as these ancient structures could host a number of modern performances that can attract the attention of the public and enhance the cultural activity of a region. On the other hand, the usage of an ancient theatre for such purposes needs to be approached with particular attention, depending on its stage of preservation (especially the preservation of the cunei (kerkides), seats and koilon) and the other monuments that might be in its vicinity. The topic is even more complicated if the theatre has not been systematically excavated and is partially covered by soil deposits.*

Geophysical prospection techniques can contribute to the preservation assessment of ancient theatres although they constitute a difficult survey target, mainly due to their topographical settings, terrain characteristics and architectural attributes. A suite of geophysical techniques such as Electrical Resistivity Tomography (ERT), Ground Penetrating Radar (GPR), Electromagnetic techniques, magnetic and electrical resistance prospection has been applied in a number of ancient theatres from various parts of Greece aiming to retrieve information concerning their status of preservation.

Keywords: *Ancient theatres - geophysical prospection - Greece - ancient maps - ERT - GPR - magnetics*

Introduction

Geophysical techniques are usually applied for mapping the horizontal extent or even the stratigraphy of archaeological sites (*Sarris et al. 2010; Lolos et al. 2012*), for investigating the geological or environmental settings of these sites and for risk assessment analysis (*Hayden et al. 2007; Papadopoulos et al. 2008*). Very few geophysical applications have been undertaken so far to acquire information regarding the preservation and integrity of monuments or historical buildings (*Soldovieri et al. 2008; Masini et al. 2010; Papadopoulos - Sarris 2011*) and even fewer are the reports dealing with the geophysical studies of theatres (*Aubry et al. 2001; Gaffney et al. 2007; Perez-Gracia et al. 2008*). This originates mainly from the intrinsic difficulty (such as abrupt slope, complexity of architecture, bad preservation status, a.o.) that the theatres impose for the application of subsurface surveying techniques.

A recent trend has been observed in Greece for the promotion and restoration of ancient theatres, stadiums, Odeons, and other venues for spectators and listeners (http://www.diazoma.gr). This effort has been also connected to the restoration of the monuments aiming, partially, to their re-use for public performances. Whatever the purpose, any kind of restoration planning needs to take into account the state of preservation and architectural integrity of the monuments. In this way, geophysical techniques can provide the means to portray the preserved architectural elements of the theatres in a non-destructive way, thereby contributing significantly to the excavation or restoration activities that can follow. This report demonstrates the potential of the geophysical methods in prospecting such monuments, by examining certain case studies from the area of Greece. Each case study has been approached in a different way, and in a few situations it was even possible to compare the geophysical survey results with plans made by historical travellers. Examples are drawn from the theatres of Dodoni, Sikyon, Ierapetra, Gortyna, a.o. and the results of the geophysical surveys – integrated and fused through GIS techniques – are discussed in correlation with the methodological approaches that have been applied in each case.

The Ancient Theatre of Dodoni, Epirus

The archaeological site of Dodoni is located in an alluvium valley about 22 km south of the city of Ioannina. The site has been inhabited since prehistoric times, flourishing during the later phases of the classical period. Relics of the ancient theatre, the temple of Dodonian Zeus and the famous oracle (the first of its kind in the ancient Greek world) constitute the most important monuments of the site.

The ancient theatre of Dodoni, one of the largest in Greece, has a capacity of 17,000 people. It was built in the 3rd century BC and consists of the auditorium, the orchestra, a Doric stoa and a proscenium. After its destruction by Aemilius Paulus in 167 BC it was turned into an arena. The theatre was established within a natural cavity, oriented towards the south and looking down the valley. A big retaining wall (analemma) was erected to hold the fill for the construction of the theatre. The east front of that wall was reinforced with two towers. The theatre itself consisted

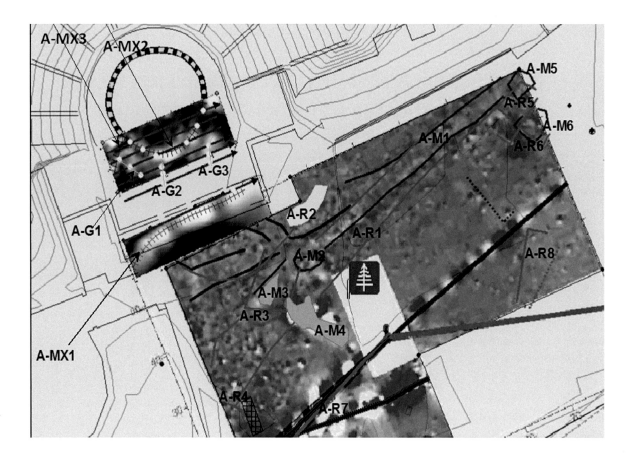

Fig. 1. Ancient Theatre of Dodoni. Presentation of the most significant geophysical anomalies identified within the orchestra and to the south of the ancient theatre. A-MX# corresponds to electrical multiplexer anomalies, A-M# to magnetic anomalies, and A-G# to GPR reflectors.

of the two-storey stage with a wooden proscenium and a Doric stoa, the semicircular orchestra and the koilon (the tiers for the spectators) (*Dakaris 1966, 76*). Outside the koilon two large staircases led the spectators to the upper landings of the theatre, while an arch opened onto the centre of the stage. The rock-cut koilon was divided into three landings (diazomata) with originally 55 rows of seats. Ten radial staircases divided the koilon into nine tiers. The upper part had intermediate staircases. At the top of the koilon was an exit for the audience. At the centre of the orchestra the base of Dionysus' altar (themele) was found.

The orchestra is encircled by a rock-cut drainage intended for the removal of rainwater from the orchestra and the koilon. The depth of the water drainage is 0.92 m and its width ranges from 0.48-0.50 m at the top to 0.60 m at the bottom. It is covered with eight stone slabs (0.65-0.75 m width) at regular distances of 3.00-3.60 m. During the performances, the gaps were covered with portable wooden constructions. The remaining part of the water drainage under the stage was subterranean and covered by big limestone slabs. The restoration of the theatre and the excavation of its surroundings are still in progress. In this context, geophysical works were undertaken in order to investigate the architectural relics that might be preserved in front of the theatre and to map the whole of the path of the water drainage below the orchestra.

Vertical magnetic gradient and soil resistance measurements acquired in the region south of the theatre were disturbed by the underlying water pipe network crossing the area of interest as well as other modern installations. On the other hand, a number of structural remains were pinpointed by the geophysical techniques, which include parts of the so-called "sacred road" (anomaly AM1 – Fig. 1) that leads from the Bouleutirion to the east entrance of the stadium. Remnants of the stone-paved sacred road have been brought to light by test trenches opened in the area between the Bouleuterion and house "O" (*Dakaris 1973, 88-89; 1985, 43*). A couple of architectural structures were also recognized at the eastern side of the sacred road (A-M5, A-M6) (*Sarris et al. 2004*).

Within the area of the ancient theatre, the projection of a well-preserved stone-built ditch of semicircular shape found at the north section of the orchestra was also explored through the use of soil resistance multiplexer (0.5, 1 and 2 m electrode spacing) and GPR techniques. A water tank was used to fill the drainage with water in an effort to detect signal differences before and after the water flux. The detected anomalies were well correlated and the ditch was found to continue its circular path within the orchestra. The absence of anomalies extending away from the theatre suggests that rainwater was concentrated inside the stone-built ditch, before being directed into the ground through karstic fissures similar to those visible at the west side of the theatre. An EKKO 1000 GPR using antennas of 225 MHz was employed for the verification of the shallow depth reflectors which may have been correlated with the theatre's drainage. After the enhancement of the original GPR data through the use of gain and high pass filters, radargrams were combined to produce a synthetic three-dimensional volumetric image representing the stratigraphy of the area of interest. The isolated slices of the subsurface verified that the drainage of the orchestra (anomaly A-MX2) most probably communicated with the drainage pipes of the stadium and the collected rainwater was directed towards lower ground formations through karstic fissures, below the stage and the proscenium. This is in perfect agreement with the results of the excavation that have not been able to find the location of any kind of artificial drainage system in the specific area (*Sarris et al. 2004*).

The Amphitheatre of Ierapetra (Ancient Ierapytna), Eastern Crete

The modern town of Ierapetra is located along the SE coast of the island of Crete. It was built over the remains of ancient Ierapytna, which flourished during the 2nd century BC. The power of Ierapytna reached its apex during Roman times, when the city was provided with monumental buildings such as theatres, temples, thermae, administrative buildings, etc. Very few of these buildings now remain, as many were destroyed either by past earthquakes or by the modern construction activities.

Evidence of the location of some of the ancient buildings is provided by plans of the British Vice-Admiral Thomas Spratt (1811-1888). Among others, Spratt pinpointed the location of the two theatres and the amphitheatre that existed in the town, even though the particular monuments were then no longer as well preserved as they were in 1590 when the Italian traveler Onorio Belli drew detailed plans of the ancient structures still standing at Ierapytna (*Falkener*

1854). Still, the rectification of Spratt's original map based on various landmarks, crossroads and the coastline, made the identification possible of the approximate location of these monuments in the current landscape, within a margin of error of less than 5 m (*Sarris et al. 2011*).

One of the targets of the geophysical prospection was the mapping of the hypothesized location of the ancient amphitheatre. According to Onorio Belli, the amphitheatre was situated between two little hills having six buttresses of solid masonry built at each extremity to provide an oval shape necessary for the construction (*Falkener 1854*). Unfortunately, Belli's plan has been lost and even worse, the recent (1960s-1970s) construction of the "Minos" oil and soap production factory has probably destroyed all the surface architectural relics. Later, the factory was demolished and the area was levelled to be used as a municipal parking lot.

Obviously, for the above reason, the magnetic results were obscured by the collapsed foundations of the factory, back-filled soil and other scattered metal fragments. On the other hand, the employment of GPR (resolution of 0.5 x 0.05 m) and ERT (resolution of 1 x 1 m) proved useful in scanning most of the area, reaching the deeper layers of the ground and providing a detailed 3D reconstruction of the subsurface in the form of slices with increasing depth. The ERT depth slices were extracted by the 3-D resistivity model in which the inversion algorithm converged after seven iterations with a RMS=3.2 %. The upper depth anomalies (less than 1 m) were attributed to the residues of the structural remains of the factory, while the deeper features were examined in detail and in correlation with the rectified amphitheatre's plan. According to the GPR depth slices, an almost semicircular area oriented in an NW-SE direction extends up to three meters below the surface (Fig. 2). Parts of this anomaly were also observed with the 3-D ERT technique and the concave shape of the feature could be correlated with the western part of the amphitheatre's

Fig. 2. Overlay of GPR and ERT depth slices on the satellite image of the area where the amphitheatre of Ierapetra is located. a) GPR depth slice 2.9-3.0 m. b) ERT depth slice 2.5-3.0 m. The ERT depth slices represent the resistivity in Ohm-m and were extracted from the 3-D final resistivity inversion model (minimum=3, maximum=1000, average=93 Ohm-m).

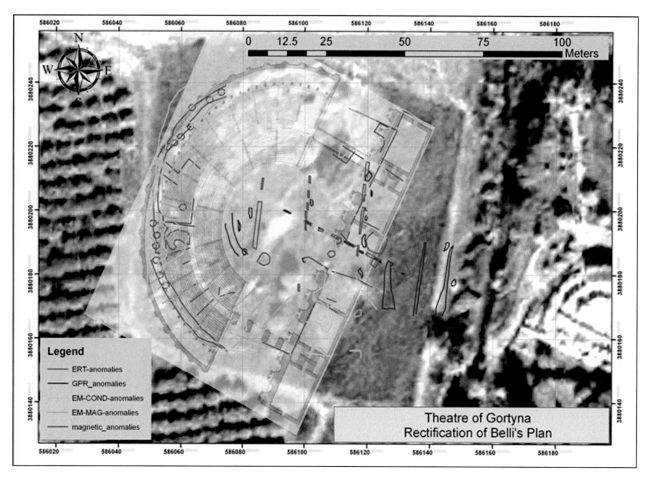

Fig. 3. Theatre of Gortyna. Superposition of the geophysical interpretation maps over Belli's plans. The fusion of the two datasets, together with the excavated or surface relics, has been able to provide a more integrated image of the current stage of preservation of the monument.

orchestra within an error margin of 5-7 metres – which equals the approximate error of the plan's rectification. Another feature to the east of this anomaly might correspond to the eastern side of the orchestra and part of the cunei. Similar kinds of reflectors, corresponding to high resistivity anomalies, were observed to radiate outwards from the centre of the orchestra, which is reminiscent of the underground drainage elements that have been found in other well-preserved amphitheatres, such as the one of Pozzuolli in Italy (*Taylor 2003,* fig. 37). The above converge to increase our confidence for finding again the position of the amphitheatre.

The Theatre of Gortyna, Central Crete

Onorio Belli also left drawings of the large theatre of Gortyna. Gortyna was one of the largest cities of Crete during Roman times, with a population of more than 100,000 inhabitants, and it became the seat of the first Christian bishop of the island. The city hosted three theatres, but Belli's drawings provide only details for the largest of these. The latter, c. 100-105 m in diameter, rested against the curved hill slopes and its koilon was subdivided into two diazomata. The radius of the orchestra was estimated to be c. 20 m and a large stage (c. 100 m long) was also outlined in Belli's plans at a distance of c. 20-25 m from

the orchestra. According to the Italian traveller, the river Lithaios shaped a curved terrace about 200 paces in size (i.e. 320 m) behind the stage, which is still visible nowadays. This curved section of the river was continuous and was shaped by big stones without mortar, in a similar way to the opposite bank of the river (*Falkener 1854, 20-21*).

Indeed, geophysical investigations proved that the koilon and the seats of the theatre are conserved for more than 10 m below the upper diazoma, which is also well preserved (Fig. 3). GPR readings provided evidence regarding the limits of the lower diazoma, while magnetic and electromagnetic measurements indicated a number of concentric linear anomalies that may be correlated to stairs between the different diazomata. The same techniques provided evidence for columns and vertical retaining walls at the upper diazoma. To the east, ERT and magnetic measurements revealed sections of a large linear anomaly that could correspond with the stage of the theatre. Further to the east, GPR and ERT data suggested two parallel features possibly outlining the direction of a N-S street (8 m wide) that seems to extend to the curvilinear terrace formed along the Lithaios river, exactly as mentioned in Belli's diaries. The above is also in agreement with the urban planning of the ancient city that followed the hippodamian system. Conductivity measurements also testified to past flooding events that could have resulted in drifting away of parts of the architecture (especially the eastern walls of the stage) that was mentioned by Belli.

The Theatre of Sikyon, Peloponnese

Beside plans and drawings, ancient visitors also provided us with some written descriptions and testimonies regarding archaeological sites and theatres. This is the case with the town of Sikyon (near ancient Corinth) whose architectural relics are known thanks to the writings of *Dodwell (1819, 293-297), Leake (1830, 355-373), Curtius (1851-1852, 483-498)* and *Frazer (1898* III, 45 and 546-549). Archaeological research was resumed in Sikyon in 2004 under the direction of the University of Thessaly, in collaboration with the 37th Ephorate of Prehistoric and Classical Antiquities, the Institute of Mediterranean Studies and the University of York. The aim of the Sikyon Survey Project is the study of the architectural remains of the ancient urban centre through a combined use of intensive surface survey, geophysical prospection, geo-archaeological survey and rescue excavations. The vast (33 hectares) geophysical survey was able to reconstruct the urban plan of the Hellenistic and Roman city, providing details of the structural remains of temples, porticoes, a basilica, street lines, houses and industrial installations. It is worth mentioning that the location and characteristics of all these monuments match the description of modern travellers.

The theatre of Sikyon, which constituted one of the main targets of the geophysical survey, was constructed at the end of the 4th century BC against the natural and relatively abrupt slopes of a hill to the west of the agora. With an orchestra c. 20 m in diameter and a cavea c. 120 m wide, it is one the largest ancient theatres to be preserved. It comprises about six tiers of seats, while the auditorium is divided by two diazomata into three sections. Two vaulted passages (c. 16 m long and 2.6 m high) erected at both sides of the theatre were intended to provide access to the upper series of seats (diazoma). Most of the seats were carved into the rock and they are considered to have porous slabs on top (*Fossum 1905*).

In order to examine the state of preservation of the seats, which are currently covered by a thin layer of soil eroded from the upper plateau, the main cavea was investigated through the use of GPR techniques. It was hoped that seats having a porous slab cover could produce reflection anomalies at the interface between the porous slabs and the carved seats. For this reason, nineteen GPR transects were laid out, starting from the upper level of seats towards the lower section up to the wall that separates the cavea from the orchestra. Adjacent transects were c. 5-7 m apart on the upper level, while they converged in the orchestra. Due to the high slope of the cavea, the GPR NogginPlus cart with 225 MHz antennas was tied with a rope, sliding slowly towards the bottom, while two persons were driving it along the proper direction and holding it in contact with the ground.

Processing of the individual radargrams was carried out on the basis of a 0.09 m/nsec estimate of the propagation velocity of the GPR electromagnetic waves. In order to avoid deformations due to the interpolation of measurements (large separation between transects compared to the 0.05 m sampled along the transects), the construction of depth slices was avoided. Instead, each radargram was independently rectified and overlaid on the topographical plan thanks to the GPS measurements that had been taken at the beginning and the end points of each profile (Fig. 4). A detailed study of each radargram led to the identification of specific reflectors that were marked on

Fig. 4. Theatre of Sikyon. Left: Details of the survey in the cavea of the theatre. The abrupt sloping surface of the cavea was scanned with almost concentric GPR profiles, having the cart of NogginPlus GPR unit tied to a rope for sliding slowly downhill towards the orchestra of the theatre. Right: Diagrammatic representation of the GPR reflectors (in white) identified in each GPR profile within the cavea of the theatre of Sikyon. The particular anomalies were overlaid on the topographic plan of the theatre indicating that a large section of the porous covered seats are in situ and located along the different levels (as is suggested by the iso-elevation lines) of the diazomata.

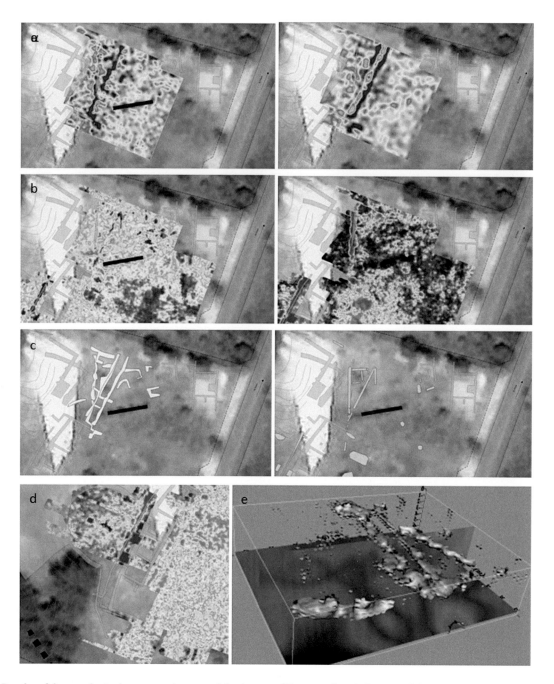

Fig. 5. Results of the geophysical survey to the west of the theatre of Demetriada: a) Horizontal depth slices (depths z=0.5-1 m (left) and z=1-1.5 m (right)) of the 3D geoelectrical inversion model. b) Horizontal slices of the GPR at depths of Z=0.32-0.42 m (left) and Z=0.76-0.85 m (right). c) Diagrammatic representation of the geoelectric (left) and GPR (right) anomalies. d) GPR reflectors for the region of the stage. Strong reflectors appear in front of the entrances of the stage and behind it (representing most probably earlier construction phases. e) The 3D geoelectric volumetric model of the double wall found at the NE projection of the southern wall of the stage.

the plan of the theatre. Most of these reflectors originate from subsurface disturbances within the first 0.5-1 m from the current inclined surface of the cavea. A diagrammatic representation of these anomalies indicated that most of them are located along different iso-elevation lines, which suggests that a large number of the seats of the theatre remain in situ (with or without a small lateral displacement).

The Theatre of Demetriada, Volos

The city of Demetriada was constructed around 294-292 BC to support the Macedonian navy fleet. The strategic

importance of the city is still evident today nowadays by the strong fortification walls that enclose a large area in the region of Pefkakia and Nees Pagases. The city experienced significant growth and blossoming in the Roman period. W. Leake was the first to recognize the existence of the theatre in 1809 and excavations took place periodically from 1907. The theatre was constructed at the same time as the foundation of the city, it went out of use during the 1st century BC and the 1st century AD, and it was definitely abandoned after the 4th century AD to be used only as a quarry for extraction of building material for Christian basilicas in the area (*Intsesiloglou 2010*).

Magnetic, GPR and ERT techniques were employed for mapping the subsurface in the orchestra and the stage of the theatre, together with the area extending to the south of the building. A number of features were recognized by the magnetic techniques, including older excavation trenches and a series of pillars of the stoa of the proscenium. The different occupation phases of the area were reconstructed through the employment of various geophysical techniques and, more particularly, through the use of GPR and 3D ERT (Fig. 5). Orthogonal features oriented in a S-N direction can be correlated to the excavated ceramic workshop, which was probably constructed over a large section of the theatre after its final abandonment. The suspected built space forms a triangular complex, c. 28 by 14 m in size and located between 2 and 2.5 m below the surface. Similarly, linear features oriented in a NE-SW direction seem to run parallel to the stage of the theatre, suggesting therefore earlier phases of construction. GPR measurements testified to the existence of the altar of Thymele in the centre of the orchestra and various internal divisions inside the stage, probably also pointing to an earlier construction phase. Furthermore, a series of strong reflectors around the northern side of the theatre proved the projection and the relative good conservation of a supporting wall that was constructed at the northern side of the koilon.

Final Remarks

The examples presented here demonstrate clearly the potential of geophysical approaches in mapping the architectural relics of ancient theatres. Either well preserved or not, completely buried or still standing, the geophysical techniques make it possible to identify structural elements, evaluate the degree of preservation of the monuments, and rediscover the location of the associated features that form the theatrical complex. Obviously, a single methodology is not sufficient to clarify all the subsurface features, as these may vary in terms of dimensions, depths, and composition or typology. For this reason, the efficiency of geophysical prospection relies on the combined use of different techniques and fieldwork procedures that provide a chance to recover a maximum of information regarding these complex structures. It is only through this manifold approach (*Sarris 2012*) (with a non-destructive intervention) that we can obtain the necessary feedback for any kind of subsequent excavation or restoration work aimed at the promotion of these significant monuments.

References

Aubry, L. - Benech, C. - Marmet, E. - Hesse, A. 2001: Recent Achievements and Trends of Research for Geophysical Prospection of Archaeological Sites. Journal of Radioanalytical and Nuclear Chemistry 247(3), 621-628.

Curtius, F. 1851-1852: Peloponnesos I-II, Gotha.

Dakaris, I.S. 1966: The Sanctuary of Dodoni. Arxaiologiko Deltion 22, 71-84.

Dakaris, I.S. 1973: The Sanctuary of Dodoni. Arxaiologiko Deltion 29, 87-98.

Dakaris I. S. 1985: Anaskafi Dodonis, Praktika Archaiologikis Etaireias, 140: 39-44.

Dodwell, E. 1819: Tour through Greece, II. London.

Falkener, E. 1854: A Description of some important Theatres and other remains in Crete, from a MS. History of Candia by Onorio Belli in 1586, Being a Supplement to the "Museum of Classical Antiquities, London, Trubner & Co., 12 Paternoster Row, 1854, 20-21.

Fossum, A. 1905: The Theatre at Sikyon. American Journal of Archaeology 9(3), 263-276.

Frazer, J.G. 1898: Pausanias's Description of Greece, I-VI, London, 1989.

Gaffney, C. - Goodchild, H. - Harrison, S. 2007: Geophysical and Topographical Survey of the Theatre at Ancient Sparta. Birmingham Archaeology Report, PN 1643.

Hayden, B. - Bassiakos, Y. - Kalpaxis, Th. - Sarris, A. - Tsipopoulou, M. 2007: A New Exploration of Priniatikos Pyrgos: Primary Harbor Settlement and Emporium of the Vrokastro Survey Region, In: P.P. Betancourt – M.C. Nelson – H. William eds, Krinoi kai Limenes: Studies in Honor of Joseph and Maria Shaw, Instap Academic Press, Philadelphia, Pennsylvania, 93-100.

Intsesiloglou, M. 2010: Archai Theatra in Thessaly, Volos.

Leake, W.M. 1830: Travels in the Morea III. London.

Lolos, A. - Gourley, B. - Sarris, A. - Hayward, C. - Trainor, C. - Kiriatzi, E. - Papadopoulos, N. 2012: Surveying the Sikyonian Plateau: integrated approach to the study of an ancient cityscape, Πρακτικά 5ου Συμποσίου Ελληνικής Αρχαιομετρικής Εταιρείας. In: Ν. Ζαχαριάς - Μ. Γεωργακοπούλου - Κ. Πολυκρέτη - Γ. Φακορέλλης - Θ. Βάκουλης eds, Εκδόσεις Παπαζήση, Αθήνα 2012, 101-116.

Masini, N. - Persico, R. - Rizzo, R. 2010: Some examples of GPR prospecting for monitoring of the monumental heritage. Journal of Geophysical Engineering 7, 190-199.

Papadopoulos, N. - Sarris, A. 2011: Integrated geophysical survey to characterize the subsurface properties below and around the area of Saint Andreas church (Loutraki, Greece), Proceedings of the 14th International Congress "Cultural Heritage and New Technologies", 643-652.

Papadopoulos, N. - Yi, M.-J. - Sarris, A. - Kim J.-H. 2008: Archaeological Investigations in Urban Areas through Combined Application of Surface ERT and GPR Techniques, Korean Conference on Geophysics.

Pérez-Gracia, V. - García, F. - Pujades, L. - Drigo, R.G. - Di Capua, D. 2008: GPR survey to study the restoration of a Roman monument. Journal of Cultural Heritage 9 (1), 89-96.

Sarris, A. 2012: Multi+ or Manifold Geophysical Prospection? Computer applications and Quantitative methods in Archaeology 2012. University of Southampton.

Sarris, A. - Papadopoulos, N.G. - Stamatis, G. - Kouriati, K. - Elvanidou, M. - Katifori, M. - Kaskanioti, M. 2004: Geophysical Investigations at the ancient theatre of Dodoni, N. Greece. Invited paper - International Conference on Remote Sensing Archaeology, Beijing, China.

Sarris, A. – Galaty, M. – Yerkes, R. – Parkinson, W. – Gyucha, A. – Billingsley, D. – Tate, R. 2010: Investigation of Hungarian Early Copper Age Settlements through Magnetic Prospection and Soil Phosphate Techniques. In: F. Niccolucci – S. Hermon eds, Beyond the Artifact: Digital Interpretation of the Past, Proceedings of CAA2004, Prato, Italy, 13-17 April, 2004, Archaeolingua, 469-472.

Sarris, A. - Seferou, P. - Kokkinou, E. - Papadopoulos, N. 2011: Geophysical Prospection as a way of confirming older topographic plans and descriptions of archaeological sites. Proceedings of the 14th International Congress "Cultural Heritage and New Technologies", 234-245.

Soldovieri, F. - Bavusi, M. - Giocoli, A. - Piscitelli, S. - Crocco, L. - Vallianatos, F. - Soupios, P. - Sarris, A. 2008: A comparison between two GPR data processing techniques for fracture detection and characterization. 70th EAGE Conference and Exhibition incorporating SPE EUROPEC 2008, Rome.

Taylor, R. 2003: Roman Builders: A study in architectural process. Cambridge University Press.

Mapping the Archaeological Landscape of Palaepaphos through Remote Sensing Techniques

A. Sarris, N. Papadopoulos, M.C. Salvi, E. Seferou and A. Agapiou

Abstract: *The archaeological landscape of Palaepaphos in S.W. Cyprus has been the subject of topographical, geophysical surveys and archaeological excavations for the past five years. The latest fieldwork campaigns were carried out under the auspices of an applied research project funded by the University of Cyprus, entitled "A Long-Term Response to the Need to Make Modern Development and the Preservation of the Archaeo-Cultural Record Mutually Compatible Operations - Pilot Application at Kouklia-Palaipaphos (CYPRUS)". During the geophysical surveys of 2007 and 2010, more than 70,000 square metres located at various sections of the site were covered through the combined use of Ground Penetrating Radar (GPR), soil resistance and magnetic techniques. Most striking of all the detected geophysical disturbances was a number of very intense magnetic anomalies (measured and confirmed by two different fluxgate gradiometers). However, a number of geophysical anomalies resulting from the geophysical surveys were of no archaeological value since excavations indicated that most of the particular targets were of geological origin or were caused by heavily disturbed layers.*

In the light of the results of these preliminary excavations, a different approach has been applied. First, a large area at Arkalon, one of the most promising areas from a geophysical point of view, was re-surveyed through a combination of methods including GPR and magnetic methods, the latter producing exactly the same signature as the previous surveys. Second, spectral signatures - covering both visible and near-infrared spectrum- were retrieved using a handheld spectroradiometer. These measurements were obtained in specific grids and were compared to the geophysical maps. Although geophysical results have been able to pinpoint again areas of archaeological interest, they have raised more questions regarding the origin of the anomalies observed in the site of Palaepaphos.

Keywords: *Palaepaphos Cyprus - remote sensing - geophysical prospection - GPR - magnetics - spectroradiometer*

Introduction

The diverse remote sensing methods applied in the site of Palaepaphos in S.W. Cyprus (Fig. 1a) comprise an individual research module completed under the framework of a three-year (2007-2010) scientific project: "*A Long-Term Response to the Need to Make Modern Development and the Preservation of the Archaeo-Cultural Record Mutually Compatible Operations. Pilot Application at Kouklia-Palaipaphos (CYPRUS)*", funded by the Department of History and Archaeology, Archaeological Research Unit, of the University of Cyprus. The aim of the project was to determine a number of procedures for an effective management of the archaeological landscape in Palaepaphos where development plans that may significantly alter the environmental regime are foreseen.

The area of Palaepaphos comprises the pilot region that integrates a number of different methodologies. These range from the application of geophysical methods to reconstruction of buried archaeological structures, the execution of small-scale excavations in selected sites, the compilation of three-dimensional digital base maps and digital elevation models, and the construction of a multidimensional GIS platform in order to combine the mapping with the archaeological information through a geo-database. This will result in an effective tool for the cultural resources management and development of the area.

A remote sensing survey consisting of geophysical and spectroradiometer methods was completed in two field seasons during 2007 and 2010. The geophysical investigations covered an area of more than 70,000 square metres in various places (*Marchello, Mantissa, Evreti, Arkalon, Hadjiabdullah, Laona*) employing electrical resistance, magnetic gradiometry and ground penetrating radar (GPR) methods (Fig. 1a, b). The geophysical survey emphasized the detailed subsurface mapping utilizing high density sampling (1 m for electrical resistance, 0.5 m for magnetic gradiometry, and 0.1 m for GPR). In situ spectroradiometric measurements were also applied to measure the canopy/soil reflectance over a specific area which aroused significant archaeological interest during the 2010 season.

The GPP package (*Kalokerinos et al. 2004*) was used to process the gradiometer and resistance data. Processing options of the GPP include geometry correction of the grids, evaluation of statistical parameters, mutation of dummy values and shifting of the X, Y coordinates, application of de-spiking techniques based on the noise level, grid equalization and line equalization. At the last processing

Fig. 1. a) Location of the pilot region in Palaepaphos in the southwest of Cyprus (Eastern Mediterranean). b) Area that was covered by the diverse geophysical methods during the 2007 field season. c) Layout of the geophysical grids in the area of Arkalon that was surveyed in 2010.

stage kriging interpolation was used for gridding the data and compiling the final maps.

Initially the GPR sections were calibrated by estimating the first peak in order to define the initial useful signal from each line. The line equalization of the radargrams based on the selected first peak was followed, trying to bring the first reflections of each line in a common starting time. Then the application of AGC, Dewow and DCshift filters enhanced the reflected signal, while rejection of the background noise and data smoothing was accomplished by a trace-to-trace averaging filter. Finally, horizontal depth slices at different depth levels were created by the original vertical sections assuming a velocity for the electromagnetic waves equal to 0.1 m/nsec.

Results of the Geophysical Survey

Marchello

The western part of *Marchello* hill was surveyed with the magnetic gradiometry method and the GPR technique was also applied to part of the area. The vertical magnetic gradiometry values ranged from -1032 to 974 nT/m, indicating possible metallic objects and after the application of de-spiking filters the values were compressed to +/- 50 nT/m. The majority of the linear anomalies came from the magnetic measurements. However the soil cultivation and erosion contaminated the magnetic data with noise, and among the geophysical anomalies MAR-30 and MAR-31 areas were considered to be the most prominent to indicate buried architectural relics (Fig. 2c).

Architectural relics of a 3.5 metre wide wall were excavated at the north-western part of *Marchello*. The most intense magnetic anomalies are located around the areas MAR-8, 9, 11, 16, 17, having a dipole nature and affecting an area of 30-50 square metres around the dipole. The systematic NE-SW orientation and the intensity of these dipole anomalies are either correlated with burned residues or with the presence of metal fragments. Ploughing and cultivation activities were the cause of the linear anomalies MAR-10 and MAR-14 recorded on magnetic and GPR maps. The inner and outer part of anomaly MAR-8 appears

with a square and round shape respectively which is also confirmed by the resistance and GPR readings. Anomalies MAR-5 (also evident on the resistance map) and MAR-7 are caused by the roots of a nearby tree and a pile of stones respectively. The high intensity reflectors MAR-21 and MAR-20 coincide with the direction of paths leading to the archaeological site (Fig. 2a, b). Furthermore, GPR was applied in areas where scattered metal fragments prevented the application of the magnetic method. MAR-22 shows the continuation of the excavated wall, while MAR-24 indicates an even longer and larger wall. This latter wall reaches an area to the east with indications of strong reflectors probably related to poor conservation residues (Fig. 2d).

Mantissa

The hill of Mantissa was surveyed with magnetic and resistance methods, while GPR covered only a small portion of the site without any significant results (mapping mainly the superficial rocky basement). The measurements of the vertical magnetic gradient in the site exhibited a noteworthy phenomenon, where the registered values exceeded the dynamic range of two different fluxgate magnetometers (Bartington G601 range +/- 3000 nT/m; Geoscan Research FM256 range +/- 207.4 nT/m.). There is no clear justification for the particular measurements since the area was clear of any modern surface features (e.g. metal fences or objects) or any other archaeological features (e.g. kilns). One possibility is that they are caused by large quantities of metal artefacts in underground tombs. However, this cannot explain the large size of the anomalies and their extensive distribution. An alternative explanation lies in the geological origin of the anomalies due to the existence of volcanic rocks rich in ferrous minerals. Preliminary measurements of the magnetic susceptibility tend to support the latter hypothesis. The distribution of the various magnetic anomalies with its codes in Mantissa is shown in figure 3a.

Evreti

The superficial anthropogenic layer, up to 30 cm below the ground surface, was disturbed due to ploughing which has having similar effects to the underlying architectural relics.

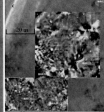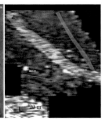

Fig. 2. a) Diagrammatic interpretation of the geophysical anomalies in the north of Marchello where the arrows indicate the most prominent anomalies. b) Electrical resistance map of the area of Marchello. c) Combined diagrammatic interpretation of the magnetic, resistance and GPR anomalies in the western part of Marchello overlain on the magnetic map. d) GPR slice at a depth of 100 cm below the surface in the area of Marchello.

Fig. 3. a) Diagrammatic interpretation of the magnetic anomalies in the area of Mantissa where the arrows indicate the most probable archaeological features. b) Magnetic anomalies and diagrammatic interpretation in the area of Evreti.

Older excavations in this area revealed the foundations of a large building occupying an area of 25 by 20 metres. To the east in the outer area of the building a Late Bronze Age grave was (*Maier and Wartburg 1985*, 113-117).

The magnetic measurements seem to be noisier to the west where the elevation decreases and the degree of erosion increases. Anomalies EV-1 (~42 m), EV-5, EV-6, EV-7 (~54 m), EV-9 (~26 m) and EV23 are linear without indicating a regular orientation. Some of them extend over a large distance and some others (EV-5, EV-23 and EV-6/EV-9) cross each other. Furthermore, anomalies EV-16 and EV-17 show a continuation of architectural relics revealed by older excavations. Some isolated anomalies (EV-2, 3, 8) affect an area with a 5 m diameter and are probably caused by metal fragments buried very close to the ground surface. Among the geophysical anomalies, the areas indicated by EV-5, EV-7, EV-9 and EV-23 are considered of high priority for future investigation with excavation trenches (Fig. 3b).

Hadjiabdullah

The past excavations in *Hadjiabdullah* have revealed parts of a fortification wall (length ~ 60 m) in a S-N direction, including a rectangular tower. The tower was constructed in

the inner side of the wall during the Cyprus-Archaic Period (c. 600 - 475 BC) covering an area of 42 by 43 metres which is rather unusual for these kinds of buildings. During Classical times it was renovated and finally destroyed around 300 BC (*Maier and Wartburg 1985,* 106-107).

The magnetic results (Fig. 4a) show similarities with those in *Mantissa* since there are magnetic regions where the magnetic instruments recorded over-ranged magnetic gradient values caused most probably by outcrops of rocks rich in ferrous minerals. The most significant anomalies in terms of archaeological interest are recorded in HA-3, HA-8, HA-7, HA-10 and HA-11, where HA-10 shows a more geometrical shape. Anomalies HA-12 and HA-13 in the NE and NW also exhibit a particular interest. On the other hand, GPR results were quite disappointing since the superficial rocky basement masked any linear anomalies that could be attributed to archaeological structures (Fig. 4b).

Arkalon

The experimental magnetic measurements during the 2007 field campaign resulted in significant information regarding the mapping of archaeological remains. A NE-SW rectangular structure measuring 10 by 12 metres

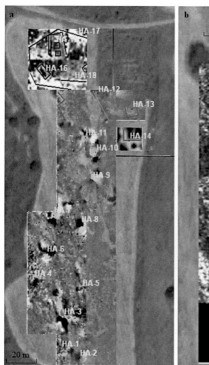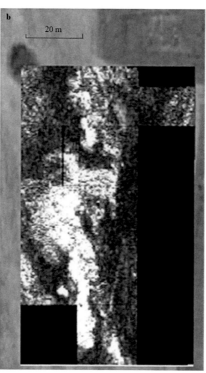

Fig. 4. Hadjiabdullah area: a) Interpretation of the magnetic anomalies in the area. b) GPR depth slice of 50cm below the ground surface.

(AR-1) extends to the north. The linear characteristics AR-3 and AR-5 form a rectangular feature extending to more than 70 metres in a northerly and easterly direction, in a similar orientation as AR-1. In the south of the AR-2 linear anomaly, a 10 by 15 metre magnetic anomalous region (dynamic range +/- 80 nT/m) is recorded, indicating probable burning residues (Fig. 5).

Despite these encouraging geophysical anomalies the initial excavation trenches which were opened during 2010 did not yield the anticipated results, apart from the location of some isolated rocks. To address this issue, a more extensive survey was completed during 2010 which covered again the same area as the 2007 survey (Fig. 5). Magnetic results of the 2010 season were of comparable accuracy to those of the 2007 survey regarding the overlapped region, while similar linear northeast-southwest anomalies are outlined in the central area of *Arkalon*. The central region appears with intense magnetic anomalies and the linear segments outline a large rectangular area measuring 41 by 41 metres. The registered dipole magnetic anomalies are probably caused by older terraces or other geological or modern characteristics (Fig. 5a).

GPR results partly confirmed the magnetic prospection survey regarding the overlapped area of the 2007 and 2010 field campaigns, and at the same time the GPR survey was quite successful in mapping some small-scale archaeological targets. Two areas aroused most interest due to a larger density of detected anomalies. The first of these (Area A) is located in the northern and central part of the investigated section. This part shows some interesting strong reflection signals forming a fuzzy picture. This can lead to the conclusion of either a great stratigraphic disturbance

or a poor preservation status of the subsurface structures. On the other hand, Area B is composed of a substantial number of linear anomalies in a NE-SW direction and with the same orientation as the already excavated features. These structures show a further continuation to the south and are probably related to the extension of the structured environment in the specific region (Fig. 5b).

Ground Hyperspectral Data

Ground spectroradiometric techniques have been applied already in a number of remote sensing approaches such as vegetation canopy reflectance modelling, spectral mixture analysis, classification techniques or even predictive modelling for a range of applications. Field spectroscopy involves not only the acquisition of accurate reflectance measurements but also the study of the interrelationships between the spectral characteristics of objects and their biophysical attributes in the field environment (*Milton 1987*). Therefore, it can provide valuable information on an area, considering the fact that the human eye senses only a small part of the electromagnetic spectrum, from approximately 400 to 700 nm, whereas field spectroscopy in support of remote sensing operates in a wider spectral range to include the near infrared. In situ spectroradiometric measurements can be used for measuring the canopy/soil reflectance over areas with archaeological interest. These instruments measure the amount of energy (radiance) reflected from a ground area for a range of wavelengths and these measurements can then be converted to reflectance values using calibration panels.

A calibrated hand-held spectroradiometer was used to retrieve ground "truth" data from a single grid of the

Fig. 5. a) Overlay of the magnetic map composed of the 2010 field survey on the aerial photo of Arkalon area, and diagrammatic interpretation of the linear magnetic anomalies. The white polygon outlines the overlapped area which was surveyed during the 2007 and 2010 field campaigns. b) Overlay of the GPR slice of 50 cm depth from the 2010 field survey on the aerial photo of Arkalon area, and diagrammatic interpretation of strong GPR reflections. Grid 50 where the experimental ground spectroradiometric measurements were taken is outlined with the black square.

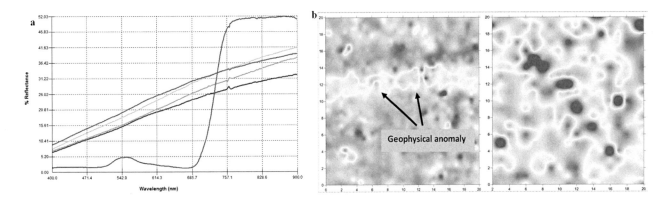

Fig. 6. a) Soil spectral signatures from the Arkalon locality. b) Geophysical anomalies (left) and TSAVI images (right) resulting from spectroradiometer measurements related to Grid 50.

geophysical squares. These data were acquired with a GER 1500 field spectroradiometer covering a range from 400 nm – 1050 nm. A reference calibrated spectralon panel was used to measure the incoming solar radiation. The spectralon panel ($\approx$100% reflectance) measurements were used as a reference. In order to avoid any errors due to significant changes in the prevailing atmospheric conditions, the measurements over the panel and the target were taken within a short time of each other. In this case it is assumed that irradiance had not significantly changed which is true for non-hazy days (*Milton et al. 2009*).

The primary aim of these measurements was to compare the results with the geophysical anomalies and therefore to detect any possible soil marks since the measurements were taken over dry soil before the seeding period. Crop marks had been verified already with previous geophysical surveys (see *Agapiou et al. 2010*). In this field campaign more than 400 spectroradiometric measurements have been acquired at a specific grid (Fig. 5a). All the measurements were taken from nadir view, from a height of 1.2 m using a 4° FOV lens. The measurements were acquired between 10 am and 2 pm (local time) in order to minimize the impact of illumination changes on the spectral responses.

The spectral signatures profiles taken over bare soil did not reveal any sub-surface anomalies. As indicated in figure 6a, soil profiles are similar to each other, without any difference at the VIS and VNIR spectrum. Moreover, although different equations and filtering algorithms were applied (e.g. Normalized Difference Vegetation Index - NDVI, Simple Ratio - SR, Transformed Soil Adjusted Vegetation Index – TSAVI, etc.), spectroradiometric results were not able to confirm the geophysical anomalies. This may be a result of the soil composition of the area since soil marks are formed whenever a different soil is used to fill in a ditch or road, and this "filler" soil is different enough in composition to distinctly contrast with the in situ soil. Soil marks are therefore related to soil chemistry, organic material content and soil texture. All these characteristics affect the reflectance taken from a spectroradiometer (Fig. 6b). In our case, the bare soil and the absence of vegetation seem not to have created any substantial signal to register radiometrically.

Final Remarks

The survey in Palaepaphos through remote sensing methods managed to provide an integrated picture of the buried archaeological structures for an area covering more than 70,000 square metres. The combined application of diverse geophysical methodologies (magnetic gradiometry, electrical resistance, ground penetrating radar) complemented with experimental ground hyperspectral data was crucial in the integrated interpretation of the geophysical anomalies, the reconstruction of the settlement of the region and the assessment of their preservation degree. The results are encouraging in terms of the valuable archaeological information that was retrieved and can be used in future excavation activities. Besides the geophysical anomalies which exhibited a clear archaeological signature, the extreme magnetic anomalies in *Mantissa* and *Hadjiabdullah* are probably caused by rocks or soils rich in ferrous minerals. The geological origin of these anomalies can be justified by their non-geometric shape, the lack of a specific orientation and the absence of any dipole nature, but further investigation through chemical analyses of samples should be made to verify this hypothesis. Finally, the spectroradiometry method proved insufficient to distinguish any archaeological targets, probably due to the presence of bare soil and absence of vegetation.

References

Agapiou, A. - Hadjimitsis, D.G. - Sarris, A. - Themistocleous, K. - Papadavid, G. 2010: Hyperspectral ground truth data for the detection of buried architectural remains. Lecture Notes of Computer Science 6436, 318-331.

Kalokerinos, G. – Kokinou, E. - Sarris, A. - Vallianatos, F. 2004: GPP: A Program To automate the geophysical data processing of the 1st International Conference on Advances in Mineral Resources Management and Environmental Geotechnology, AMIREG 2004, Chania – Crete, Greece.

Maier, F.G. - Wartburg, M.L.V. 1985: Reconstructing history from the earth, c. 2800 B.C. - 1600 A.D.: Excavating at Palaepaphos, 1960–1985. In: V. Karageorghis ed., Archaeology in Cyprus 1960-1985, 142-172, Nicosia: A.G. Leventis Foundation.

Milton, J. 1987: Principles of field spectroscopy. Remote Sensing of Environment 8, 12, 1807-1827.

Milton, J. - Schaepman, M.E. - Anderson, K. - Kneubühler, M. - Fox, N. 2009: Progress in field spectroscopy. Remote Sensing of Environment 113, 92-109.

Non-destructive Survey on Fortified Settlement in Wicina, Jasień Commune, Lubuskie Voivodeship, Poland

Michał Bugaj

Abstract: *The paper presents the results of a non-destructive survey performed in November 2010 on the Early Iron Age fortified settlement in Wicina, Jasień commune, Żary county, lubuskie voivodeship. The scope of fieldwork consisted of: geophysical prospection, geodetic measurements (including microrelief of the site), aerial photographs and a digital 3D model of the prehistoric settlement relic. The research results constitute a significant contribution to our knowledge about this unique archaeological site. Verification of its extent showed a great discrepancy in relation to what had been determined so far. The registered geophysical anomalies and the humidity determinants are evidence of the still existing relics of the hillfort superstructure. The author attempts also to reconstruct the settlement layout.*

Keywords: *archaeology – Poland – Early Iron Age – Lusatian culture – fortified settlement – Non-destructive survey*

Introduction

The fortified settlement in Wicina, Jasień commune, Żary county, lubuskie voivodeship, Poland – site I, AZP 64-10/1 (Polish Archaeological Record) – has been one of the best recognized Lusatian culture settlements. Due to the ongoing archaeological excavations, which were carried out here for more than three decades and which resulted in numerous spectacular discoveries, this site is mentioned in every synthetic archaeological book which deals with the Early Iron Age period in Poland. Calling this place "the second Biskupin" or "The Pompeii of the North" might be perceived a slight exaggeration, yet some historical resemblance still remains.

The defensive settlement in Wicina (Figs. 1, 2) was built by the Lusatian culture people and existed in the Early Iron Age, Hallstatt C-D period (*Kołodziejski 1975*, 19). The archaeological research provides evidence of the settlement's dramatic fate: most probably it was destroyed by a Scythian raid (*Kołodziejski 1970*; *1993*, 11; *1998d*, 50, 52).

In November 2012, the site was subjected to a non-invasive archaeological survey with the purpose of preparing specific documentation of a historical area with its own terrain shape. The research included geophysical recognition, geodetic survey, aerial photography and the creation of a digital 3D model of this settlement.

Earlier research

We shall present first a short history of the settlement survey. The first excavations were carried out by Carl Schuchhardt in July 1920. These were merely a reconnaissance, performed in only 14 days (*Schuchhardt 1926*, 184-188).

Over 40 years later, in the autumn of 1966, Adam Kołodziejski initiated the next stage of research (*Kołodziejski 1971a*, 93; *1974*, 78; *1998c*, 48). He became head archaeologist and supervised all works undertaken in this area for the next 30 years, until 1998 (*Kołodziejski 1998a*, 7; *1998b*, 129). Undoubtedly, these were one of the longest lasting excavations ever accomplished in Poland. Unfortunately, all that research carried out here was not followed by the proper number of publications.

The most recent archaeological excavations in this site took place after a 10-year-long brake – in 2008 and 2009, and again in 2011 and 2012 (*Kałagate - Jaszewska 2009*, 51; *Kałagate 2011*, 101). The research was led by *Sławomir Kałagate* and *Julia Orlicka-Jasnoch* (*2010*, 147, 150). The work was started in order to complete the exploration of the site and to fill in the two archaeological trenches left by Kołodziejski (*Kałagate - Jaszewska 2009*, 51; *Kałagate - Orlicka-Jasnoch 2010*, 147; *Kałagate 2011*, 101).

It is not an easy task to determine precisely the range of the investigated area. It is the non-invasive research, the analysis of the written sources and the general plan, made by Kałagate (*Kałagate - Orlicka-Jasnoch 2010*, 148, fig. 3), that allows us to ascertain that *Schuchhardt* (*1926*, 186, fig. 2) had explored an area of c. 2.5 ares (1 ar = 100 m² = 0.01 ha); Kołodziejski, most probably, investigated an area of c. 60.5 ares (Fig. 6:3).

The trenches, made by Schuchhardt and Kołodziejski, partly overlay each other, making the whole reconnoitred area close to c. 62.5 ares. This is approximately 28.4 % of

Fig. 1. Early Iron Age fortified settlement in Wicina, commune Jasień (photo M. Bogacki).

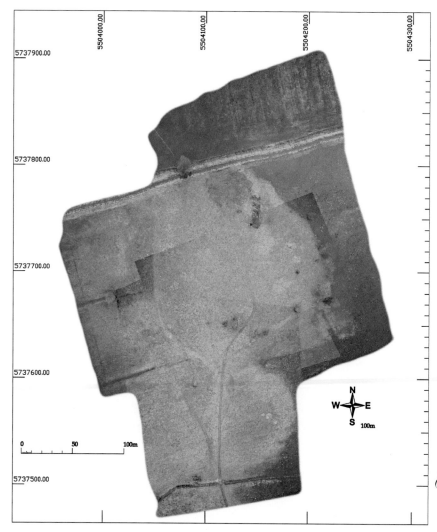

Fig. 2. Orthophotomap of the fortified settlement in Wicina, commune Jasień (prepared by M. Bogacki, W. Małkowski).

the whole settlement's surface (which covers a total area of 220 ares). In fact, the site in Wicina has been one of the most thoroughly excavated defensive settlements of the Lusatian culture.

The fortified settlement

Before we proceed to the non-invasive research issues, we will provide some more details about the settlement itself. The state of preservation, characteristic features of the preserved constructions, their surroundings and the strata depths are key factors to the geophysical survey final outcomes (*Misiewicz 2006*, 31-35). As already stated by *Kołodziejski* (*1971a*, 93, 96; *1974*, 79) – in reference to the settlement's state of preservation – the long-term agricultural activities "significantly" damaged the top layers. In his opinion, the maidan (central square) strata and the upper parts of the settlement's rampart suffered the heaviest devastation. At the same time, removing the top part of the rampart helped to save the layout of layers located in the adjacent area. *Kołodziejski* (*1971a*, 96) provides us with a noteworthy report by F. Dziegciarz – the former landowner – who claimed that the inner slopes of the ramparts had still been high and steep in the mid-1940s. This formation hampered farming activities, which is why Mr. Dziegciarz lowered the rampart in the southern part by removing the earth (*Kołodziejski 1971a*, 96). He then pushed the earth down and relocated it towards the settlement's interior.

The excavation works proved clearly that all conditions have been relatively propitious here and allowed wooden elements to be preserved. The area abutting the site is periodically flooded (Figs. 1, 2), which helps preserve organic relics. The maintained cultural strata abound with relics – a single are yielded around two tonnes of pottery remains (*Kołodziejski 1971a*, 96; *1971b*, 74; *1974*, 79). Kołodziejski discerned six different layers; the recorded wooden constructions were not officially marked as separate stratigraphic units. The number of layers as well as their depth varies in particular ares. The shallowest strata arrangements are found in the maidan with 60-80 cm thick layers respectively (*Kołodziejski 1970*, 6; *1971b*, 74; *1974*, 79). The deepest strata layout is recognized in the eastern part of the settlement – are 237 in particular. The layers reached as deep as 3 metres here (*IA 1972*, 102, 103). In the neighbouring ares, 217 and 196, the layers were significantly shallower – approximately 2 metres thick (*IA 1997a*, 62). Apart from the cultural strata, numerous archaeological features, up to 20 – 30 in a single are, were uncovered within the fortified part of the settlement (*Kołodziejski 1971a*, 96; *1974*, 79). An archive documentation shows that the recorded features were mainly circular in shape, not very large (c. 1 metre in diameter) and not deep (maximum depth of 1 metre). Summing up, despite both the human-related and natural destruction, we shall confirm the relatively good state of preservation of this site.

The fortified settlement is an archaeological monument. Just as every monument, this settlement is also a source. To use this source as much as possible we shall begin with the simplest things, such as the measurements and a description. In his several short publications Kołodziejski unfurled some imprecise or even false information into the scientific air. His estimations of the settlement's total area varied. At the beginning, it was assessed to be 400 ares – not clearly and constantly though. One time it included the ramparts and the moat (*Kołodziejski 1971a*, 95, 96; *1971b*, 73), another time it was only the ramparts (*Kołodziejski 1974*, 79) that demarcated the area. Later, Kołodziejski reduced the size of the fortified settlement together with its ramparts to "more than 300 ares, out of which 150 ares occupies the internal area" (*Kołodziejski 1984*, 185; *1998c*, 107). The latter estimation was recently supported by *Kałagate* and *Orlicka-Jasnoch* (*2010*, 147). Incidentally, it is difficult to determine what the width of the moat itself was, according to Kołodziejski; no trial trenching was undertaken, as can be seen in the general plan (Fig. 6:3).

The non-invasive measurements and research, carried out in November 2010, allowed us to verify the size of the settlement. Today, its remains encompass an area of 22008 m² with the circumference of the destroyed ramparts measuring 541 m – a Roman numeral I marks its outlines in figure 3 (Fig. 3). The monument has an oval, slightly triangular shape, with the following dimensions: length (collegially approved) – 163 m (section A-B), width – 168.5 (section C-D). Alternative dimensions are as follows: 176 m (section E-F) to 172.5 (section G-H). Due to erosion of the site, it was not possible to measure this area precisely nor to determine the exact extent of the "maidan", which is scarcely visible today – II in (Fig. 3). We can conventionally assume that the discussed area covers 5573 m², with the circumference of the inner part of the destroyed ramparts being equal to 267 metres. The inner "square", or rather the "lowered part", is oval in shape, measuring 85 m (section I-J) to 81-85 m (section K-L).

In fact, the original 400 ares large settlement, as stated by Kołodziejski, is almost twice as large as the actual area. The overstated data has been quoted in the relevant literature (*Niesiołowska-Wędzka 1974*, 192; *Purowski 2007*, 75; *Kałagate - Orlicka-Jasnoch 2010*, 147), and that is why we shall repeat again: the destroyed site encompasses not 400 nor 300 but only 220 ares. The real area of the settlement must therefore have been smaller.

63500 measurement points were set up and analysed. The highest – marked P1 – is located on the rampart, in the southern part, near cross-section trench Y-Z (Fig. 4). Its altitude is 80.67 MASL with the precise location determined by the following coordinates: W-E 5504130, N-S 5737644. The lowest point (P2) nearest to the settlement area is located exactly on the U-W section line, east of the rampart (Fig. 4). It is 73.90 MASL and the coordinates are: W-E 5504222.4, N-S 5737703.08. The difference between these two points is 6.77 m. Altitudes are given in the Kronstadt

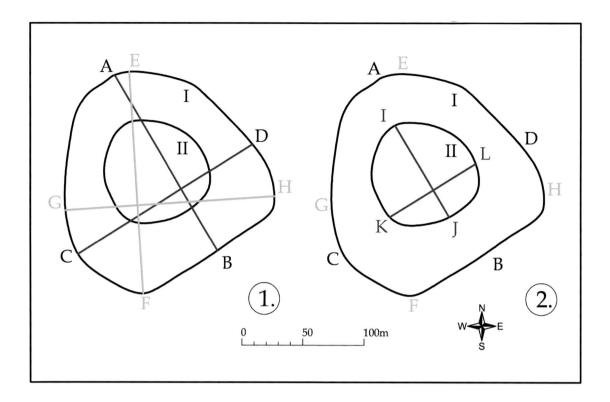

Fig. 3. Plan of the fortified settlement in Wicina, commune Jasień (1-2): I – outline of the relics of the ramparts; II – outline of the depression inside the ramparts ("maidan").

86 system; the location is given in coordinate system 2000, zone 5.

As can be seen on the situational-altitude plan (Fig. 4) and on the presented cross-sections (chosen out of hundreds possible), today the highest parts of ramparts are located in the southern part and reach over 80 MASL. The zone of 79.5-80 MASL, C-shaped, extends a bit farther, along the ramparts line, from the south-west to the south-east part of the site. Northern parts of fortifications are scarcely visible, with recorded altitude points not exceeding 79 MASL.

Partial removal of the rampart resulted in a raising of the maidan level. Presently, most of the maidan area is located at 78-79 MASL, and only 1.5 m lower than the highest parts of the rampart. Thus, looking from the internal part of the settlement, one realises that the fortifications are not impressive. The presented cross-sections (Fig. 4), as well as the single image of the 3D model of the site (Fig. 5), show plainly that the present form of the settlement is relatively flat.[1]

Geophysical research

Coming to the geophysical research we should realise that its aim was not only to locate the archaeological trenches and excavations made by Schuchhardt and Kołodziejski but also to gain new information about this historic site. A pursuit to identify old trenches may seem unintelligible, yet in the case of sites which have already been excavated

but have not yielded enough information, such actions appear reasonable, considering the matters pertaining to the protection of monuments as well as scientific issues.

The geophysical surveying was implemented with the use of the magnetic method; two different devices were used: the Bartington Grad 601-2 Dual fluxgate gradiometer and the Geometrix G-858 Cesium magnetometer. The first one helped reconnoitre only the central part of the settlement, with an investigated area of 1.15 hectare (Fig. 6:1); the second device was used to reconnoitre an area of 3.23 hectare (Fig. 6:2). The whole area of the settlement was investigated, together some smaller parts outside the site outline. Due to particular limitations, which are always inherently connected with every geophysical research (*Misiewicz 2006*), an electrical resistivity tomography was proposed. However, because of unfavourable weather conditions, i.e. potent ground dampness, this idea was soon abandoned. Eventually, against all odds, the outcomes were fruitful and clear even for outsiders. Nonetheless, as often happens, there were more questions than answers.

As for the old and buried archaeological trenches, which cannot be seen at the site, the first device (Grad 601-2 Dual fluxgate gradiometer) brought distinct results. Figure 6:1 (Fig. 6:1) clearly shows the outlines of the main trench, made by Kołodziejski, situated in the central part of the settlement. In some places, the outlines and edges of particular ares can be observed, being the result of this archaeologist's methods of archaeological exploration. A geophysical survey proved that the excavations had covered an area of 5.5 are, larger than was ascertained by *Kałagate*

---

[1] The popular-science 3D model (PDF version) can be downloaded from http://e-zabytek.nid.pl/Zabytek/szczegoly.php?ID=188.

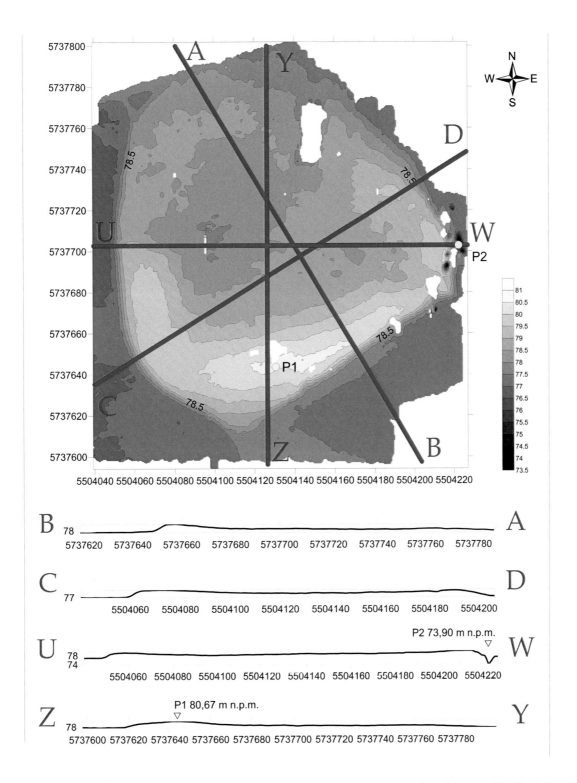

Fig. 4. Situational-altitude plan and sections in the fortified settlement in Wicina, commune Jasień (prepared by W. Małkowski).

and *Orlicka-Jasnoch* (*2010*, 148, fig. 3). The buried trenches made by Kołodziejski can also be spotted in the northern part of the settlement. In this zone, however, only their southern range can be detected. As the gradiometer was less often used, – the trenches had been laid out in a slightly chaotic way and several metal objects and waste were detected – it was more difficult to achieve a full reconnaissance in this sphere. The measuring devices did not detect the trial trenches made by Schuchhardt and, in

any event, they are not recognisable after digital processing. It should be added here that the undertaken surface microrelief was also used to locate the archaeologically excavated grounds.

There are, apart from traces made by archaeologists, at least three interesting anomalies which presumably can be linked with the discussed hillfort. In the southern part, we have a distinct irregularity, caught by the geophysical

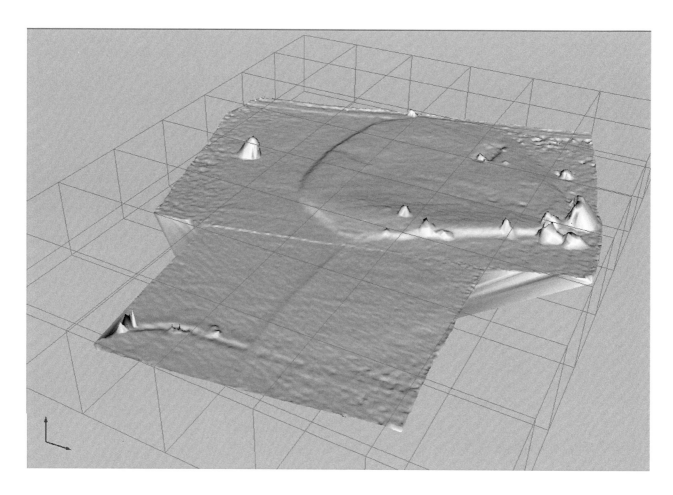

Fig. 5. Digital 3D model of the fortified settlement in Wicina, commune Jasień (prepared by M. Bogacki, W. Małkowski).

reconnaissance, marked A (Fig. 6:3). It is, most probably, caused by the preserved construction elements of the rampart; apparently they were burned, thus making them "clearer" for detection instruments. On the basis of anomaly A the inner rampart line was demarcated, together with the internal area of the settlement (outline III – Fig. 8:1, 2). This anomaly can be clearly observed in the southern part of the settlement (over a distance of c. 130 m); the farther to the north the less visible it becomes. This mainly results from the destruction caused by excavations.

There are four, short perpendicular anomalies, A1-A4 (Fig. 6:3), radiating from anomaly A. Presumably, these are the burnt inner parts of the rampart's construction and have the following dimensions: A1 – 6.7 m long, 5.5 m wide; A2 – 16.4 m long, 8.7 m wide; A3 – 12 m long, 7 m wide; A4 – 12.9 m long, 5.4 m wide. If we assume that the recognised structures (A1-A4) are the real rampart's construction elements, then its length may indicate the width (the second stage?). The distance between particular structures is as follows: A1-A2 – 17.3 m; A2-A3 – 46 m; A3-A4 – 22.2 m. One can instantly see a large gap between anomalies A2 and A3, as well as a relatively close distance between A1-A2 and A3-A4. Additionally, in the gap between structures A2 and A3, just after A2, there is a slight but distinct "depression" in anomaly A. At this stage of research, it can be perceived as an over-interpretation, yet considering

its location, we can risk the hypothetical observation that a hillfort gate once stood here. Kołodziejski assumed that in an earlier stage the gate was located in the north-east part of the settlement (*IA 2006*, 130), while in a later (?) stage it probably was in the eastern, partly excavated "top" of the settlement (*IA 1997b*, 44, 45; *IA 1998a*, 48). It should also be mentioned that during the documentation analysis doubt arose whether anomalies A1-A4 were simply the trial trenches made on the rampart by Schuchhardt. Consulting Misiewicz and Małkowski allowed us to eliminate such a possibility and the comparison of geophysical outcomes and the general plan of the German archaeologist *Schuchhardt (1926*, 186, fig. 2) confirmed this observation.

The second anomaly, B, was recorded in the western part of the investigated area (Fig. 6:3). The length of structure B – from the north side to the edge of the excavation trench – is 170 m, the width 5-6 m. This long anomaly is situated exactly on the external edge of the rampart, what might indicate the existence of some type of construction. It is possibly a wooden or stone reinforcement of the rampart's lower part and the adjoining area. Nevertheless, the interpretation should rather remain moderate. In practice, such outcomes can only be verified by archaeological excavations (*Misiewicz 1998*, 181-183). It is certain that this anomaly was not caused only by the depression. If it had been, it would have been recorded along the whole

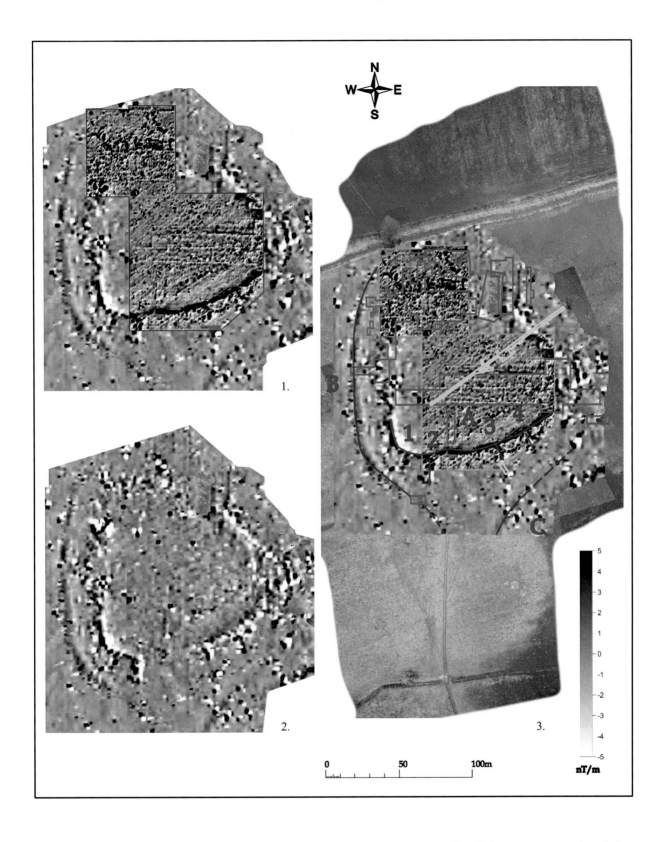

Fig. 6. Results of the geophysical reconnaissance of the settlement in Wicina, commune Jasień: 1 – prospection made with the Bartington device – surrounded area in the centre; 2 – prospection made with the Geometrix device; 3 – interpretation of results: recorded anomalies A, B, C together with the plan of archaeological trenches by C. Schuchhardt and A. Kołodziejski (prepared by W. Małkowski, K. Misiewicz, M. Bugaj).

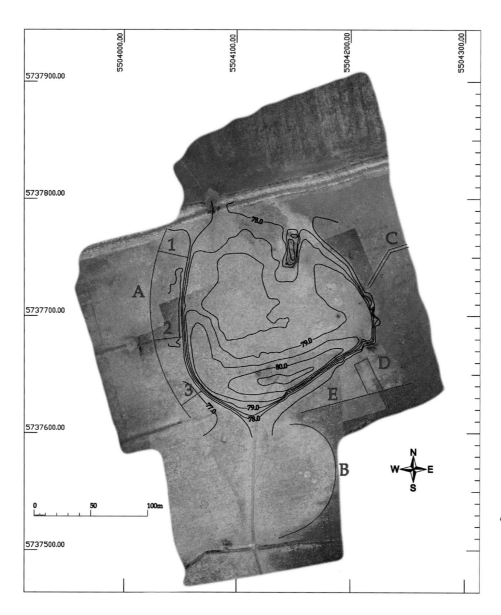

Fig. 7. Orthophotomap of the fortified settlement in Wicina, commune Jasień, together with the interpretation of aerial photographs (prepared by M. Bogacki, W. Małkowski, M. Bugaj).

rampart line. Evidently, this is not a moat either; aerial photography confirmed that the moat was probably much wider (Figs. 1, 7:A). Despite Kołodziejski's conclusions (*Kołodziejski 1998d*, 50; *IA 2005*, 145; *IA 2006*, 130) not being entirely explicit, he still claimed there had been an adjacent, narrow wooden road and some oblique wooden stakes located outside the rampart.

The last anomaly, C (Fig. 6:3), is situated in the south-east part and extends beyond the investigated area. It is about 75 m long and about 4 m wide. A similar anomaly is seen on the other side of today's road; presumably, it is a part of structure B which is less observable below the archaeological trench. It appears that anomalies B and C share common features.

The geophysical devices also recorded the parallel anomalies caused by the modern (?) and contemporary farming activities mentioned above.

I have to add that we should beware when talking about the real dimension of the described structures, as the dimensions of recorded anomalies do not simply reflect the real size of an original structure.

Aerial Photography

The non-invasive survey was supplemented by aerial photographs (Figs. 1, 2) for which a helium balloon with photo camera was used. These are the first aerial images of the hillfort in Wicina. In fact, the very first aerial photographs of Biskupin were made from a hydrogen balloon and occurred 75 years ago in 1935 (*Bukowski 2005*, 74, 75; *Kobyliński 2005*, 29, 33; *Piotrowski 2005*, 29, 30). Pictures of the settlement in Wicina were used to create an orthophotomap (Fig. 2) and a 3D model (Fig. 5).[2]

Having taken over 300 vertical and diagonal pictures, today we can have a bird's eye view of the hillfort. Due to some partial flooding of the site's foreground, it was possible

---

[2] More information can be found in the following links: http://e-zabytek.nid.pl/Zabytek/szczegoly.php?ID=188 and http://www.youtube.com/watch?v=iO4qfIPXCdI. A short film, a 3D model, and photos give us an idea of the final results of the work performed by Bogacki and Małkowski.

to record several interesting facts. The ground conditions which occurred during the survey partly resembled those of the time of the settlement's existence – it had probably been surrounded by wet meadows (*Kołodziejski 1993*, 8; *1998d*, 50). Outside the western part of the rampart, due to the existence of the so-called wetness marker, a wide structure was discovered (Fig. 7:A) Presumably, this is a moat. However the recognized streak is large, c. 25 m wide. Possibly, this newly observed structure may also contain other elements of the rampart and fortification system.

In the southern part of the photographed zone, there emerged a not very large area with a clear curved edge line running from the east side; from the west side a small elevation peters out just behind the presently existing road (Fig. 7:B). The middle part of this area is slightly depressed. Possibly, this area can illustrate the real extent of the settlement adjacent to the hillfort – i.e. site IV (AZP 65-10/4) excavated by Kołodziejski (*IA 1973*, 111; *IA 1997b*, 45). It may have been separated from the wet meadows by a small embankment, which cannot be seen at ground level today. As we can see, contemporary tillage has not erased it. This area, starting from the presently existing road, extends to about 60-65 ares; *Kołodziejski* (*1998b*, 107) estimated the size of this neighbouring settlement to be around 120 ares.

On the east side of the hillfort there is an interesting, partly visible, curved dike (Fig. 7:C). It is difficult to determine its connection with the fortified settlement, but we must not exclude this plausibility. As it is a relatively large structure – approx. 50 m long and 2-4 m wide – it cannot be associated with any archaeologically-related remains, such as old spoil heaps.

Most probably the other structures are not connected with the settlement (Fig. 7:D, E). Structure D is a rectangular area (30 x 12.5 m), flooded at its edge lines, which can be identified as the remains of an archaeological trench (possibly measuring 3 ares?). Structure E is a straight line which can be seen to run near the rampart's southern part. Based on the analysis of diagonal photographs, this structure runs along the canal system to the edge of the photographed area. It is probably a drainage canal.

Discussion

The non-invasive survey allows us to reconstruct the layout and to estimate the size of the defensive settlement in Wicina. Obviously, it would be preferable if we could refer to the results of previous archaeological work. Unfortunately, due to the poorly published outcomes, that is now not possible.

According to Kołodziejski the hillfort has a "rounded triangle" shape, with an entrance gate at its eastern "apex" (*IA 1997b*, 44, 45; *IA 1998a*, 48). It was the shape of the destroyed site that contributed to the hypothesis – which is false, in my opinion – that "the defensive object was built on the triangle-form plan" (*IA 1997b*, 45),

and that the 45° bend of the rampart was an intentional construction, which would enhance the defensive aspects of the settlement (*IA 1998a*, 48). The performed research challenges those statements. Analysis of the geodetic and geophysical documentation proves that this hillfort was partly transformed into a triangle-shaped object by intense tillage. The ground microrelief confirms such a conclusion. Agricultural works led to the "cutting" and lowering of the rampart from the south-east side.

The triangle-shaped fortified settlement theory may have originated under the influence of Schuchhardt who claimed that the nearby settlement in Starosiedle, Gubin commune, dating to the same period, was built on such a triangular plan (*Schuchhardt 1926*, 188-201, fig. 1). His theories have recently been discredited by *Kobyliński* and *Nebelsick* (*2010*, 159-164). The triangular shapes in defensive architecture originated together with the rise and development of artillery and rarely occur. A fortification built on a triangular plan has the following disadvantage: it does not meaningfully shorten the total length of the defensive wall but significantly reduces the internal area instead. We shall abandon the idea of the existence of regional variants of defensive settlements from the Early Iron Age arranged on triangular plan.

The outcomes of the geophysical survey allow us to put forward the theory that the settlement's interior, distinguished on the basis of recorded anomaly A (Fig. 6:3) – presented as outline III (Fig. 8:1, 2) – had originally covered an area of 10869 m². The circumference of the internal part of the ramparts was 380 m. It has an oval-shaped perimeter, with the following dimensions: 115 (section M-N) to 123 (section O-P) metres. The interior area of the settlement would be much smaller than assumed by *Kołodziejski* (*1984*, 185), or *Kałagate* and *Orlicka-Jasnoch* (*2010*, 147) who believed it had encompassed around 150 ares. Defining the usable space of a specific area is a substantial help, among other things, towards estimating the population size of a particular settlement. *Kołodziejski* (*1984*, 185; *1998c*, 107) claimed that the central part of the settlement had not been a built-up area. He also deduced that there had been around 40-50 houses, covering approx. 60 to 72 m², arranged in two rows, and located in the rampart-neighbouring zone. This would give a total of 2400-3600 m² as living area. Just to compare, *Rajewski* (*1950*, 244) calculated that houses in Biskupin occupied approx. 8250 m² of a total area which is two or three times larger. Considering that the interior of the settlement in Wicina is more than 40 ares smaller (27.5 %) than was assumed by Kołodziejski, we should verify his conclusions.

Kołodziejski (*1993*, 10; *1998c*, 50, 51, fig. 2) claimed that the rampart base was over 10 metres wide, and *Kałagate* and *Orlicka-Jasnoch* (*2010*, 150) shared this opinion. Based on this information, outline IV (Fig. 8:1) was drawn. It depicts the hypothetical outer line of the rampart, which was located exactly 10 m from the recorded edge line of the settlement's interior (outline III). With this theoretical assumption of

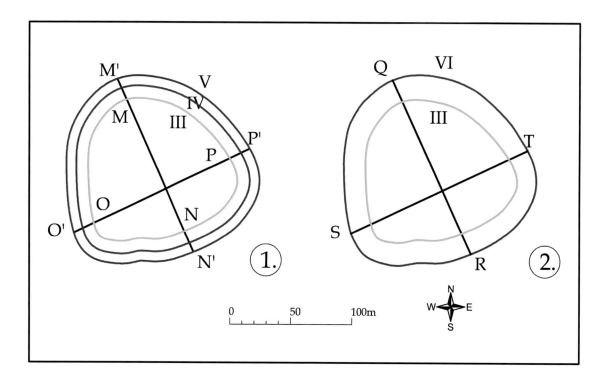

Fig. 8. Attempt at the reconstruction of the original foundation of the fortified settlement in Wicina, commune Jasień (1-2): III – outline of the utilitarian space – the inner border of the ramparts, based on the geophysical survey; IV – theoretical plan of the settlement assuming that the base of rampart was 10 m wide; V – theoretical plan of the settlement assuming that the base of rampart was 18 m wide; VI – reconstruction of the settlement plan with its theoretical, maximum size (outline V adjusted on geophysical survey and terrain elevation measurements).

the width of the rampart base, the settlement's area would measure 14981.5 m², with a circumference of 442.5 m, and total dimensions of 135 to 143 m (elongation of sections M-N and O-P). However, the geophysical survey seems to confirm that the rampart base could have been much wider, namely up to 18 metres. We should remember though that according to Kołodziejski's conclusions (*Kłodziejski 1998c*, 108; *1998d*, 50; *IA 1998b*, 50) the rampart line had been rebuilt. The obtained outcomes could be problematic though, as the geophysical devices recorded two stages of fortifications, which may have run in slightly different ways. Assuming, hypothetically, that the rampart base had been 18 m wide at any point, and remembering the distinguished internal edge of the rampart (outline III), the hillfort would have encompassed an area of 18724 m². The settlement's shape is depicted in outline V (Fig. 8:1). The oval-shaped hillfort would have had the following dimensions: 151 (M'-N') to 159.5 (O'-P') metres, with a circumference of 493 m.

Outline VI, shown in figure 8:2 (Fig. 8:2), illustrates the partly modified – based on the geophysical and geodetic survey – theoretical shape of the settlement marked as V (Fig. 8:1). This outline has been an attempt to reconstruct the original shape of the settlement in its virtual maximum size. Consequently, the settlement would originally have had an oval, to circular shape. The area would have covered 18684 m², with a circumference of 491 m and total dimensions of 152 (Q-R) to 158 (S-T) metres. Obviously, this is not the final reconstruction. However, the conducted research allows us to assume that outlines IV and VI depict

the hypothetical shape of the hillfort in its minimal and maximal sizes.

At this stage of the research, it would be essential to refer to the documentation of the excavations which would allow verification and a more precise elucidation of the above data. It mainly concerns the course of the internal edge of the rampart line (outline III) and its width (outlines IV-VI). The question of the rebuilding of the fortifications and their course in the early and late stage renders the whole issue even more problematic. We should also remember that the real location of trenches, set up with traditional methods, will be slightly different from the idealized general plan of Kołodziejski. Measurement errors would most probably impede the final reconstruction attempt.

Conclusions

Summing up, we should add that the data presented in this article are somewhat relative and subjective. This ensues from the fact that not all recorded bordering lines are unequivocal and clearly recognisable along all their courses. In practice, we are dealing here with an interpretation accomplished over a very narrow range. It should be stressed that the two particular edge lines are clearly visible and thus objectively demarcated. These are the present outer edge line of the rampart's destroyed area (Fig. 3:1) and the southern edge line of the settlement's interior, recorded during the geophysical survey (Figs. 6:3A, 8:III).

The obtained data bring new perspectives and set a new starting point for future analyses. The new documentation has been created. Only a small part of this new documentation has been presented in this article as it gives an opportunity to reconstruct a piece of the Early Iron Age environment. Due to the conducted research, the settlement in Wicina is today the best surveyed historical monument with its own terrain form in Poland. From a conservation point of view, the up-to-date documentation is an essential element of the protection and management of a specific monument. The achieved outcomes lead to the conclusion that an analogical scientific procedure should be obligatory in cases of planned excavations which are to be carried out at such precious historic sites, in particular of hillforts.

Acknowledgements

The research was conducted, on the initiative of the author of the present article, by Krzysztof Misiewicz PhD, Wiesław Małkowski and Miron Bogacki. I would hereby like to express my deep appreciation and thank them for all their work and remarks provided. The recorded documentation was used as a crucial material for an unpublished work "The fortified settlement in Wicina – protection of the archaeological heritage in practice" (*Bugaj 2012*); the present article comprises of several modified parts of this work.

The research was financed by the Voivodeship Office for the Protection of Historical Monuments in Zielona Góra and the National Heritage Board of Poland, Warsaw. The accommodation in Wicina was provided by the Archaeological Museum of the Middle Oder Riverside in Zielona Góra, Świdnica department.

References

Bugaj, M. 2012: Grodzisko w Wicinie – ochrona dziedzictwa archeologicznego w praktyce. Warszawa (an unpublished work in National Heritage Board of Poland, Warsaw).

Bukowski, Z. 2005: Działalność Wojciecha Kóčki w Biskupinie. In: A. Grossman, W. Piotrowski eds, Badacze Biskupina (Biskupińskie Prace Archeologiczne 4), Biskupin, 71-84.

IA, 1972: Informator Archeologiczny. Badania rok 1971. Warszawa.

IA, 1973: Informator Archeologiczny. Badania rok 1972. Warszawa.

IA, 1997a: Informator Archeologiczny. Badania rok 1991. Warszawa.

IA, 1997b: Informator Archeologiczny. Badania rok 1992. Warszawa.

IA, 1998a: Informator Archeologiczny. Badania rok 1993. Warszawa.

IA, 1998b: Informator Archeologiczny. Badania rok 1994. Warszawa.

IA, 2005: Informator Archeologiczny. Badania 1996. Warszawa.

IA, 2006: Informator Archeologiczny. Badania 1997. Warszawa.

Kałagate, S. 2011: Sprawozdanie z badań grodziska ludności kultury łużyckiej w Wicinie, stan. 1, gm. Jasień, woj. lubuskie w sezonie 2011. Lubuskie Materiały Konserwatorskie, t. VIII, 101-107.

Kałagate, S. – Jaszewska, A. 2009: Wicina – uzupełniające badania archeologiczne na grodzisku ludności kultury łużyckiej. Zapiski Archeologiczne 7, 51-53.

Kałagate, S. – Orlicka-Jasnoch, J. 2010: Gród obronny kultury łużyckiej w Wicinie. Z otchłani wieków 65(1-4), 147-156.

Kobyliński, Z. 2005: Archeologia lotnicza w Polsce. Osiem dekad wzlotów i upadków. Warszawa.

Kobyliński, Z. – Nebelsick, L.D. 2010: Gród z wczesnej epoki żelaza w Starosiedlu na Ziemi Lubuskiej: mit naukowy i jego obalenie. Z otchłani wieków 65(1-4), 157-165.

Kołodziejski, A. 1970: Najeźdźcy zjawili się jesienią. Z otchłani wieków 36(1), 5-10.

Kołodziejski, A. 1971a: Badania zespołu osadniczego ludności kultury łużyckiej z okresu późnohalsztackiego w Wicinie, pow. Lubsko, w latach 1966-69. Sprawozdania Archeologiczne 23, 93-108.

Kołodziejski, A. 1971b: Kultura łużycka na Ziemi Lubuskiej. In: W. Hensel ed., Materiały do prehistorii ziem polskich, cz. IV, Epoka brązu i wczesna epoka żelaza, z. 1, Warszawa, 49-110.

Kołodziejski, A. 1974: Problematyka kultur okresu halsztackiego na Ziemi Lubuskiej. Zielonogórskie Zeszyty Muzealne 4, 67-105.

Kołodziejski, A. 1975: Próba nowego podziału chronologicznego okresu halsztackiego i lateńskiego w północnej części Dolnego Śląska na tle przemian kulturowych. Zielonogórskie Zeszyty Muzealne 5, 5-42.

Kołodziejski, A. 1984: Wicińska „aglomeracja łużycka". Z otchłani wieków 50(3-4), 180-190.

Kołodziejski, A. 1993: Wicina. Osada obronna sprzed 2500 lat w zbiorach Muzeum Archeologicznego w Zielonej Górze, Zielona Góra.

Kołodziejski, A. 1998a: Muzeum Archeologiczne Środkowego Nadodrza. Archeologia Środkowego Nadodrza 1, 5-11.

Kołodziejski, A. 1998b: Muzeum Archeologiczne Środkowego Nadodrza w Zielonej Górze u progu XXI wieku. Rocznik Lubuski 24(1), 117-137.

Kołodziejski, A. 1998c: Wstępne wyniki badań archeologicznych makroregionu osadniczego kultury łużyckiej z okresu halsztackiego we wschodniej części Dolnych Łużyc. Archeologia Środkowego Nadodrza 1, 101-119.

Kołodziejski, A. 1998d: Kultura łużycka i kultura pomorska na Środkowym Nadodrzu w badaniach archeologicznych końca XX wieku. Rocznik Lubuski 24(1) 41-81.

Misiewicz, K. 1998: Metody geofizyczne w planowaniu badań wykopaliskowych. Warszawa.

Misiewicz, K. 2006: Geofizyka archeologiczna. Warszawa.

Niesiołowska-Wędzka, A. 1974: Początki i rozwój grodów kultury łużyckiej. Warszawa-Wrocław-Kraków-Gdańsk.

Piotrowski, W. 2005: Wykopaliska biskupińskie z lotu ptaka – próba podsumowania. In: J. Nowakowski et al. eds, Biskupin... i co dalej? Zdjęcia lotnicze w polskiej archeologii, Poznań, 27-49.

Purowski, T. 2007: Przedmioty szklane odkryte na grodzie ludności kultury łużyckiej w Wicinie, stan. 1. Archeologia Środkowego Nadodrza 5, 75-172.

Rajewski, Z.A. 1950: Budowle grodów kultury łużyckiej na półwyspie jeziora biskupińskiego w powiecie żnińskim. In: J. Kostrzewski ed., III Sprawozdanie z prac wykopaliskowych w grodzie kultury łużyckiej w Biskupinie w powiecie żnińskim za lata 1938-1939 i 1946-1948, Poznań, 239-285.

Schuchhardt, C. 1926: Witzen und Starzeddel, zwei Burgen der Lausitzer Kultur. Praehistorische Zeitschrift 17, 184-201.

A Combined Archaeological Survey of the Historical Landscape Surrounding the Prominent Hillfort of Vladař, Czech Republic

Ladislav Šmejda

Abstract: This article presents the results of the application of combined survey methods on the prehistoric site of Vladař hillfort in the Czech Republic. During the survey of this extensive hillfort, we undertook fieldwalking, a geophysical survey, a metal detector survey, analysis of aerial photography and small-scale test excavations. The broad range of methods adopted by the research project allows drawing conclusions about the validity of the individual survey results and methods when they are applied in this specific type of natural environment. The main outcome of the survey is represented by the record of spatial data which put the site in context with its surroundings and reveal spatial properties in greater detail. The digitalised survey results can now be used by other researchers and modified in a GIS environment to help answer further research questions.

Keywords: surface survey - remote sensing - data digitalisation - metal detectors - GIS - prehistoric hillfort sites

Introduction to the site

This paper discusses the role of archaeological prospection in a research project which focused on a prominent prehistoric hillfort of Vladař located in the region of West Bohemia in Central Europe. It primarily aims to highlight the advances brought by the combined survey methodology. The site is one of the largest and most complex ancient fortifications in the Czech Republic. Its foundation could have been related to early attempts to extract gold in the nearby auriferous sediments (*Chytráček - Šmejda 2005*), although this hypothesis has not been fully confirmed as yet. The site is located away from the old settlement zone and outside the most favourable climate zone when compared to regions typically settled by prehistoric agriculturalists. However, there is some fertile land available in its vicinity (*Chytráček et al. 2012*). The site has long been known as very ancient (*Foedisch 1867*), but a systematic research was only started here around the year 2000.

Any large-scale project today necessarily involves a number of professionals and institutions who focus on various aspects of the site and its vicinities. In our case, several institutions from the Czech Republic contributed to the research on the project. Perhaps most importantly I should name here the Institute of Archaeology in Prague (Czech Academy of Sciences), The Museum in Karlovy Vary and University of West Bohemia in Plzeň. The respective authors will be cited in the following text wherever it draws on their results.

The archaeological site of Vladař is located on and around a hill of volcanic origin, which prominently stands out in the surrounding landscape (Fig. 1). Its flat and spacious top remind us of mesa hills which have natural characteristics different from their lower neighbourhood and which is also the case of Vladař hill. The hilltop reaches 693 metres above sea level with the superelevation of 200 m above the nearby river valley which passes the hill close by on the north side and makes it a truly dominant feature of the landscape. The name "Vladař", after all, means "ruler" or "sovereign" in English and therefore is a very fitting name. Not surprisingly, it has been recorded in written sources since the Middle Ages, when the opportunity of an elevated position was taken up by the Hussite's military forces, that set up camp and defended themselves in this strategic position. The place was then mentioned in post-medieval times, when the relics of old fortifications were specifically recorded. The sheer dimensions of these fortifications continued to impress in the later periods of history; during the Thirty Years War of the 17th century they were re-used again as they could still provide an advantage for the army. Later the earthworks were depicted on all historical military maps of Bohemia produced during the 18th - 20th centuries (Fig. 2).

All this documentary evidence, however, reflects only the later reuse and shared knowledge of structures of a much earlier origin. The finds discovered on the site, as well as the obtained radiocarbon and dendrochronological dates, testify to the presence of a lightly fortified hill-top settlement in this area already in the middle Bronze Age (probably from the 15th century BC onwards), which developed through time into an impressive Iron Age hillfort (Halstatt and La-Tène periods) (*Chytráček - Šmejda 2006*).

Surface survey

New survey and precision mapping by means of GPS revealed that the complex site covers an extensive area of

Fig. 1. A ground view toward Vladař hill from the south-east.

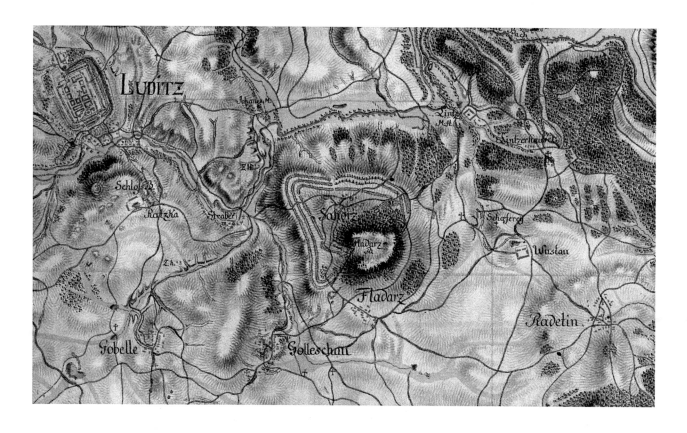

Fig. 2. The hillfort of Vladař on a historical map from the second half of the 18th century (the so-called First Military Survey, Austrian State Archive/Military Archive, Vienna).

more than 100 ha, which means that its outer line of ditches and ramparts encloses an area exceeding 1 km². The large extent of the site, together with the dense vegetation that today covers considerable parts of this region, require a combination of multiple survey techniques to be applied in order to derive further reliable data about the site.

The first stage of research in the immediate vicinities of the hillfort was by means of systematic fieldwalking and the collection of surface artefacts (*Kuna 2000*). We divided the accessible fields into a regular grid of squares of 50 x 50 m, and each square was walked by 5 surveyors spaced 10 metres apart. The navigation was aided by a hand-held GPS receiver. The results show that archaeological finds occur on the surface of arable land in a surprisingly high density. Every surveyed field yielded finds of prehistoric date of up to 50 pieces per each 50 x 50 m square. Unfortunately, the chances of a more precise chronological assignment of these highly fragmented objects, which were mostly potsherds, are very limited. We can only make the general statement that the great majority of the pottery can be dated to the Late Bronze Age Urnfield period, and somewhat smaller quantities can be ascribed to the Iron Age Hallstatt and La-Tène periods (*Chytráček - Šmejda 2005*).

Geophysical survey

The next stage of research in our project consisted of a geophysical survey, which was seeking to detect possible anthropogenic anomalies in the subsurface layers on site. We applied several methods with variable results. Magnetometry survey proved to be virtually useless, because magnetic volcanic bedrock hinders the discrimination of archaeological features. The electric resistivity survey provided much better results, but due to the difficult undulating terrain with many subsurface rocks and stones, it could only be carried out on smaller areas, preferably those located in context with the planned test excavations.

One more successful example of the geoelectrical survey application was conducted around the unique find of a well-preserved water management structure, most probably a cistern, built in several successive phases during the 5th century BC as a kind of dam consisting of wooden boxes filled with clay. The survey probably recorded differences in soil moisture as well as possible subsurface concentrations of stones. Furthermore, it has been possible to obtain results from Ground Penetrating Radar, but due to the inherent limitations of the mentioned methods and the specifics of the local geological and soil conditions, the geophysical survey always yielded rather inconclusive results. The excavation of detected anomalies seems necessary in such particular conditions to evaluate their significance.

Now I will briefly describe an application of another survey technique that in principle belongs to the family of geophysical prospection methods, namely a metal detector survey. We have tested this approach in selected parts of

the hillfort interior with the aim to develop a workable methodology of metal detector prospection as a tool of academic research (*Šmejda 2007*). In many countries the metal detectors have a negative reputation today because of their popularity among treasure hunters who frequently cause an irreversible damage to the integrity of archaeological deposits (*Křivánek 2006*). Our approach was based on a predefined set of rules describing what has to be recorded when the detector signals the presence of a metallic find. We thus systematically collected information on the position of a find by means of GPS, its depth, provisionally determined its material and age, the type of the item and other contextual observations. Even the clearly modern artefacts were recorded in this way, although such items as food cans were not collected for subsequent laboratory examination. Having followed this procedure during the survey we can now make use of a spatial database comprising hundreds of data points (Fig. 3). Their spatial distribution and recorded attributes can be analysed in the Geographical Information System. Among the objects retrieved we have identified at least a dozen finds made of iron, which could be attributed to the late Iron Age La-Tène culture. They provide a completely new insight into the multi-layered history of Vladař hill, as they are unparalleled in the material collected from the site before our survey. We are convinced that the careful methodology used during the metal detector survey paid off very well, especially when it turned out that approximately 95 % of all the recovered finds were located very close to the surface (in the zone affected by bioturbation) and we thus avoided any substantial intrusion into the deeper and more intact deposits.

Aerial reconnaissance and historical air photos

The aerial survey programme was started in 2004 as a complementary approach to the ground survey methods. We have gathered a collection of oblique photographs taken from small hand-held cameras, which provided general views of the hill, its individual parts and the features visible, as well as its surrounding landscape (Fig. 4). However, as the local environmental conditions are not favourable to the production of cropmarks (*Beck 2007*) and large tracts of the landscape are today used as pastures or covered by shrubs and trees, we needed imagery that would potentially provide more information. We found it in the archive of the Czech military reconnaissance (located in Dobruška, Czech Republic) where the collection is kept of vertical aerial photographs taken in the country since the 1930s. It proved to be the key source of accurate photogrammetric data. Luckily for our project, the oldest photographs held in the archive show the landscape in its state before the political changes and communist agricultural reforms that took place after the Second World War (*Hanson 2012*). This era of modern agricultural intensification introduced many profound changes to the traditional land use, heavily affected the structure of field systems and disturbed the subsoil by the construction of extensive drainage systems. As a result, many traces of the historical cultural landscape

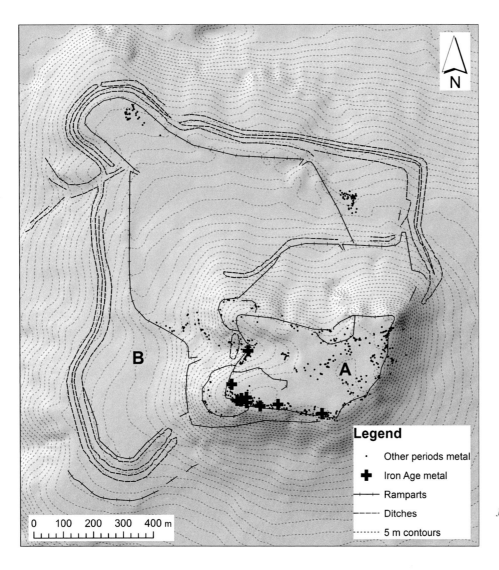

Legend

· Other periods metal

✛ Iron Age metal

|—|— Ramparts

----- Ditches

········· 5 m contours

0 100 200 300 400 m

Fig. 3. Layout of the hillfort of Vladař on a contour map. The image shows the extent of the ditches and ramparts, the location of two Iron Age cisterns (A, B) and of the finds located during the metal detector survey.

have been lost or unavailable for study by remote sensing; their shape and position nevertheless is still noticeable on old photographs. We aimed to extract as much information as possible from old aerial photographs and transcribe them into accurate digital maps, using the appropriate computer hardware and software (Leica Photogrammetry Suite, ArcGIS Desktop). It was possible to distinguish a number of ramparts and ditches, other types of artificial elevations and depressions, terraces, former field plots, sometimes even boggy areas and other useful features (Fig. 5) that may help to interpret the current (heavily transformed) landscape (*Šmejda 2009*).

This approach draws on a long tradition of British research of this kind (*Bewley 1995; Wilson 2000*), but also on the latest computer technologies in the field of photogrammetry and mapping (*Pavelka 2003; Scollar et al. 1990*). The aim was to provide a digital record of the identified features directly in the national system of geodetic coordinates that can be displayed and analysed in a GIS. Therefore a necessary infrastructure for such aim has been developed, based on a central geodatabase (in Microsoft SQL format) located on a server (ArcGIS Server, ArcSDE) where the raw imagery and other additional data could be stored, managed and analysed, and the outputs exported in a variety

of formats according to specific research needs. Among them we can find applications such as the web map services (*Peng - Tsou 2003; Shekar - Xiong 2008; Šmejda 2010*).

In our case study the work with archival vertical photographs usually began with a basic visual inspection of individual photographs with the aid of pocket optical stereoscopes. For the areas with higher archaeological potential, where a detailed stereoscopic analysis of related pairs of aerial photos and the mapping of information relevant for archaeology was required, a digital terrain model (DTM) of the selected area was computed from the particular stereo pair of vertical photos and used in the process of orthorectification (removal of camera tilt and transformation of the central projection of a photographic camera to the orthogonal projection of a map, producing a planimetrically correct image in the end). This work was largely helped by using software packages like Leica Photogrammetry Suite and ESRI GIS Desktop.

The result was then combined with the outcomes of the previously discussed prospection methods in the GIS project, where all information layers obtained by various methods can be cross-checked and studied in a single dataset (http://eugen.zcu.cz/vladar). Our original intention was to

Fig. 4. An aerial photo of Vladař hill and the surrounding landscape from 2004 (viewed from the west).

create a versatile research tool that would include also the data from excavated test pits, augering and trenches which were excavated in parallel with the described prospection, but the different scales and the nature of the results has not made this goal achievable within the scope of our project.

Recently a quite new perspective on surveying archaeological landscapes offers airborne laser scanning (ALS, LiDAR). This technology provides terrain models of excellent resolution (*Bewley et al. 2005; Devereux et al. 2008*) and, what is perhaps more important, it provides a continuous model without gaps (unlike the DTM extracted from photogrammetric techniques), because dense vegetation and a forest canopy present no serious obstacle in this type of survey (*Chase et al. 2011; John - Gojda 2013*).

Having such high-quality plan to hand today (Fig. 6), the former laborious ground prospection and analysis of aerial photographs may perhaps seem redundant, but we have to remember that even this seemingly perfect plan produced by LiDAR scanning must be checked, confronted with the situation in the field and interpreted (*Doneus et al. 2008*). The former investment in the collection of independent prospection data will therefore make this operation much

easier and faster, and most importantly the resulting data will be more reliable.

Conclusions

The airborne remote survey, be it photographic or as a laser-scanning survey, represents a powerful base for the integration and better understanding of data resulting from a variety of field techniques. Ground-based survey techniques are perhaps more limited in their spatial catchment, but they often add the necessary finer detail to the general picture. Satellite data were not much helpful in our case, but they can play a key role in the regions where hi-resolution aerial photographs and their long time series are not available.

However, handling data so diverse in their nature requires the utilisation of efficient methodological tools. In our case study, the technology of Geographical Information Systems provided the necessary framework. A structured geodatabase then allows building specific GIS applications which meet the particular needs of different user groups.

The project's focus on the large-scale context of spatial data has made possible a more complex analysis of the changing nature of the settlement through time. While the

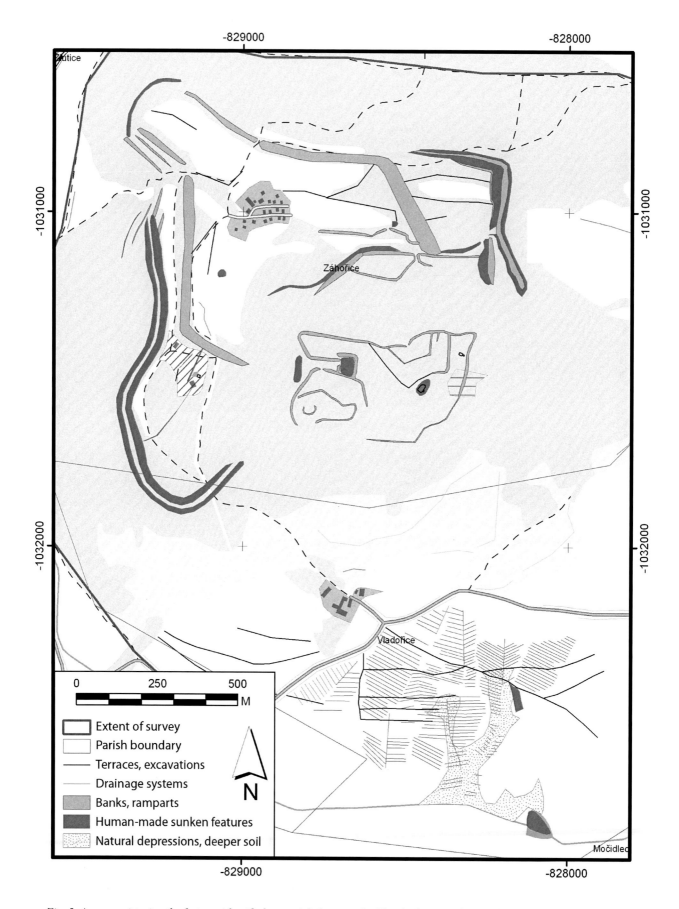

Fig. 5. A map registering the features identified on aerial photographs (Czech plane geodetic grid coordinate system S-JTSK).

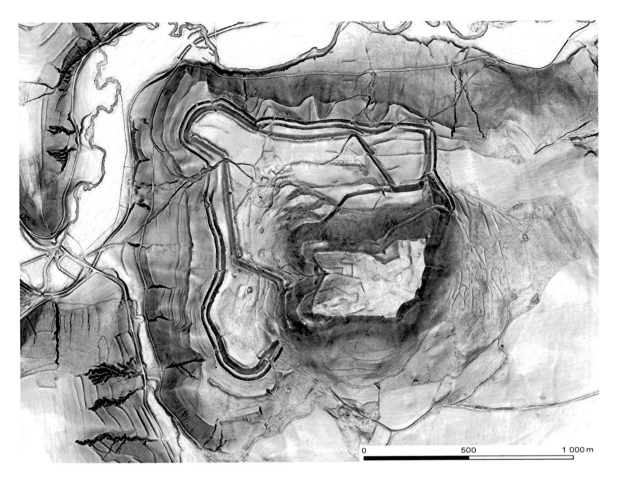

Fig. 6. A LiDAR image (visualised using sky view factor) of the site (after John - Gojda 2013, 15).

monumental character of the earthworks made it a site of interest to early archaeologists and the public alike, it is now clear that the site in fact extended over a much wider area and developed in a close-knit relationship with the surrounding landscape. The detailed study of the two well-preserved water cisterns located within the fortified settlement revealed its unique character and an exceptionally early date (*Chytráček et al. 2012*, 310; *Šmejda et al. 2010*).

The great contribution of adopted prospection methods lies in their ability to identify, delimit and characterise the spatial properties of archaeological structures (their location, size, and morphology). However, the dating and a detailed understanding of individual features discovered by the non-destructive prospection methods remains quite often impossible without an excavation, especially in the case of complex multi-period sites.

Acknowledgements

This paper was presented at the XVI UIPPS World Congress 2011 in Florianópolis, Brasil. Participation in the conference was supported by the Czech Science Foundation project No. P405-10-P145. I would like to thank Monika Baumanova for her valuable comments on the draft of this paper.

References

Beck, A. 2007: Archaeological site detection: the importance of contrast. Proceedings of the 2007 Annual Conference of the Remote Sensing and Photogrammetry Society, Newcastle University, Sept. 11-14, 2007, Newcastle.

Bewley, R.H. 1995: A National Mapping Programme for England. In: J. Kunow ed., Luftbildarchäologie in Ost- und Mitteleuropa, Forschungen zur Archäologie im Land Brandenburg; Potsdam: Brandenburgisches Landesmuseum für Ur- und Frühgeschichte, 83-92.

Bewley, R.H. - Crutchley, S.P. - Shell, C.A. 2005: New light on an ancient landscape: lidar survey in the Stonehenge World Heritage Site. Antiquity 79, 636-647.

Chase, A.F. – Chase, D.Z. – Weishampel, J.F. – Drake, J.B. – Shrestha, R.L. – Slatton, K.C. – Awe, J.J. – Carter, W.E. 2011: Airborne LiDAR, archaeology, and the ancient Maya landscape at Caracol, Belize. Journal of Archaeological Science 38(2), 387-398.

Chytráček, M. - Šmejda, L. 2005: Opevněný areál na Vladaři a jeho zázemí. K poznání sídelních struktur doby bronzové a železné na horním toku Střely v západních Čechách. Archeologické rozhledy 57, 3-56.

Chytráček, M. - Šmejda, L. 2006: Zur Bedeutung des Vladař in der Siedlungsstruktur der Hallstatt- und La-Tène- Zeit Westböhmens, Archeologická pracovní skupina východní Bavorsko/západní a jižní Čechy -

Archäologische Arbeitsgemeinschaft Ostbayern/West- und Südböhmen 15, 50-67.

Chytráček, M. - Danielisová, A. - Pokorný, P. - Kočár, P. - Kyselý, R. - Kyncl, T. - Sádlo, J. - Šmejda, L. - Zavřel, J. 2012: Vzestupy a pády regionálního mocenského centra. Přehled současného stavu poznání pravěkého opevněného areálu na Vladaři v západních Čechách. Památky archeologické 103, 273-338.

Devereux, B.J. - Amable, G.S. - Crow, P. 2008: Visualisation of LiDAR terrain models for archaeological feature detection. Antiquity 82, 470-479.

Doneus, M. – Briese, C. – Fera, M. – Janner, M.. 2008: Archaeological prospection of forested areas using full-waveform airborne laser scanning. Journal of Archaeological Science 35(4), 882-893.

Foedisch, J.A. 1867: Kamenné valy na Vladaři. Památky archeologické 7, 599-600.

Hanson, W.S. 2012: Archaeology from historical aerial and satellite archives. New York: Springer.

John, J. - Gojda, M. 2013: Ex caelo lux. Principy leteckého laserového skenování a jeho využití pro dálkový archeologický průzkum. In: M. Gojda – J. John eds, Archeologie a letecké laserové skenování krajiny. Plzeň: Katedra archeologie, Západočeská univerzita v Plzni.

Křivánek, R. 2006: Nelegální využívání detektorů kovů není problém několika jednotlivých lokalit. Archeologické rozhledy 58(2), 313-321.

Kuna, M. 2000: Surface Artefact Studies in the Czech Republic. In: J.L. Bintliff – M. Kuna – N. Venclová eds, The Future of Surface Artefact Survey in Europe, Sheffield Archaeological Monographs, Sheffield: Sheffield Academic Press, 29-44.

Pavelka, K. 2003: Fotogrammetrie. Plzeň: Západočeská univerzita v Plzni.

Peng, Y.-R. - Tsou, M.-T. 2003: Internet GIS: Distributed Geographic Information Services for the Internet and Wireless Networks. Wiley.

Scollar, I. - Tabbagh, A. - Hesse, A. - Herzog, I. 1990: Archaeological Prospecting and Remote Sensing. In: G. Hunt – M. Rycroft eds, Topics in Remote Sensing. Cambridge University Press.

Shekar, S.-X. - Hui eds 2008: Encyclopedia of GIS. Springer.

Šmejda, L. 2007: Poznámky k průzkumu lesního prostředí pomocí detektorů kovů. In: P. Krištuf – L. Šmejda – P. Vařeka eds, Opomíjená archeologie 2005-2006 (Neglected archaeology 2005-2006). Plzeň: Department of archaeology, University of West Bohemia, 233-245.

Šmejda, L. 2009: Mapování archeologického potenciálu pomocí leteckých snímků. Plzeň: Západočeská univerzita v Plzni.

Šmejda, L. 2010: Nová verze mapového serveru pro elektronickou publikaci archeologických dat. In: P. Krištuf – P. Vařeka eds, Opomíjená archeologie 2007-2008, Plzeň: Katedra archeologie Fakulty filozofické Západočeské univerzity v Plzni, 182-189.

Šmejda, L. - Chytráček, M. - Pokorný, P. - Kočár, P. 2010: Nové poznatky z výzkumu hradiště Vladař u Žlutic, okr. Karlovy Vary. In: P. Krištuf – P. Vařeka eds, Opomíjená archeologie 2007-2008. Plzeň: Katedra archeologie Fakulty filozofické Západočeské univerzity v Plzni, 46-53.

Wilson, D.R. 2000: Air Photo Interpretation for Archaeologists. London: Batsford.

APPLICATIONS OF AIRBORNE LiDAR FOR CULTURAL HERITAGE MANAGEMENT INITIATIVES IN NORTHERN IRELAND

Rory McNeary

Abstract: *The Northern Ireland Environment Agency (NIEA): Built Heritage is the statutory body charged with the protection of Northern Ireland's cultural heritage. In recent years it has commissioned a number of high-resolution (0.125 m) airborne LiDAR surveys of select archaeological landscapes. In addition to these high-resolution datasets the NIEA have also compiled lower resolution (1 m) datasets flown ostensibly for flood mapping. This further study hopes to prove the usefulness of utilizing archived LiDAR data for archaeological prospection and improved cultural heritage management (CHM). The principal objectives of these two studies include: an assessment of the archaeological resources of select landscapes using LiDAR (in conjunction with other non-intrusive data sources); the compilation of robust georeferenced datasets that collate information describing the archaeology of these areas and ultimately, the inputting of this information into the Northern Irish Monuments and Buildings Record (NIMBR) to inform future CHM. To-date project results have been significant with LiDAR analysis leading directly to new archaeological discoveries and an improved understanding of monuments and their landscape setting. LiDAR clearly has a useful future role to play in Northern Ireland, both to support archaeological research and reconnoitre areas earmarked for development or other types of invasive land-use change; particularly in upland contexts where relict feature survival is often greater. But its application has also highlighted the limitations of traditional site-based systems for managing archaeological data when confronted with the complexity of landscape character so richly reflected in LiDAR visualizations.*

Keywords: *Aerial Photography – Archaeology – Cultural Heritage Management (CHM) – Data Integration – Geographical Information System (GIS) –LiDAR – Northern Ireland*

Introduction

Airborne LiDAR (an acronym for Light Detection and Ranging) is an aerial remote sensing technique that rapidly measures the height of the ground surface by the application of a laser. These data can be used to build detailed and accurate topographic maps at metre and sub-metre resolution which have an obvious application for archaeological landscape survey (see for example *Bewley et al. 2005*; *Crutchley 2006* and *Challis et al. 2008*). The previous ten years has seen an ever increasing uptake in the use and awareness of airborne laser scanning (ALS) by archaeologists and cultural resource managers with the data being incorporated, both informally and formally, into an array of heritage-related projects (see, for example, *Barnes 2003*; *Powlesland et al. 2006*; *Opitz - Cowley 2013*). In an Irish context there have been a number of high-resolution (sub-metre) LiDAR surveys of discrete archaeological landscapes commissioned by, for example, the Northern Ireland Environment Agency (NIEA): Built Heritage[1] (e.g., Devenish Island and Kiltierney Deerpark in Co. Fermanagh and Dunluce and Lindford in Co. Antrim); and in the Republic of Ireland: the Department of the Environment, Heritage and Local Government (DoEHLG) (Skelling-Michael, Co. Kerry and the Boyne Valley, Co. Meath); The Discovery Programme (Tara, Co. Meath; see *Corns

et al. 2008*) and others (for example, University College Cork and University of Cambridge's joint study of the landscape of Loughcrew, Co. Meath; see *Shell - Roughley 2004*). But systematic application and evaluation of LiDAR data for archaeological research in an Irish context is still in its infancy and rarely, if at all, do archaeologists actually engage with these data themselves, preferring to leave the data processing and subsequent raster visualizations to 'experts'. Much remains to be done to fully assess the archaeological uses of LiDAR in the Irish landscape and incorporate it into meaningful cultural heritage management (CHM) strategies.

The author is currently engaged in a study that is utilizing high resolution LiDAR data, commissioned by the NIEA, in order to re-assess the archaeological resource of an area of the Antrim uplands at Linford. Ultimately the results will be inputted into the Northern Irish Sites and Monuments Record (NISMR) and will inform future CHM in the study area. Some preliminary results from this work are introduced as a case study alongside a more general background to cultural heritage management, aerial archaeology and the recent development of LiDAR for archaeological research in Northern Ireland.

Cultural heritage management in Northern Ireland

Cultural heritage management (CHM) in Northern Ireland is the responsibility of the NIEA. The current approach to

---

[1] The Northern Ireland Environment Agency (NIEA): Built Heritage is an agency within the Department of Environment; hereafter referred to as the NIEA.

statutory protection of the historic environment is based on two principal pieces of legislation. Firstly, historic monuments or archaeological sites are scheduled under the Historic Monuments and Archaeological Objects (Northern Ireland) Order 1995 according to several criteria, including period, rarity, group value, diversity, fragility and excavation potential. Scheduled Monument Consent is required for any activities which would result in their demolition, destruction or disturbance, or for any removal, repair or alteration. Secondly, buildings of special architectural or historical interest are protected by listing under the Planning (Northern Ireland) Order 1991. Any proposed changes that might affect the character of either the exterior or interior of these buildings are controlled by statute and require listed building consent and/or planning permission. Both pieces of legislation are administered by the NIEA. Sites and monuments and cultural landscapes can receive some further degree of protection within various landscape designations like Environmentally Sensitive Areas (ESAs), Areas of Special Scientific Interest (ASSIs) or through agri-environmental schemes, such as the Northern Ireland Countryside and Management Scheme (NICMS).

In addition to the above legislation, protection and management of the historic environment is achieved through the planning system. This is particularly important with respect to sites which lack the statutory protection of listing or scheduling. Regional policies on particular aspects of land-use planning that apply to the whole of Northern Ireland are prepared by the Planning Service (an Agency within the Department of the Environment) and normally issued through Planning Policy Statements (PPSs). PPSs of specific importance to the conservation of archaeology include: PPS 6 '*Planning, Archaeology and the Built Heritage*' which sets out regional planning policies for the protection and conservation of archaeological remains and elements of the historic landscape.

In practice, protection is achieved through consultation between the Planning Service and the NIEA. This allows statutory sites and features to be identified in development plans and where appropriate, local designations and policy statements prepared. Historic landscapes and sites may be included within Areas of Significant Archaeological Interest (ASAIs) designated in development plans. Such designations seek to identify particularly distinctive areas of the historic landscape which are likely to include a number of individual and related archaeological sites and monuments. Local policy statements are normally included in plans to protect the overall character and integrity of these distinctive areas.

Where development proposals for any new built development have the potential to impact on the historic environment, the NIEA gives advice to the Planning Service on how to respond to these proposals. Careful consideration is given by the NIEA to the implications of development proposals. The general presumption is that archaeological

sites and their settings should, where possible, be preserved. In cases where development affecting archaeological remains is considered acceptable, the NIEA will advise on required archaeological mitigation. Certain large-scale development projects and developments likely to have a significant impact may require an Environmental Impact Assessment (EIA) under the Planning (Environmental Impact Assessment) Regulations (Northern Ireland) 1999. EIAs assist Planning Service and the NIEA in reaching decisions regarding the environmental impacts of proposed developments. All the above measures are well-established and have played a major role in ensuring the protection and conservation of Northern Ireland's historic environment to-date.

Aerial archaeology in Northern Ireland

The most significant curatorial tool for CHM that the NIEA possesses is the Monuments and Buildings Record (MBR). This comprises the Sites and Monuments Record (SMR), the historic and listed buildings register, the Maritime Archaeology Record, as well as information on industrial heritage, heritage gardens, defence heritage and built heritage at risk, in the form of databases, written records, maps and photographic, drawn and digital material. The record holds a range of air photographic material and this collection comprises prints of relevant photographs from a variety of archive sources (notably Ordnance Survey Northern Ireland (OSNI) and Cambridge University Committee for Air Photography (CUCAP)) which are mainly black-and-white (both vertical and oblique) with some oblique colour photography. They are held, together with ground-level photographs, within the individual site files in the MBR. The earliest photography was commissioned in 1927 by a special sub-committee on aerial archaeology set up by the Ancient Monuments Advisory Council (AMAC). This work demonstrated the value of air photography in identifying, recording and illustrating earthwork sites in the context of a range of key monuments in Northern Ireland and several of the photographs were published in *A preliminary survey of the ancient monuments of Northern Ireland* (*Chart 1940*). Further notable surveys were undertaken by CUCAP under the direction of Professor J.K. St. Joseph between 1951-55 and 1963-73. In the 1980s archaeologists working for the Department of the Environment (NI) studied the vertical aerial photographic coverage held by OSNI looking for new archaeological sites (*Williams 1992*) and this project did much to supplement the SMR. Approximately 9 % (1,458 of 16,431) of the archaeological sites in the SMR have been identified from aerial photography (Fig. 1). However, the majority of these AP-derived sites are still poorly understood in terms of context and many are simply classified as 'earthwork', 'enclosure' or 'AP Site' in the records.

The University of Ulster (UU) and Queen's University Belfast (QUB) have also been active in aerial archaeological research and both hold collections of aerial photography relating to particular research programmes and the interests

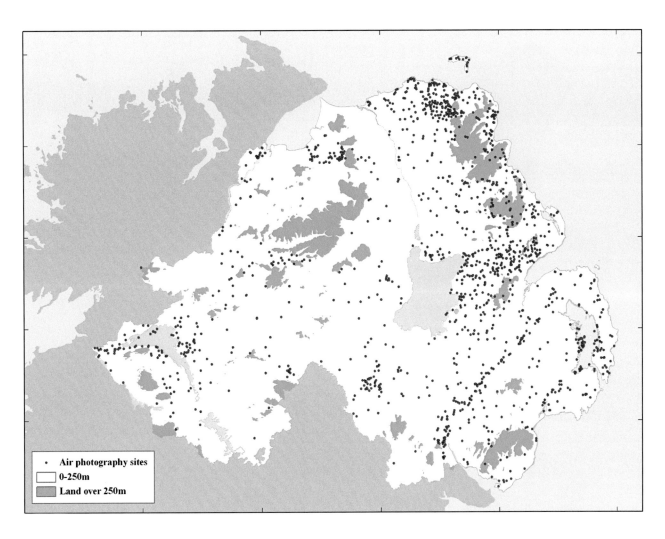

Fig. 1. The distribution of archaeological sites identified from air photography in Northern Ireland (distribution derived from NISMR).

of research staff. Dr. Barrie Hartwell of QUB has built up a substantial collection of material covering Northern Ireland related to a number of archaeological research projects (*NAPLIB 2001*). Archaeologists at the Centre for Maritime Archaeology (CMA, UU) also utilized air photography as one of several techniques used to explore the archaeology of Strangford Lough, Co. Down (*McErlean et al. 2002*) and Rathlin Island, Co. Antrim (*Forsythe - McConkey 2012*). These various research projects were more often than not carried out in close partnership with the NIEA who continue to undertake a significant amount of low-level oblique aerial photography of important sites, particularly those in State Care, for the purposes of condition monitoring as well as generating illustrative and publicity material, especially connected with publication of County surveys (for example Co. Armagh, see *Neill 2009*). Inspection of the air photographic archives held by the NIEA is part of the routine process for desk-based assessments for areas earmarked for development.

LiDAR in Northern Ireland – first steps...

Until 2008 aerial archaeology in Northern Ireland was synonymous with air photography but after the publicity

generated by the Hill of Tara[2] LiDAR Project undertaken by the Discovery Programme (*Corns et al. 2008; Corns - Shaw 2009*) the NIEA began to commission their own projects often in consultation with the Discovery Programme (*Shaw - Corns 2011*, 83). Once again the focus was on discrete localities that would feed into current programmes of research, such as Dunluce castle (*Breen 2012*; Fig. 2) and County survey publications being compiled at that time (*Neill 2009; Foley - McHugh* forthcoming). These surveys were carried out principally to allow NIEA archaeologists the chance to better contextualize the known archaeology of these areas and check micro-topographic features that may have been missed through traditional ground-survey and/or usage of aerial photography. The NIEA employed a specialist company Fugro-BKS Ltd. to undertake these LiDAR surveys along similar specifications to the Hill of Tara LiDAR Project. These surveys used the helicopter mounted laser mapping sensor FLI-MAP 400.[3] All point

---

[2] The Hill of Tara located near the River Boyne in Co. Meath is an archaeological complex associated with pre-Christian sacral kingship rituals and according to tradition was the seat of the High King of Ireland.
[3] This sensor system consists of: three 150 kHz LiDAR sensors (forward, nadir and aft); two RTK GPS receivers – which provide accurate locational information when used in conjunction with RTK base stations; Inertial Navigation System (INS) - which continuously tracks the position,

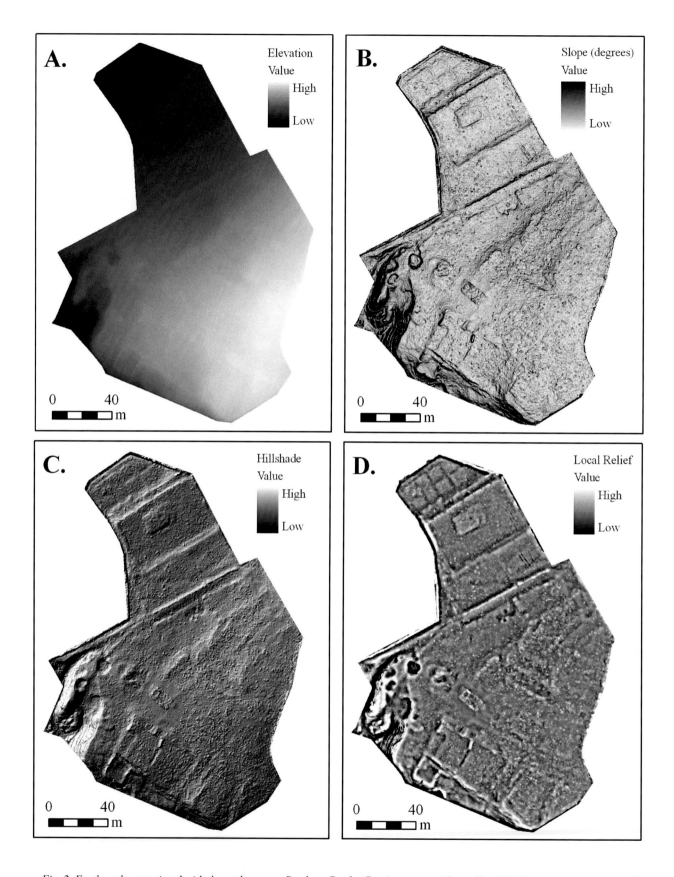

Fig. 2. Earthworks associated with the settlement at Dunluce Castle, Co. Antrim as evidenced by LiDAR data using a variety of visualizations, a) elevation, b) slope severity, c) hillshade, d) local relief.

cloud data processing and final surface model creation were carried out by Fugro-BKS Ltd. This included several stages of data processing: transformation of data to WGS84 and Irish Grid coordinates; production of tiled ASCII Digital Surface Models (DSMs); removal of vegetation, buildings and above-surface features using a combination of intensity and video inspection and the production of tiled ASCII Digital Terrain Models (DTMs) (*Corns et al. 2008*, 37-38). Both DSM and DTM ASCII datasets are tiled to more readily allow for the production of surface models. One of the first published archaeological studies to utilize LiDAR data to come out of Northern Ireland was focused on a medieval inauguration mound at Cornashee, Co. Fermanagh (*Fitzpatrick et al. 2011*).

Independently of this action researchers at the CMA were also beginning to grow interest in the research applications of LiDAR.[4] The CMA provides a contractual maritime archaeology service for the NIEA and has specialist expertise in underwater remote sensing, including the application of high-resolution multi-beam data for underwater CHM (see for example, *Westley et al. 2011* and *Plets et al. 2011*). In 2009 the remit of the CMA was extended by the NIEA to include freshwater archaeology. A first task was the creation of a GIS-based resource inventory of the archaeology associated with Northern Ireland's rivers (see *McNeary 2011*). Towards the end of this desk-based study and as a result of interaction with the Rivers Agency[5] on behalf of the NIEA, some 1300 sq km of LiDAR with a raster resolution of 1m was acquired.[6] These LiDAR data were flown ostensibly for the Rivers Agency's programme of strategic flood mapping and are focused on river valley and coastal landscapes (68 % of the coverage is land classified as agricultural, the majority of which is improved pasture; 27 % is classified as artificial fabric, i.e., urban areas; Fig. 3a). Despite this the land area covered by this LiDAR holds 5267 historic environment records and 285 scheduled archaeological monuments (SAMs) (Fig. 3b), and the potential of the data for palaeo-landscape reconstruction, archaeological prospection and monument

visualization under tree-cover was recognized at CMA from initial test samples of data provided (*McNeary - Westley 2010; Forsythe - McConkey 2012, 133*). Since acquiring the 1 m-resolution LiDAR data from the Rivers Agency the CMA has utilized it for archaeological prospection; improved visualizations of recorded monuments, such as earthworks (Fig. 4); pre-survey planning and post-survey visualizations and environmental modelling (approach informed by *Kincey et al. 2008*) as part of the unit's current core brief for the NIEA which examines the potential impacts of climate change on Northern Ireland's cultural heritage (see *McErlean et al. 2011; McNeary - Westley 2013*). Because of CMA's existing background in micro-topographic data analysis, albeit bathymetric data, and the author's exposure to GI technologies as a researcher with the Discovery Programme (see for example *McNeary - Shanahan 2005; 2008; Corns et al. 2008; Brady et al. 2013*) the CMA found itself in a position to offer valued assistance to the NIEA with its own high-resolution discrete LiDAR datasets, in terms of raster model analysis, data integration, feature classification and digitization; as well as incorporate the 1 m-resolution Rivers Agency data into a number of CHM-led research projects on behalf of the NIEA.

For example, the high-resolution LiDAR survey commissioned by the NIEA of Devenish Island[7] has vastly improved upon existing earthwork surveys carried out in the past by the NIEA and provided new insights into the medieval monastic landscape surrounding the central church complex. One such new insight is the imaging of a holloway or path that leads away from the church complex to what would have been the western ferry terminal. This ferry crossing was used up until the 19th century by funerary parties. An antiquarian writing in the 1800s described it as thus, '...a very rudely constructed *tochar* or path..., leads to a port..., situated on the western side of the island.... It is composed almost entirely of small rough surface-stones, and is the only road by which funeral processions from the main land proceed to the cemeteries' (*Wakeman 1874, 62*). The LiDAR Local Relief Model (LRM) clearly images this pathway and its terminus at the former pre-drainage shoreline – the site of a potential medieval landing place or 'port'. This potential 'port' and the channel between the island and the mainland is the focus of a current research project being undertaken at the CMA. This work builds on the work of *Lafferty et al.* (*2005*) utilizing shallow water side-imaging sonar in conjunction with dive-truthing. The new airborne LiDAR and conventional aerial photography are also being used to better contextualize these crossing points as part of a wider monastic landscape. In 2012 a preliminary underwater sonar survey was conducted.

orientation, and velocity of the helicopter; as well as digital imaging and digital video capture. This technology has the advantage in that it is helicopter mounted, allowing for relatively slow air speeds and low altitude flight paths which result in the collection of extremely high resolution height data (10 cm). Flights are operated at an altitude of approximately 275 m above ground level (AGL) at a speed of 25.7 m/s and a scan angle of 60°. The scanner acquires data at a pulse repetition rate of 150,000Hz. The average point density of the dataset is about 15-30 points/m². The vertical accuracy is equal to or better than ±3cm and horizontal accuracy equal to or better than ±5 cm (see Corns et al. 2008, 36-37).

[4] Attendance at the Training and Research in the Archaeological Interpretation of LiDAR (TRAIL) International Workshop at Bibracte in 2011 and subsequent inclusion in the ArchaeoLandscapes Europe network also focused the CMA to the potential of the technology.

[5] The Rivers Agency acts on behalf of the Department of Agriculture and Rural Development (DARD) and is responsible for drainage and flood defence in Northern Ireland.

[6] This data was also flown by Fugro-BKS Ltd. Vertical accuracy is +/- 150 mm. The raw data has been gridded and the point cloud data interpolated to a raster surface stored in grid format and provided as ASCII files. Major 'artefacts' have been processed out already, such as buildings and trees, providing a 'bare-earth' model or DTM (Digital Terrain Model). However, in a few instances DTM and DSM (Digital Surface Model) CSV grids and original point clouds exist for some areas.

[7] Devenish, an island in Lough Erne, Co. Fermanagh, is one of the greater Irish medieval ecclesiastical sites (McKenna 1931; Radford 1970) and is considered to be the most important of Lough Erne's many island church settlements. The ruins are in State Care. The church site was founded in the sixth century AD and functioned until the early seventeenth century (burial practice continuing into the nineteenth century). It was raided by Vikings in AD 837 and burned in AD 1157, but in the middle ages flourished as the site of a parish church and St. Mary's Augustinian Priory. The site was also a likely stop-over for waterborne medieval pilgrims en route to St. Patrick's Purgatory in Lough Derg, Co. Donegal.

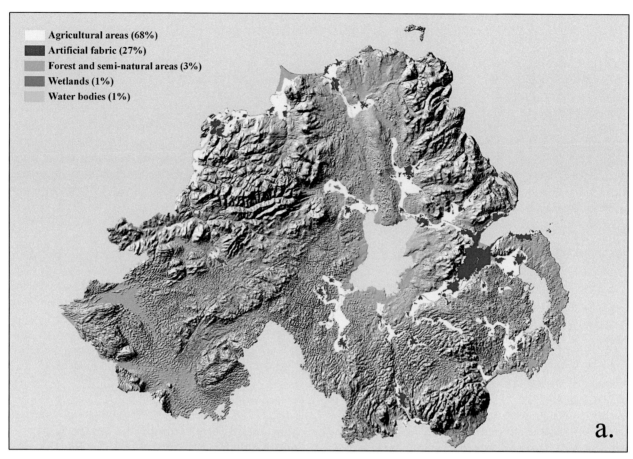

Agricultural areas (68%)
Artificial fabric (27%)
Forest and semi-natural areas (3%)
Wetlands (1%)
Water bodies (1%)

a.

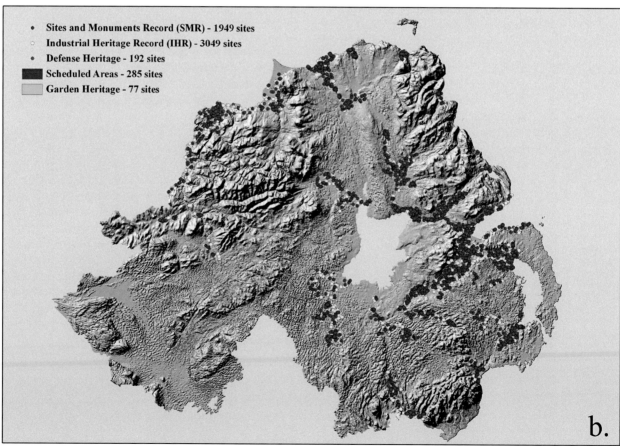

•   Sites and Monuments Record (SMR) - 1949 sites
○   Industrial Heritage Record (IHR) - 3049 sites
•   Defense Heritage - 192 sites
Scheduled Areas - 285 sites
Garden Heritage - 77 sites

b.

Fig. 3. Area coverage of Rivers Agency's 1m spatial resolution LiDAR data, a) land cover type, b) historic environment records falling within.

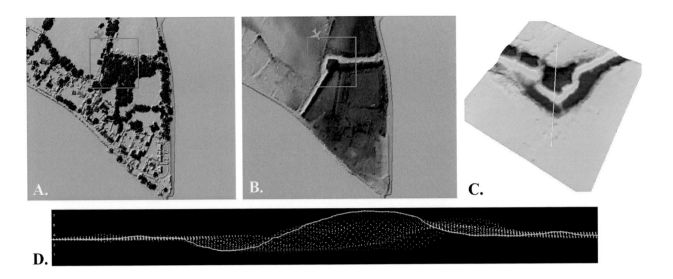

Fig. 4. Earthworks of a Plantation-era bastion fort at Culmore, Co. Londonderry as evidenced by 1m spatial resolution Rivers Agency LiDAR data, a) LiDAR first pulse DSM, b) LiDAR second pulse DTM, c) 3D visualization of bastion and ditch, d) DTM point cloud profile of bastion and ditch.

From the data collected it has been possible to render the underwater terrain and identify and mark anomalous features imaged on the bottom. These potential targets have been mapped in a GIS and will inform a future programme of diving at the site (Fig. 5). The combined results from this study will lead to improved decision-making concerning the ongoing management of not only the terrestrial environment of this site but also the underwater cultural landscape of the associated ferrying location.

Similarly the 'rediscovery' by the author of an early seventeenth-century earthen star-shaped fortification on the banks of the River Foyle at Dunnalong[8] utilizing the archived 1 m resolution LiDAR data allowed for the earthwork remains of the fort to be mapped for the first time since the cartographic efforts of the Ordnance Survey in the 1830s and proved that there was still a topographic signature of the fort surviving in the fields adjacent to a modern farmstead. This rediscovery helped initiate an interdisciplinary archaeological research project in 2012 that brought together professional archaeologists and members of the local public to learn more about the site and celebrate a 'shared' history and archaeology in the context of post-conflict Northern Ireland. The field project integrated terrestrial and underwater remote sensing with limited test excavation, and while from a social perspective the real success of the project was the community engagement aspect of the project, from an archaeological perspective the principal success has been the level of digital data integration (Fig. 6). The LiDAR topographic model helped inform the terrestrial geophysical survey

strategy, the results from which have considerably enhanced our knowledge of the monument. In fact the LiDAR model has proved the foundation for all subsequent analyses as well as forming the basis for the spatial database within the project GIS (*McNeary 2013*, 42-45).

Case study: the Linford uplands

In addition to these 'integrated' surveys of discrete locations, the author has been working on a more expansive high-resolution LiDAR dataset on behalf of the NIEA and as part of the author's current Doctoral studies. The study site is located in north-east county Antrim and is represented by a 9 km² area of LiDAR coverage (Fig. 7a). The principal aim of this LiDAR-based study is the transcription, recording and interpretation of all archaeological features visible. It is intended that the results will not only enhance the existing information in the SMR but also act as a planning and curatorial tool to inform future landscape management decisions and detailed field recording and/or excavation in the area. The LiDAR survey was commissioned by the NIEA because of the area's recognized archaeological importance. Within the study area, 42 archaeological monuments are recorded, ranging from Neolithic flint mines to post-medieval settlements and field systems, and 11 scheduled archaeological monuments (SAMs); these SAMs include the enigmatic 'Linford earthworks' (Fig. 7b), the inland promontory fort at Knockdhu (Fig. 7c) and the Anglo-Norman motte in Corkermain townland, known as Ballyhackett motte (Fig. 7d).

The LiDAR data takes in an upland zone (Antrim plateau) and a lowland zone (coastal strip) but the area of archaeological interest is very much focused on the transitional zone and the uplands themselves where relict feature survival is highest and agricultural improvement and modern ploughing has had less impact on rates of survival.

---

[8] Dunnalong was the site of a Gaelic Irish towerhouse belonging to a sept of the O'Neill lords. It was strategically placed to control an important ferry crossing and prolific salmon fishery on the River Foyle. In 1600 as part of the campaign against the Gaelic lords, English crown forces garrisoned the site and created an earthwork bastion fort. Although occupation was short lived, this was a pivotally important site during the latter stages of the Nine Years War (1593-1603).

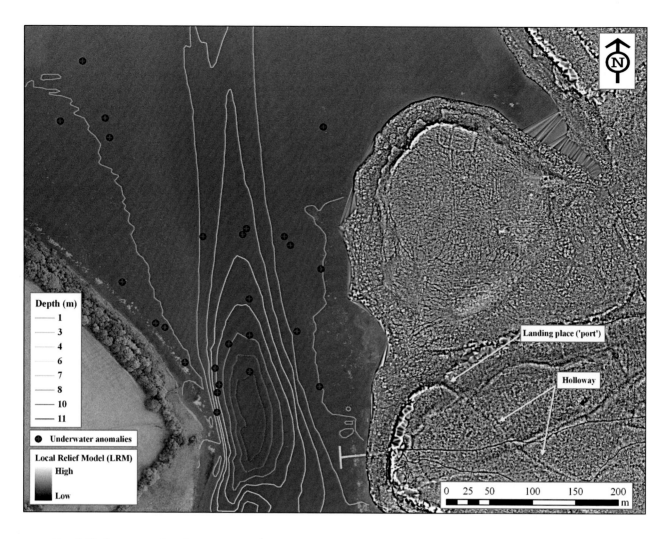

Fig. 5. Underwater archaeological survey results and LiDAR local relief model (LRM) combined at Devenish Island, Co. Fermanagh.

The uplands are characterized by a series of structural plateaux, which include Knockdhu promontory and are largely given over to pasture with sheep grazing dominating as the major land-use.

Research methods

A GIS project (ESRI ArcGIS v9.3) was created to provide a platform for co-registering existing datasets, both historical and modern, with the acquired LiDAR data for the study area. Contemporary OSNI® vector product (1:2500 and 1:50,000 scale), OSNI® orthophotography (Version 1: flown between March 2003 and July 2006), digital Geological Survey Northern Ireland (GSNI) maps and georeferenced historical mapping dating from the 1830s were added. These data were acquired from Land and Property Services (LPS) through the Northern Ireland Mapping Agreement (NIMA). In addition digital historic environment records from the NIEA and high-resolution (0.1 m) vertical aerial orthophotography, also flown by Fugro-BKS Ltd., were incorporated into the project.

For this study a number of now established techniques for the visualization and analysis of airborne LiDAR elevation data were experimented with using existing tools within ESRI ArcGIS v9.3 software. In addition an ArcGIS-compatible 'LiDAR DEM visualization' toolbox was incorporated into the project GIS and a stand-alone version of Sky-View Factor Computation code (SAV) (version 1.11, Feb. 2011) run with IDL Virtual Machine was used (10 m search radius; 8 directions); both developed at the Institute of Anthropological and Spatial Studies ZRC SAZU (*ZRC SAZU, 2010; Kokalj et al. 2011*).

For digital transcription of archaeological features, both established and previously unrecorded, the local relief modelling technique (*Hesse 2010*) proved to be the most expedient as there is negligible horizontal shift in the position of positive and negative features (*Bennett et al. 2012*, 45). In this case the local relief model (LRM) was derived by resampling the original DEM to a lower resolution (the trend DEM) which was then subtracted from the original DEM. This procedure separates local small-scale features from large-scale landscape forms (*Štular et al. 2012*, 3356) and was effective in its own right for feature detection. It clearly identified positive and negative features in both low- and high-relief landscapes within the study area and even subtle low-intensity earthworks, such as

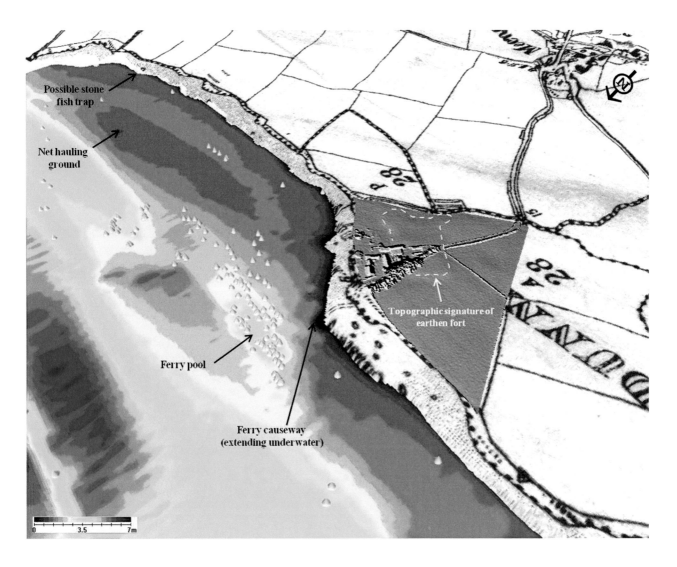

Fig. 6. Digital data integration as part of the Dunnalong Archaeology Project undertaken in 2012.

cultivation ridges, could be readily delineated and digitized. This visualization was given context by comparing other raster visualization techniques, aerial observation from recent vertical orthophotos and nineteenth and twentieth century historic maps. A 3D visualization of the study area was also created in ArcScene in order to provide another perspective. This 3D scene incorporated a standard LiDAR hillshade and local relief model (LRM), as well as the orthophotos and historic mapping. A lack of contemporary ground observations limits the absolute reliability of all the feature detection and transcription carried out and a programme of future field verification is required.

First Results: Overview and examples

Preliminary analysis of the LiDAR data for the study area has revealed a wealth of new archaeological features as well as better quantifying and qualifying the known record. Stand-out discoveries include the sheer number of potentially new hut sites on the promontory itself (a total of 48; whereas before only 18 were known – see Fig. 8) and the large number of potential open-caste mining scars

and trackways. In addition the LiDAR visualisations have allowed for the delineation of relict boundaries, cultivation ridges, settlements, enclosures and cairns. 3-D models have also aided our understanding of monument morphologies and provided a better appreciation of their landscape setting in relation to other relevant relict features. This new information is to be incorporated into the existing SMR and recommendations made for protection in certain cases under the Historic Monuments and Archaeological Objects (NI) Order 1995. A further benefit of the LiDAR data is that they have revealed potential threats to the cultural heritage, such as, arterial drainage, overgrazing, erosion and inappropriately sited development; all of which can now be better managed in the future (Fig. 9). The following examples of house sites, trackways and possible mining pits provide an impression of the range of archaeological sites detected from the initial LiDAR analysis.

Aside from the large number of potential new hut sites on Knockdhu promontory, the LiDAR data has also revealed over one hundred and fifty potential relict buildings that pre-date the OS 6-inch map of 1829-33 (Fig. 10a). These

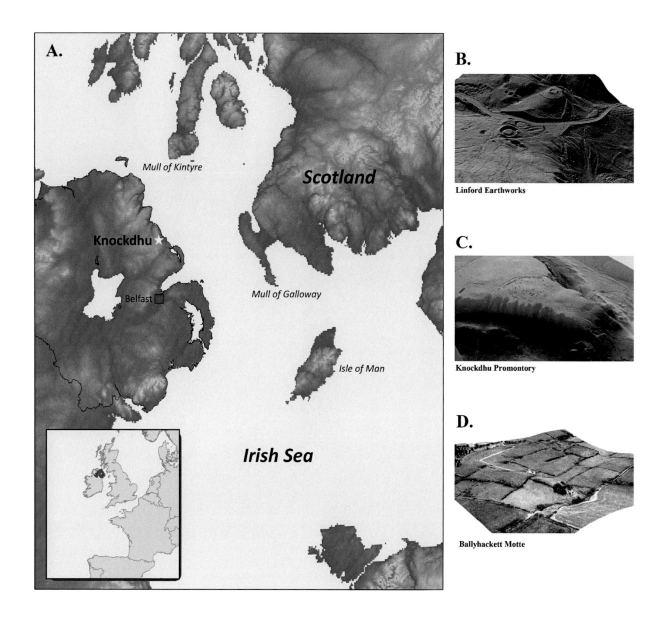

Fig. 7. a) map showing the location of LiDAR project at Knockdhu, Co. Antrim, b) LiDAR 3D hillshade of 'Linford earthworks', c) 3D visualization of Knockdhu promontory with relict features highlighted, d) high-resolution LiDAR height data and aerial photography combined at Ballyhackett motte.

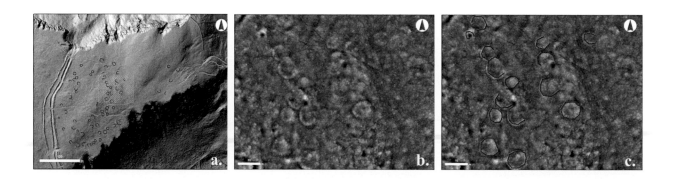

Fig. 8. Distribution of potential Bronze Age hut sites on Knockdhu Promontory identified from LiDAR survey, standard hillshade with hut sites digitized in red.

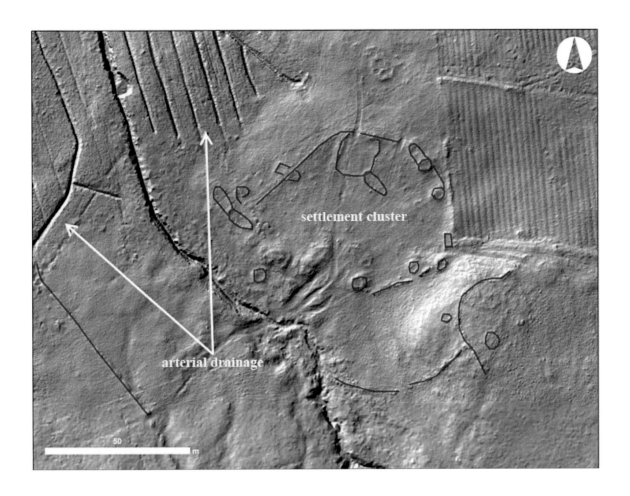

Fig. 9. Relict settlement cluster mapped in relation to encroaching arterial drainage in Linford townland, Co. Antrim.

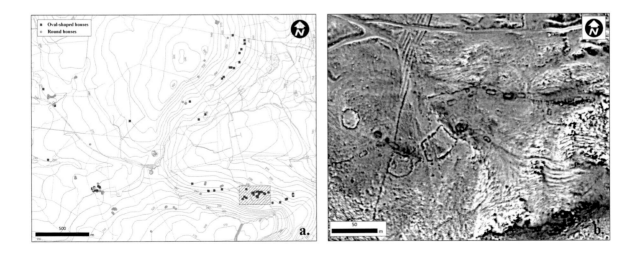

Fig. 10. a) distribution of possible relict house sites in the study area as identified from LiDAR survey, b) example of a settlement cluster associated with animal enclosures and relict cultivation displayed as a local relief model (LRM).

remains are most likely associated with the practice of *Buailteachas* (Anglicised to 'booleying');[9] that is, the seasonal movement of people with their livestock between fixed summer and winter pastures. But the sheer number of potential house sites identified above 250 m AOD creates the very real possibility of medieval and prehistoric settlement horizons encompassed in this relict farming landscape. These buildings predominate on the lower slopes but further concentrations occur on the plateau. They are found singly, in loose groupings, and lying inside (and sometimes abutting) circular and sub-circular walled 'compounds'. These structures are separated into two broad types: 'round houses' and 'oval-shaped' (rounded rectangular) structures (after *Gardiner 2012*).[10] One distinct clustering of relict buildings is ranged along the lower slopes of the northern face of Knockdhu promontory and to the south of an extensive east-west braided trackway at a height of 240 m AOD (Fig. 10b). The LiDAR survey has revealed up to thirty-five potential individual buildings along this ridge, the majority of which are oval-shaped. *Hodges (1975)* recognized a portion of these buildings and he described them as follows: *'On a N-facing spur beneath the N. cliff of Knockdhu are ten elliptically shaped structures... Their walls are two-stones thick and 2 ft across, and there is regularly one entrance about 2 ft wide. This must be the summer settlement of a group of shepherds or cattle-herders working on the top of the Sallagh Braes'* (*Hodges 1975*, 22). *Hodges' (1975)* assumption that the structures he viewed represented the remains of 'booleys' is probably correct as the overall morphology of the settlement, the size of the buildings and their association with animal folds would suggest a settlement linked with seasonal pastoral farming activity. These clustered buildings and their association with animal enclosures suggest that this north-facing spur seems to have been designated as a stock-focused farming zone, probably used as a location where herd animals could be brought from the uplands for

shearing, milking, readying for market/consumption, etc. However, at the western end of this ridge there is ephemeral evidence for relict cultivation on either side of the braided trackway where crops of oats or rye may have been sown and harvested in addition to this dairy activity. Another smaller area (1,824 m²) of broad ridge and furrow is located to the immediate north of the large cluster of buildings.

Interpretation of the LiDAR data has also revealed evidence for extensive trackways. Before the construction of the principal vehicular road in the latter part of the nineteenth century, access to the plateau appears to have been provided by two distinctive concentrations of trackways or holloways clearly evidenced in the LiDAR visualizations (Fig. 11). The first group of holloways is located in the north of the study area and provides access to the upland plateau. They appear to be linked with isolated farmsteads on the lower slopes. The LiDAR standard hillshade reveals that a number of the principal trails have in places become heavily braided where the erosion of tracks through continuous use on these slopes has necessitated the creation of further new paths. It is probable that these paths are primarily linked to past and even current herding activities (wear paths from cattle and sheep). The second major concentration of braided tracks runs beneath the northern flank of Knockdhu promontory; at one end they appear to merge into a modern farm track before continuing past Ballyhackett motte and onto Carncastle church. At the other end the trails pass up through the Linford Gap[11] where they radiate out in all directions. A standing stone and a cross-incised boulder[12] located alongside one of these tracks on the plateau appear to corroborate the antiquity of these trackways.

In addition, concentrations of possible extractive pits are evident (Fig. 12a); with the largest concentration in the area immediately west of the Linford Gap. These pits are situated either side of the modern vehicular road, with some pits cut by the thoroughfare. These pits are both singular and conjoined, averaging c. 2.5 m-3 m deep. A particularly large concentration (90 m E-W x 25 m N-S) is situated to the north of the road, c. 140 m west of the Linford cairn. These pits have been variably explained as natural sink holes or 'dolines'; further evidence of flint mining; and, probably most convincingly by *Hodges* (*1975*, 19, 22), as iron ore extraction pits. *Hodges (1975)* noted iron staining and residues on the exposed sides of the pits and observed the fact that some of these pits held water while others did not, ruling out the possibility that all were sink holes (*Hodges 1975*, 22). And because of their relatively small size, in comparison to other nineteenth-century workings in north Antrim, he thought them likely to be medieval or even Iron Age in date (*Hodges 1975*, 19). The underlying basalt

---

[9]   The practice of 'booleying' refers to the exploitation of seasonal pastures (often in uplands) and their associated temporary dwellings ('booley huts') and was often an integral part of 'rundale' (an infield/outfield system of mixed farming). The word 'booley' is an anglicisation of the Irish word buaile ('a temporary milking place'). In an Irish context this practice dates back to the Early Medieval period, or even older, and continued in use up until the nineteenth century. The practice was known in Scotland as Sheiling (see Miller 1967, 193-221).

[10]   While round buildings continued to be constructed in Ireland until c. AD 1000 (Lynn 1978, 37; Gardiner 2012, 22) there is every chance that some of the buildings imaged by the LiDAR at Linford may be relics of the warmer and drier climates of the Early and Middle Bronze Age; particularly those on the plateau closest to Knockdhu promontory fort and in the vicinity of possible flint extraction pits. Gardiner (2012, 23-24) places the oval-shaped buildings he has identified on the Garron plateau, Co. Antrim in the later medieval period (c. thirteenth or fourteenth century AD until the seventeenth century AD). However, circular, oval, rectangular and square-shaped house-plans have been presumed to be the remains of booley huts in other parts of Ireland (O'Sullivan - Downey 2003, 35) and evidently in use up until the eighteenth and nineteenth centuries and so caution must be exercised when attempting to ascribe a date to these types of buildings whose function, seasonal utilization and date remain debatable. It can also be assumed that not all the buildings identified from the LiDAR survey were dwellings, as some may have served as stores, barns or small animal folds; it is also possible that in a very few cases clearance cairns and other small mounds have been misinterpreted as hut sites. Clearly extensive field verification is needed to ascertain the true morphology, function and nature of construction of many of these buildings.

[11]   The Linford Gap is located where the modern road ascends onto the upland plateau.

[12]   The cross-incised boulder has been referred to as 'The Priest's Grave' (O'Laverty 1887, 582) and known locally as 'The Mass Rock' (Hamlin 2008, 443). Evans (1966, 47) called the standing stone situated c. 800 m to the south-east of this stone (and also situated on this routeway) 'The Headless Cross'; a name derived from the OS Memoirs (Hamlin 2008, 443).

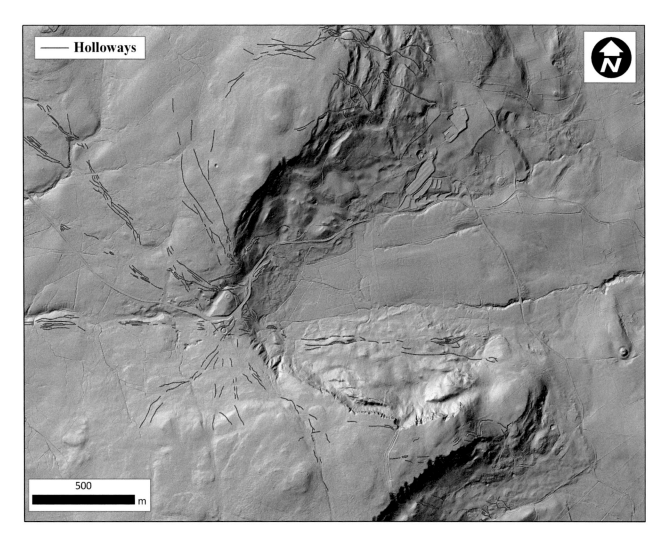

Fig. 11. Distribution of paths or holloways identified from LiDAR survey overlain on standard hillshade (Linford LiDAR Project).

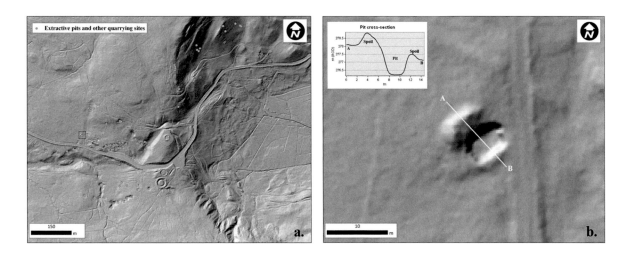

Fig. 12. a) distribution of potential quarrying sites, note detailed study marked by red box, b) example of a 'quarry hole' and associated spoil located on the plateau (Linford LiDAR Project).

geology, as mapped by the GSNI, seems to corroborate this. It is tempting to link the lumps of iron ore and possible hammer stones found in a souterrain[13] at the foot of Knockdhu (*Lawlor 1916*, 35-36; *Neill 2011*, 31) in the early 1900s with these suggested iron ore extraction pits. However, a note of caution is sounded as profiles across these pits, extracted from the LiDAR DEM, do not appear to always show clear signs for the associated spoil that one would expect to see alongside these types of extractive features. It is possible that stone and/or earth were being extracted and removed from site for more conventional building purposes. An example of a pit or quarry with associated spoil, located on the plateau, is presented in Fig. 12b.

Future Directions

The primary thrust of this research has been CHM-led with emphasis on the verification and extension of the existing SMR and the identification of threats to it. To this end, the LiDAR survey has been a success and offers cultural heritage managers in the NIEA a resource to draw upon for some time; particularly as any new features identified will have to be ground-truthed and more fully recorded in the field. However, the full research potential of the dataset has yet to be realised and further data analysis and integration in conjunction with documentary research is ongoing. A programme of field verification is also envisaged. The LiDAR data has the potential to be utilised as part of wider landscape driven studies examining themes, such as, resource exploitation, movement and control, territoriality, rural settlement, land-use and the changing nature of the agricultural economy.[14] It would appear from the preliminary results of this study that airborne LiDAR may provide the key to a fuller understanding of the extent of relict archaeological features in Northern Ireland's uplands. An important consideration in light of a recent upsurge in applications for upland-sited wind farms in Northern Ireland.

Conclusion

It is obvious that LiDAR has an important role to play in revealing patterns of change and hence threats to the archaeological resource at a landscape level in Northern Ireland. It also has an obvious application in supporting archaeological research, particularly that which is concerned with rural settlement, field patterns and environmental change. And while the implications of LiDAR for enhancing, understanding, conserving and

managing the archaeological resource is still clearly in its infancy in Northern Ireland, there is no doubt its use will increase as practitioner competency improves within the archaeological community, more archived data becomes available and bespoke surveys become less expensive. In the short term an obvious way to overcome the expense of commissioning LiDAR surveys is to not only utilize archived data, but promote the cost of ownership across government agencies. A strong case should be made for archaeology to be considered when LiDAR is commissioned for environmental protection, strategic development planning and agri-environment planning and monitoring purposes.

In the meantime intensive reviews of existing archived LiDAR data will undoubtedly lead to new discoveries; for example, the Linford LiDAR project has led to significant increases in known archaeology in what is a relatively small area (9 km²). But a very real challenge remains in translating the complexity of historical features and landscape character so richly reflected in the LiDAR visualizations into traditional site-based systems for managing archaeological data; overcoming what Dimitrij Mlekuz has termed 'messy landscapes' or 'messy entanglements' that LiDAR is bringing to bear on the practice of landscape archaeology (*Mlekuz 2011*). A major problem lies in the fact that many relict features imaged from LiDAR might be better classified as '…elements of the cultural landscape rather than archaeological sites in a traditional sense…' (*Bofinger - Hesse 2011*, 167) and yet often these 'elements' (such as field boundaries, cultivation ridges, trackways, etc.) provide contextual evidence for relationships between archaeological sites and how modern landscape change relates to longer term patterns of change. Under current legislation in Northern Ireland (and elsewhere) the SMR is essentially a list of known and potential monuments but this should not preclude the development of other non-statutory interpretive mapping and characterization projects and the conscious use of LiDAR (when and where it exists) as a means of ensuring fuller and earlier recognition of archaeological constraints for strategic assessments of land-use policy and development, particularly in areas of complex relict landscape survival.[15] LiDAR will undoubtedly force recognition amongst cultural heritage managers across Europe that information about the historic landscape environment will have to be managed in increasingly more sophisticated ways.

Acknowledgements

The author is grateful to the Rivers Agency who facilitated the transfer of LiDAR data to the NIEA and have allowed

---

[13] A souterrain is an artificial underground structure most commonly built of dry-stone walling and associated with the end of the first millennium AD and start of the second millennium AD. Because of the inbuilt defensive features it is thought that these structures were built mainly for use as places of refuge and not as storage areas (Aalen et al. 1997, 49).

[14] One theme the author is particularly interested in exploring further is the potential for medieval rural settlement survival in this landscape, the evidence for which is limited within the context of research in Irish archaeology as a whole (Barry 2009, viii), and future research will target relict settlement remains for detailed field analysis and Carbon-14 sampling.

---

[15] This is particularly relevant in light of The Strategic Environmental Assessment (SEA) Regulations (2004), brought into practice in Northern Ireland by the Environmental Assessment of Plans and Programmes Regulations (Northern Ireland) 2004, which try to ensure that environmental issues (including archaeology) are taken into account at every stage in the preparation, implementation, monitoring and review of plans, programmes and strategies. The requirement for assessment has come from the EU Directive on Strategic Environmental Assessment (2001/42/EC).

its subsequent use for archaeological research and cultural heritage management (CHM) initiatives; to Claire Foley and John O'Keeffe (NIEA: Built Heritage) for providing the Devenish, Dunluce and Linford LiDAR datasets and to colleagues at the Centre for Maritime Archaeology (CMA), especially Colin Breen, Wes Forsythe and Rory Quinn who commented on an earlier draft of this paper; a further thanks to colleague Kieran Westley who has assisted me greatly with the technical aspects of LiDAR visualizations. The above summary *Cultural heritage management in Northern Ireland* is drawn from the report: *McNeary, R. and Westley, K. 2013.* Climate change and Cultural Heritage. Report prepared for the Northern Ireland Environment Agency: Built Heritage Division. pp. 233; reproduced by permission of the authors and NIEA: Built Heritage. This work has been carried out in cooperation with NIEA: Built Heritage and the author would like to take the opportunity to thank Claire Foley, John O'Keeffe and Rhonda Robinson for ongoing assistance and guidance.

References

Aalen, F.H.A. - Whelan, K. - Stout, G. eds 1997: Atlas of the Irish Rural Landscape. Cork University Press.

Barnes, I. 2003: Aerial remote-sensing techniques used in the management of archaeological monuments on the British army's Salisbury Plain training area, Wiltshire, UK. Archaeological Prospection 10, 83-90.

Barry, T. 2009: Foreword. In: C. Corlett – M. Potterton eds, Rural Settlement in Medieval Ireland in light of recent archaeological excavations. Bray: Wordwell.

Bennett, R. - Welham, K. - Hill, R.A. - Ford, A. 2012: A Comparison of Visualisation Techniques for Models Created from Airborne Laser Scanned Data. Archaeological Prospection 19, 41-48.

Bewley, R.H. – Crutchley, S.P. – Shell, C.A. 2005: New light on an ancient landscape: lidar survey in the Stonehenge World Heritage Site. Antiquity 79 (305), 636-647.

Bofinger, J. - Hesse, R. 2011: Laminar analysis of LiDAR detected structures as a powerful instrument for archaeological heritage management in Baden-Württemburg, Germany. In: D. Cowley ed., Remote Sensing for Archaeological Heritage Management, EAC Occasional Paper No. 5, 161-171.

Brady, N. - McNeary, R. - Shanahan, B. - Shaw, R. 2013: Unravelling medieval landscapes from the air. Peritia 22-23, 295-316.

Breen, C. 2012: Dunluce Castle: History and Archaeology. Dublin: Four Courts Press.

Challis, K. – Kokalj, Z. – Kincey, M. – Moscrop, D. – Howard, A.J. 2008: Airborne lidar and historic environment records. Antiquity 82(318), 1055-1064.

Chart, D.A. 1940: A preliminary survey of the ancient monuments of Northern Ireland. Belfast: HMSO.

Corns, A. - Fenwick, J. - Shaw, R. 2008: More than meets the eye. Archaeology Ireland 22(3), 34-38.

Corns, A. - Shaw, R. 2009: High resolution 3-dimensional documentation of archaeological monuments and landscapes using airborne LiDAR. Journal of Cultural Heritage 10(1), e72-e77.

Crutchley, S. 2006: Light detection and ranging (lidar) in the Witham Valley, Lincolnshire: an assessment of new remote sensing techniques. Archaeological Prospection 13(4), 251-257.

Evans, E.E. 1966: Prehistoric and Early Christian Ireland: A Guide. London.

FitzPatrick, E. - Murphy, E. - McHugh, R. - Donnelly, C. - Foley, C. 2011: Evoking the white mare: the cult landscape of Sgiath Gabhra and its medieval perception in Gaelic Fir Mhanach. In: R. Schot – C. Newman – E. Bhreathnach eds, Landscapes of Cult and Kingship. Dublin: Four Courts Press, 163-191.

Foley, C. - McHugh, R. forthcoming: An Archaeological Survey of County Fermanagh (Vol. 1). Stationery Office Books.

Forsythe, W. - McConkey, R. 2012: Rathlin Island: An Archaeological Survey of a Maritime Landscape. Stationery Office Books.

Gardiner, M.F. 2012: Medieval settlement on the Garron Plateau of Northern Ireland: a preliminary report. *Medieval Settlement* 27, 20-28.

Hamlin, A.E. 2008: The Archaeology of Early Christianity in the North of Ireland. British Archaeological Reports, British Series 460.

Hesse, R. 2010: Lidar-derived Local Relief Models – a new tool for archaeological prospection. Archaeological Prospection 17, 67-72.

Hodges, R. 1975: Knockdhu Promontory Fortress: An Interpretation of its function in the light of some preliminary fieldwork. Ulster Journal of Archaeology 38, 19-24.

Kincey, M. - Challis, K. - Howard, A. 2008: Modelling selected implications of potential future climate change on the archaeological resource of river catchments: an application of geographical information systems. Conservation and Management of Archaeological Sites 10 (2), 113-131.

Kokalj, Ž. - Zakšek, K. - Oštir, K. 2011: Application of Sky-View Factor for the Visualization of Historic Landscape Features in Lidar-Derived Relief Models. Antiquity 85 (327), 263-273.

Lafferty, B. - Quinn, R. - Breen, C. 2005: A side-scan sonar and high-resolution Chirp sub-bottom profile study of the natural and anthropogenic sedimentary record of Lower Lough Erne, northwestern Ireland. Journal of Archaeological Science 33, 756-766.

Lawlor, H.C. 1916: Some notes on the investigation of dwelling places of prehistoric man in N.E. Ireland. Proc. Belfast Nat. Hist. and Phil. Soc. 31-61.

Lynn, C. 1978: Early Christian period domestic structures: a change from round to rectangular plans? Irish Archaeological Research Forum 5, 29-45.

McErlean, T. - McConkey, R. - Forsythe, W. 2002: Strangford Lough: An Archaeological Survey of the Maritime Cultural Landscape. Blackstaff Press.

McErlean, T., McNeary, R. and Westley, K. 2011: Climate Change and Coastal Archaeology in Northern Ireland. NIEA, Coast, Issue 7, 46-49.

McKenna, J.E. 1931: Devenish (Lough Erne): Its History, Antiquities, and Traditions. Dublin/Enniskillen.

McNeary, R. 2011: Riverine Archaeology in Northern Ireland: an evaluation. International Journal of Nautical Archaeology 40(1), 162-170.

McNeary, R. 2013: Relocating the site of the fort using aerial survey. In: The Lost Settlement of Dunnalong. Guildhall Press, 42-45.

McNeary, R. - Shanahan, B. 2005: Medieval settlement, society and land use in the Roscommon area: an introduction. In: Discovery Programme Reports 7: North Roscommon in the Later Medieval Period: An Introduction. Royal Irish Academy, 3-22.

McNeary, R. - Shanahan, B. 2008: Settlement and Enclosure in a Medieval Gaelic Lordship: a case study from the territory of the O'Conors of North Roscommon. In: L. Leveque. – M. R. Arbol – L. Pop eds, Landmarks and socio-economic Systems: constructing of pre-industrial Landscapes and their Perception by contemporary Societies. Presses Universitaires de Rennes, 187-197.

McNeary, R. - Westley, K. 2010: Airborne LiDAR, a welcome addition to the maritime archaeologist's toolkit. Coast Magazine 6, 12-17.

McNeary, R. - Westley, K. 2013: Climate change and Cultural Heritage. Report prepared for the Northern Ireland Environment Agency: Built Heritage Division. (unpublished)

Miller, R. 1967: Land Use by Summer Sheilings. Scottish Studies 2, 193-221.

Mlekuz, D. 2011: Zmeda s krajinami: lidar in prakse krajinjenja (Messy Landscapes: Lidar and the Practices of Landscaping). Arheo 28, 87-104.

NAPLIB, 2001: Directory of Aerial Photographic Collections in the United Kingdom (2nd ed). National Association of Aerial Photographic Libraries.

Neill, K. 2009: An Archaeological Survey of County Armagh. Stationery Office Books.

Neill, K. 2011: Deer Park Farms – Regional and Archaeological Setting. In: C. J. Lynn – J. A. McDowell eds, Deer Park Farms: The Excavations of a Raised Rath in the Glenarm Valley, Co. Antrim, 14-39. Stationery Office Books.

O'Laverty, J. 1887: An Historical Account of the Diocese of Down and Connor, Ancient and Modern, IV. Dublin.

Opitz, R. - Cowley, D. eds. 2013: Interpreting Archaeological Topography: Airborne Laser Scanning, 3D Data, and Ground Observation. Oxbow Books.

O'Sullivan, M. - Downey, L. 2003: Booley huts. Archaeology Ireland 17(4), 34-35.

Plets, R. - Quinn, R. - Forsythe, W. - Westley, K. - Bell, T. - Benetti, S. - McGrath, F. - Robinson, R. 2011: Using Multibeam Echo-Sounder Data to Identify Shipwreck Sites: archaeological assessment of the Joint Irish Bathymetric Survey data. International Journal of Nautical Archaeology 40(1), 87-98.

Powlesland, D. – Lyall, J. – Hopkinson, G. – Donoghue, D. – Beck, M. – Harte, A. – Stott, D. 2006: Beneath the sand – remote sensing, archaeology, aggregates and sustainability: a case study from Heslerton, the Vale of Pickering, North Yorkshire, UK. Archaeological Prospection 13 (4), 291-299.

Radford, C.A.R. 1970: Devenish. Ulster Journal of Archaeology 33, 60.

Shaw, R. - Corns, A. 2011: High resolution LiDAR specifically for archaeology: are we fully exploiting this valuable resource? In: D. Cowley ed., Remote Sensing for Archaeological Heritage Management, EAC Occasional Paper No. 5, 77-87.

Shell, C.A. - Roughley, C.F. 2004: Exploring the Loughcrew Landscape: a New Approach with Airborne Lidar. Archaeology Ireland 18, 2 (68), 20-23.

Štular, B. - Kokalj, Z. – Ostir, K. – Nuninger, L. 2012: Visualization of lidar-derived relief models for detection of archaeological features. Journal of Archaeological Science 39 (11), 3354-3360.

Wakeman, W.F. 1874: The Antiquities of Devenish. Journal of the Royal Historical and Archaeological Association of Ireland 3 (17), 59-94.

Westley, K. - Quinn, R. - Forsythe, W. - Plets, R. - Bell, T. - Benetti, S. - McGrath, F. - Robinson, R. 2011: Mapping Submerged Landscapes Using Multibeam Bathymetric Data: a case study from the north coast of Ireland. International Journal of Nautical Archaeology 40(1), 99-112.

Williams, B. 1992: Aerial Archaeology in Northern Ireland. AARGnews 4, 8-11.

ZRC SAZU 2010: IAPS ZRC SAZU (Institute of Anthropological and Spatial Studies ZRC SAZU). Available at: http://iaps.zrc-sazu.si/en/svf#v

TESTING THE POTENTIAL OF AIRBORNE LiDAR SCANNING IN ARCHAEOLOGICAL LANDSCAPES OF BOHEMIA: STRATEGY, ACHIEVEMENTS AND COST-EFFECTIVENESS

Martin Gojda

Abstract: *This paper presents an overview of the recently acquired application of ALS in archaeology in the Czech Republic. The main focus is on a general description of the first ever project in Bohemia (western half of the Republic,) the principle aim of which was to test the potential of air-borne LiDAR in a Central European landscape (heavily affected by long-term farming, most typically by means of extensive and destructive application of tillage cultivation), both forested and open. Apart from the geographical units (14 test polygons measuring together 123 sq. kilometres, irregularly spread over the whole country), the paper also provides information on two special aspects connected with the project: on testing the accuracy of historical 18th – 19th century military maps compared to a few military defensive features still preserved in more or less ruined remains in the field, and on the comparison of cost effectiveness for getting a 3D model of a large prehistoric hillfort by means of a ground-based geodetic survey on the one hand and through ALS on the other.*

Keywords: *ALS - air-borne LiDAR - digital terrain model (DTM) - ground-based geodetic survey - historical military maps*

Introduction

Bohemia, situated in the very heart of Europe, is the principal and largest part of the historical Czech Kingdom and currently of the Czech Republic. Due to its geographical position, the country had been a crossroad of major central European – and many times pan-European – political and military events. At the same time its territory, surrounded on its perimeter by an almost continuous mountain range, is a rare example of a geomorphological unit in which various climatic and terrain environmental zones are present. The fertile lowlands of the country's core area in central Bohemia (the lower Labe/Elbe and Vltava/Moldau basins are around 180 metres above sea level (asl)) are surrounded by rising undulating low-hill regions. Beyond these are highlands which rise to a more-or-less continuous mountain range that surrounds the country like a ring on its borders, the highest peak of which is over 1600 metres asl. Thus enclosed, it represents a model country in terms of an effective investigation of diachronic (prehistoric, medieval, post-medieval, early modern) processes of settlement and landscape colonisation.

A large number of archaeological remains in many countries in the northern half of Europe have been damaged or destroyed by long-term cultivation. However, in central Europe, including Bohemia, many remains are preserved as earthworks which are now in woodlands. In the post-war period some of these may have been damaged by heavy tree-harvesters and tractors, and currently by activities of illegal metal detectors and looters (*Gojda 2011*, 1450). But these remains are generally better protected in woodland than in open landscapes (cf. *Neustupný 2010*) where cultivation, on land up to 1000 metres asl, has been actively pursued in many places since medieval times.

Large-scale mapping of features in woodland is not easy and it can also be difficult to precisely geolocate their position. For these and many other reasons the arrival of airborne laser scanning (ALS) as part of the practice of archaeological detection and mapping offers a significant innovation. In the above context it is especially the potential of ALS to operate over woodland which radically may, and hopefully will, accelerate the process of systematic recording and relatively precise mapping of not only single features and sites but also complex archaeological landscapes in Bohemia.

Objectives

The development of LiDAR technology started soon after the invention of the laser in the late 1950s (see e.g. *Chang-Chang Wang 2011*), but its application in archaeology and past landscape studies was not introduced systematically until the first half of the 2000s. This application has progressed most dynamically in a few European countries, such as Austria (*Doneus - Briese 2011*), the UK (*Devereux et al. 2008; Crutchley – Crow 2010*), Ireland (*Shaw - Corns 2011*), France (*Georges-Leroy 2011*) and Germany (*Bofinger -Hesse 2011*). Apart from in Slovenia (*Rutar - Črešnar 2011*), archaeological applications of ALS are just beginning in some countries of the former Soviet bloc.

In the context of a methodological progress in

archaeological data-gathering and data-processing which resulted from positive political shifts in the early 1990s, a two-year project, *The potential of ALS for archaeological landscape survey in the Czech Republic,* has recently been completed (*Gojda et al. 2011*). Its aims and interim results are presented in this contribution and it is of importance at least in two aspects. Firstly, our use of ALS was a pioneering job in a small central European country in which the value of non-invasive methods of remote sensing for both theoretically-based research and heritage management has been recognised during the past two decades (e.g. *Gojda 2004; Kuna et al. 2004*). Secondly, at the time when the application for the Czech Science Foundation (CSF) was being prepared, only a very small area of Bohemia had been scanned by airborne LiDAR and was available only as shaded relief digital surface/terrain models in *.tiff/*.jpg formats. Consequently, it was necessary to ask the CSF for financial support to allow us to define areas that would be scanned exclusively for the project's purposes at a standard spatial resolution. Luckily, our project application was accepted at the first attempt and the necessary money allocated so that our planned strategy did not need to be changed and the principal aims of the project could be achieved.

In brief, the effort of the project team was focused on the assessment of the effectiveness and potential of the new remote sensing method in terms of heuristics (identification and evidence of archaeological earthwork heritage), interpretation of sites and features through additional activities (such as ground observation of a range of features recorded on the LiDAR images) and mapping. Also, we wanted to find out the degree of effectiveness of LiDAR application in archaeology, especially in terms of the quality of results with respect to final costs. Comparison with traditional ground-based survey (geodetical) methods producing a similar digital terrain model was carried out. The project's duration was two years (from 2010 to 2011) and was carried out by the academic staff of the Department of Archaeology, University of West Bohemia in Pilsen.

Strategy and areas selected

The selection of areas to be scanned was subject to several factors. It was intended to examine extensive areas (regions, geomorphological units, landscape transects), medium-sized areas (hillforts, postmedieval to early modern field fortification systems) and smaller areas (deserted medieval villages, barrow sites, etc.). Areas were also chosen because they were known to include an as extensive and varied representation as possible of both prehistoric and historic sites, monuments and features. Choices were weighed against the effort needed to acquire information that would enable a comparison of ALS results with conventional mapping and documentation.

As noted above, the main reason why Czech archaeology so far has not had the opportunity to use the ALS data was the very limited coverage of the Czech Republic by LiDAR

imagery, and the high cost of new LiDAR data acquisition. The present project may therefore be considered as a certain breakthrough into field archaeological survey, documentation and mapping of archaeological heritage scattered over the countryside, as it brings with it a vast potential for complex study of extensive landscape units.

The particular regions of interest to the project can be divided into two main groups:

1. Areas that have been scanned by means of ALS for the first time. Altogether 14 test polygons were selected, in which a wide range of features of various types are situated (Fig. 1).
2. Areas that had already been scanned in the past by means of ALS, but primarily for purposes other than archaeological. Those data can be used to extract the archaeological content of such areas. This includes the area of the Bohemian Switzerland National Park with its unique dynamic geo-relief landscape characteristics that had in the past, and has to date, great influence on the evolution of demographic aspects of this region, and the quality and quantity of traces of its past human settlement activities.

Collecting and evaluating the data

Six of the selected territorial units (polygons) were scanned in late March 2010 and the remaining eight in March 2011. Most are approximately 10 sq kilometres in extent. The former were scanned by the German company *Milan Geoservice GmbH* using the laser scanning device Riegl LMS-Q560 at flight level 600 m. Raw data collection was at a density of 4 points/m² and filtered to produce a digital terrain model (DTM) with a resolution of 1x1 m². The remaining eight polygons were scanned by the Czech company *Geodis Brno* using a Riegl LMS-Q680i LiDAR at flight level 900 m with raw data at a density of 2-3 points/m² and (in one case) 10 points/m². The raw data were delivered in *.las format, the filtered data (DSM, DTM) were both submitted in ASCII/*.asc format.

Existing data for the area of the Bohemian Switzerland National Park was scanned between 2004 and 2006 as part of the international project Interreg IIIA GeNeSis (Geoinformation Network for Crossborder National Parks Bohemian-Saxon Switzerland) under the auspices of the Institute of Remote Sensing of the Earth of the Dresden University for Technology.

In the first phase of assessment, output from the ALS carried out during 2010 and 2011 was subject to heuristic analysis by comparing it with documentation of recorded archaeological sites as well as with historic maps and plans. The subsequent, very important, step is the verification on the ground of individual features by means of a surface survey. For example, a barrow burial site Hádky/Javor and medieval moated site Javor (Fig. 2) was evaluated using both visual reconnaissance and control measurements of

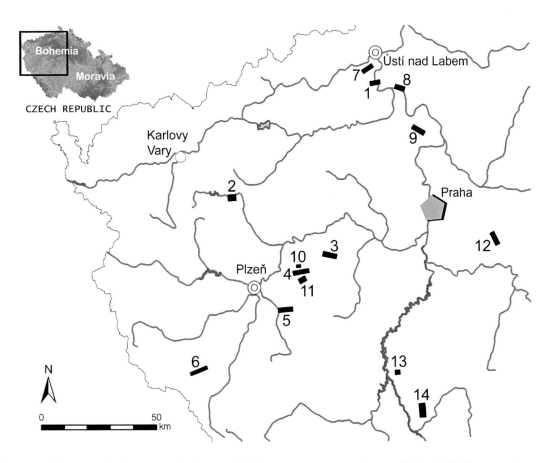

Fig. 1. Map of that part of Bohemia in which target LiDAR scanning was carried out in 2010 – 2011. The scanned areas are numbered 1 – 14 and their size and shape are marked by black rectangular polygons. All of them are rich in archaeological earthworks, and the majority of them are situated in woodland.

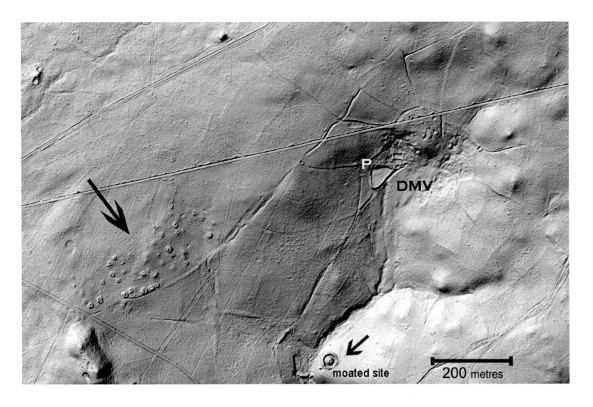

Fig. 2. An extremely well-preserved archaeological landscape, both prehistoric and historic, near Pilsen, western Bohemia with visible Bronze Age barrow cemetery (bottom left corner), deserted medieval village (DMV) including its field system attached around its perimeter and a pond (P), and a contemporary moated site of the medieval owner of the village. The whole area is covered by mixed forest. Shaded relief DTM, project polygon no. 5.

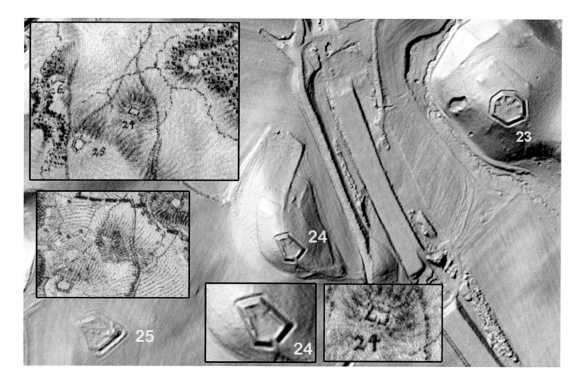

Fig. 3. Žim, northwest Bohemia (project polygon no. 7) showing part of a complex defensive system dating to the end of the 1770s. For a detailed description see text.

selected archaeological key points. Comparison of the terrestrial survey results with those achieved by ALS proved the sufficient precision of this innovative method. This raises the question whether, in future, ALS may effectively replace terrestrial survey, if suitable conditions of data recording can be met.

A similar verification technique was applied also in the area of the National Park Bohemian Switzerland during a two week terrain survey of the area. This focused mainly on the production areas of the region, detected by DTM (glassworks, tar workshops), and the settlement structures, in particular the Hely village deserted after 1945, where the ALS results enabled us to map and record both the built-up areas and the surroundings of the site.

Applying the LiDAR-derived digital terrain model to testing the accuracy of old maps: a case study

Airborne LiDAR data, with its accurate representation of the ground surface, can also be compared with the earliest modern military maps of medium to large scales that were produced by surveyors working in the field. In Bohemia, three sets of the so-called *Military Mapping* were produced between 1760 and 1870. In this case study, the first two sets were used to compare the accuracy of ground plans of military defensive features as illustrated on these maps with those documented by the ALS-derived DTM. These types of remains are spread in relatively large numbers over the Bohemian countryside: some in a more-or-less ruined form, and perhaps even more in a completely levelled/ buried state.

For the purpose of this article an example of just one site is used from project polygon no. 7. This is a group of three well-preserved fortified artillery battlements near the small village of Žim, in northwest Bohemia. These form part of a complex defensive system constructed in the second half of the 18th century as a result of repeated offensive military campaigns by the Prussian army against the Habsburg Monarchy, of which the Czech Kingdom was then an integral part. Currently all of these are covered by trees and dense bushes. In the top left corner of Fig. 3 a section from the *First Military Mapping* (FMM) is shown in which a group of three fortlets can be clearly identified. The FMM was produced between 1763 and 1787 as an 'à la vue', rather than by means of proper triangulated measurements, and the maps were produced on a 1:28,000 scale. Interestingly, the ground plan of feature no. 23 corresponds almost precisely with the ground plan from the ALS-derived shaded relief DTM. Note the earth ramps around the structure's perimeter on which guns were placed. Both ALS and the FMM show feature no. 25 to have a pentagonal plan, although each of them differs in the setting and length of individual sides. The greatest differences are apparent in the plans of fortlet no. 24. On the map it is depicted as a rectangular feature with an entrance gap near the centre of its southwest side, whereas the DTM indicates that in reality this fortlet has a pentagonal plan with the entrance placed at the convergence of two sides on its southeast side (see the more detailed view at the bottom centre of Fig. 3). It is not easy to interpret these differences, but they may reflect the results of the work of more than one group of licensed military surveyors, mapping the terrain, whose ability and/or professional responsibility was not the same.

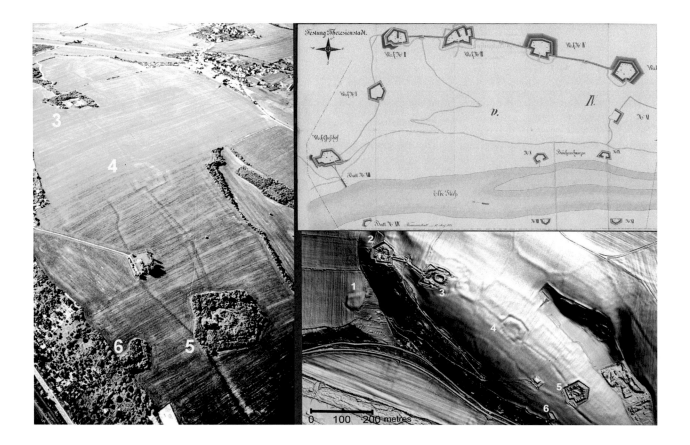

Fig. 4. Partly buried early modern (mid-19th century) fortification near the district town of Litoměřice, northern Bohemia. The site was almost completely preserved until the 1960s since when the forts no. 1, 4 and partly also 3, and the line of a rampart and ditch connecting individual forts have been levelled. Currently they are recordable through cropmarks (image to the left, excluding fort 1). Although the area has been regularly cultivated (ploughed annually) for some five decades, and its remains are almost invisible on the ground, the LiDAR 3D relief shaded DTM (bottom right) shows them clearly, as well as a network of many former roads and ditches. The evidence of the original plan (upper right) as compared with the relief-shaded DTM shows no visible differences either of the overall structure or in details; just one exception may be a sort of ditch/bank that seems to be located along the break in the slope to the SW which is visible on the DTM, but not on the map. The site lies in project polygon No. 8.

The smaller map on the left is a section of the *Second Military Mapping* which was produced between 1836 and 1852 and based on trigonometric measurements of the land surface. In comparison with the FMM no numbers denominating individual fortlets have been inserted in this map and, more significantly, feature no. 24 is not depicted at all. These differences can perhaps be explained by the fact that the defensive system was by then 50 - 60 years old and had lost its significance in the period between the end of 18th and middle of the 19th centuries when there were no wars and military campaigns. However, the complete absence on the map of a fortlet is hardly explicable other than as intentional omission for unknown reasons.

On the contrary, project polygon no. 8 includes a fortified line of artillery bases erected close to Terezín / Theresienstadt (one of two huge brick late 18th century forts and garrisons in Bohemia) in the 1860s, seven to eight decades after the military nodal point Terezín was constructed (Fig. 4). Here, the LiDAR-derived DTM shows practically no difference in the ground-plans of individual fortlets from as they are mapped on the original plan (Fig. 4, top right).

ALS or ground-based geodetic survey? Comparing the cost effectiveness of mapping a large prehistoric hillfort and its surroundings

Project polygon no. 1 includes Hrádek, one of the most impressive ancient Czech hillforts the defensive double ditch and rampart of which are completely covered by deciduous forest (Figs. 5 and 6). As a detailed ground-based (geodetical) survey of the hillfort and its surrounding area was carried out five years before the ALS survey, this provided us with a very good opportunity to compare the cost-effectiveness of both methods and to analyse how far mapping accuracy achieved by the two methods is conditioned by cost (dependent primarily on time and labour demand).

The geodetical ground-survey of the Hrádek hillfort including surrounding area was carried out as contract work by the private company *GeoNet Praha*. Mapping of the site was one of the objectives of the project "The Labe/ Elbe Valley in Prehistory" carried out by the contracting authority – the Institute of Archaeology of the Czech

Fig. 5. Hrádek district Litoměřice, northern Bohemia (project polygon no. 1). Woodland canopy almost completely obscures the huge double ditch and rampart of one of the largest and most heavily defended hillforts in Bohemia (aerial images to the left and bottom right), while the LiDAR shaded relief DTM (top right) shows it properly including some details (number of small ramparts crossing the bottom of the inner ditch, and modern diggings at the top of the outer rampart marked here by a black circle).

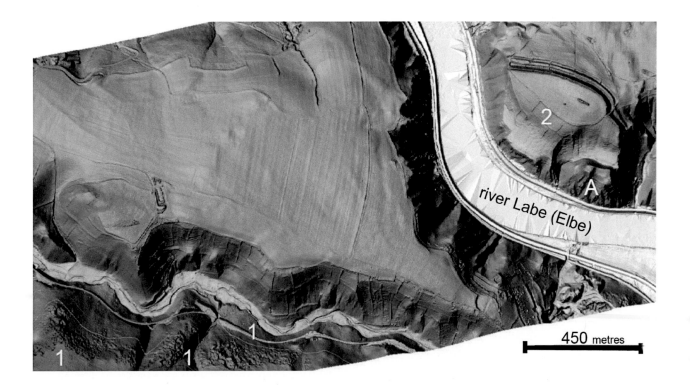

Fig. 6. 3D surface DTM of the prehistoric and early medieval hillfort Hrádek and its surroundings. 1: large area of a Late Iron Age stone extraction (material for the local production of Celtic rotary hand-mills which had been distributed over distant parts of Central Europe) located on the southern slopes of a valley whose bottom stream is a tributary to the Labe/Elbe river 2: the Hrádek hillfort, A: the so-called acropolis of the hillfort, probably its focal place.

Academy of Sciences in Prague. The following are principal data on the ground survey campaign and its cost:

1. A territory of 57.5 hectares was mapped in 3D (x, y, z axes) of which approximately a third (20 hectares) constitutes the hillfort itself. The territory has varied elevation differences and character including sloping terrain of most of the hillfort's area, natural local terrain elevation of the Three-Cross Hill, which is believed to have served as focal point in the site (the so-called *acropolis*) constituted by steep (in a part vertical) rocky slopes, and the Elbe valley bottom banks.
2. The whole area was mapped with a high-standard total station in the course of two months (not continuously, but depending on weather conditions) by a team of five to ten persons. These figures include data processing.
3. The final product of the ground geodetical survey of the selected territory is a plan on a 1:500 scale and a digital terrain model in which the accuracy of georeferenced points is within 5 centimetres in both plan (x, y) and altitude (z). The relatively low accuracy is due to the (unstable) terrain surface, which would otherwise have been higher.
4. The total cost of undertaking the ground-based mapping today can be guessed at only in general terms rather than as a definite figure. This is especially due to the fact that the sum total reflects various aspects influencing its value, such as actual (market) demand for geodetic works conditioned by the economic situation of society and of the potential customer, the number of currently existing geodetical companies, the season of the year in which the works (contracts) are required, etc. With respect to these determinants it is possible to express the current cost of ground-based detailed 3D mapping of the hillfort Hrádek and its surroundings as between € 5600 and 6000 (personal information P. Hulík, director of the *GeoNet Praha*).

Compared to this, the cost we had to pay for LiDAR-derived data (both raw and filtered) of the Hrádek territory can be expressed as an average cost of a square kilometre within the whole area scanned in 2010 (60 sq km), and this amounted to € 210. The LiDAR-derived DTM's absolute accuracy is 30 cm in plan and 10 cm in altitude. It should be stressed that the total cost of delivered data is also conditioned by the distance between the home air-base and polygons to be scanned and between individual polygons. For this reason it is important to properly design the polygons in terms of their ground plan and distance relative to each other (basically, the longer and narrower the better, as it means fewer parallel flights to fully scan a polygon, shorter flying time and – consequently – lower costs).

Concerning spatial resolution, it is obvious that although the absolute accuracy in x - y is much higher in the case of ground-based measurements, in the case of height accuracy the resulting difference between the two methods is much smaller. The importance of absolute spatial accuracy must be considered in terms of the size of the mapped archaeological feature: the larger the mapped site, the (relatively) less important it is. In the case of a 20 hectare hillfort, such as the Hrádek, the accuracy difference in terms of a few tens of centimetres is not significant. If we compare – in this context – the price of a (traditional) ground-based survey with that for ALS we can see that the latter is considerably cheaper. Spatial (3D) mapping of a one hectare area of the hillfort by a team of surveyors using total station amounts to € 120. On the other hand, the LiDAR data scanned over the hillfort and surrounding landscape, which represents an area of four square kilometres, costs approximately € 840, i.e. € 210 per square km, or € 2.1 per hectare.

Apart from cost demands, another factor that significantly supports the effectiveness of 3D mapping by means of ALS is time. Scanning a site such as the Hrádek hillfort and its surroundings would take no more than two hours (including transit from the home airfield to the scanned polygon and back). Comparing this with a ground-based geodetical survey which took two months, the difference in timescale is more than obviously in favour of ALS. Also, LiDAR data processing, including filtration, is a matter of a few days rather than weeks.

To conclude: the possibility to compare the costs to produce an elevation plan (DTM) of an ancient hillfort by means of ground-based mapping and ALS showed the following results: although the absolute spatial accuracy is higher in the case of geodetical measurements, it is the lower cost and time consumption which distinctly indicates much lower demands and consequently higher effectiveness of ALS.

Conclusion

The project, as the first of its kind in the Czech Republic, demonstrated the potential of ALS and its effectiveness to identify and document archaeological heritage of various kinds, situated in a variety of landscape types. During the two-year project, ALS data from representative sample areas that included known prehistoric and medieval to post-medieval features and sites was collected and compared with existing records.

The huge potential of data derived from airborne laser scanning for the identification and recording of archaeological sites and features preserved in the form of earthworks has been recognised. A consequence of this is that it enables 3D mapping of whole archaeological landscapes. There is no doubt that in this respect ALS is changing current investigation, recording and complex documentation of isolated archaeological features on the one hand, and of archaeological monuments adjoining local architectural and urban heritage on the other. For instance, some kinds of earthworks of historical (medieval, post-medieval and early modern) origin, whose occurrence in some parts of the countryside is extremely high, can only be studied seriously (recorded and mapped) under current circumstances provided by airborne LiDAR potential in terms of speed and accuracy of data gathering. This is, for example, the case with remains of charcoal production platforms (usually preserved as ruined lower bases of charcoal piles, circular in plan) of which groups ranging from ten to many hundreds are spread over woodlands situated most typically in hilly landscapes and highlands. Due to their high number, very little attention has been paid to their systematic study, because mapping them – which obviously is the first step in any effort to analyse their spatial distribution, the relation to environmental conditions and to contemporary settlements and road networks – by any kind of ground-based survey would take a lot of time. In Bohemia there are a large number of territories with plenty of charcoal piles more or less well conserved, datable to the period of 15th – 20th centuries. A systematic investigation of these extremely important production areas, neglected until recently, can now be easily launched.

Also, a DTM derived from ALS data is often used for monitoring the state of preservation of archaeological earthworks (either simple, such as medieval moated sites whose standing constructions have been completely destroyed, or combined with architectural remains, such as ruined castles) and as such this usage of processed LiDAR data has its significance in heritage management and protection.

It seems pointless to give exact numbers of new archaeological components identified in the Bohemian ALS data as it is difficult to interpret seriously large areas full of surface depressions and elevations without further ground-based field survey and investigation. It is primarily this way which can bring us properly to closer understanding of the origin (man-made or natural), function and age of each of them. Raw LiDAR data acquired from territorial units, whose area totals 123 sq. kilometres, at a relatively high spatial resolution constitutes a valuable basis for modern recording and 3D documentation of georeferenced traces of past human settlement activities in Bohemia. During the project's course, the information potential of this dataset was utilised just in a limited way. Its further evaluation is currently under way and our results will be published soon in a special volume and in archaeological journals.

The project also aimed at a critical evaluation of the effectiveness and potential of applications of ALS in archaeology and in particular in situations where a number of aspects influencing the final dataset must be taken into account (scanning parameters, raw data processing techniques, software and hardware requirements that are necessary to manage these large amounts of data, complementarity of applied analytical methods, landscape type of investigated area). These are included in current work on the project's results and their evaluation is a part of studies published recently (*Gojda – John et al. 2013*).

Acknowledgements

On this occasion I would like to thank my team collaborators who participated in the project headed by me: Jan John, a teaching research assistant who was involved in particular in the transformation of raw LiDAR data from ASCII/*. asc format into DTM and in field work including ground-based survey and plotting of assorted sites and monuments recorded by LiDAR; and Lenka Starková, a former post-graduate/PhD student whose task was to cover all the work in the National Park Bohemian Switzerland. My thanks are also addressed to Anthony Harding for his comments on the manuscript, and to Rog Palmer for his language revision of the text and useful notes to the content of the work.

References

Bofinger, J. - Hesse, R. 2011: As far as the laser can reach… Laminar analysis of LiDAR detected structures as powerful instrument for archaeological heritage management in Baden-Württemberg, Germany. In: D. Cowley ed., Remote Sensing for Archaeological Heritage Management. EAC Occasional Paper No. 5, Budapest, Archaeolingua, 161-172.

Chang-Chang Wang ed. 2011: Laser Scanning. Theory and Applications. Intech: Open Access Publisher.

Crutchley, S. - Crow, P. 2010: The light fantastic: using airborne laser scanning in archaeological survey. Swindon: English Heritage.

Devereux, B.J. – Amable, G.S. – Crow, P. 2008: Visualisation of LiDAR models for archaeological feature detection. Antiquity 82, 470-479.

Doneus, M. - Briese, C. 2011: Airborne laser scanning in forested areas – potential and limitations of an archaeological prospection technics. In: D. Cowley ed., Remote Sensing for Archaeological Heritage Management. EAC Occassional Paper No. 5, Budapest, Archaeolingua, 59-76.

Georges-Leroy, M. 2011: Airborne laser scanning for the management of archaeological sites in Lorraine (France). In: D. Cowley ed., Remote Sensing for Archaeological Heritage Management. EAC Occasional Paper No. 5, Budapest, Archaeolingua, 229-234.

Gojda, M. 2011: Archaeology in current society. A Central European Perspective. Antiquity 85, 1448-1453.

Gojda, M. ed. 2004: Ancient landscapes, settlement dynamics and non-destructive archaeology. Prague: Academia.

Gojda, M - John, J. - Starková, L. 2011: Archeologický průzkum krajiny pomocí leteckého laserového skenování. Dosavadní průběh a výsledky prvního českého projektu. Archeologické rozhledy 63, 680-695.

Gojda, M. – John, J. et al. 2013: Archeologie a letecké laserové skenování krajiny. Archaeology and Airborne Laser Scanning of the Landscape. Plzeň: University of West Bohemia.

Kuna, M. – Benes, J. – Dobes, M. 2004: Nedestruktivní archeologie: teorie, metody a cíle [Non-destructive archaeology: theory. methods and goals]. Prague: Academia (in Czech with English summaries).

Neustupný, Z. 2010: Cover is not shelter: archaeology and forestry in the Czech Republic. In: S. Trow - V. Holyoak

- E. Byrnes eds, Heritage Management of farmed and forested landscapes in Europe. *EAC Occasional Paper* No. 4, EAC, Brussels, 69-73.

Rutar, G. - Črešnar, M. 2011: Reserved optimism: preventive archaeology and management of cultural heritage in Slovenia. In: D. Cowley ed., Remote Sensing for Archaeological Heritage Management. EAC Occasional Paper No. 5, Budapest, Archaeolingua, 259-263.

Shaw, R. – Corns, A. 2011: High resolution LIDAR specifically for archaeology: are we fully exploiting this valuable resource? In: D. Cowley ed., Remote Sensing for Archaeological Heritage Management. EAC Occasional Paper No. 5, Budapest, Archaeolingua, 77-86.

Studying Prehistoric Dryland Agricultural Systems in Central Arizona through Aerial LiDAR, Pedology, Hydrology, and Paleobotany

Robert M. Wegener, Richard Ciolek-Torello, Jeffrey A. Homburg and Michelle Wienhold

Abstract: *Statistical Research Inc. (SRI) conducted phased data recovery at two large dryland agricultural fields and associated Hohokam habitation sites along U.S. Highway 60 in central Arizona. The agricultural fields consisted of cross channel and contour rock alignments and rock piles covering many acres within and outside of a newly proposed highway right-of-way along Queen Creek. Nearby were small, seasonal habitation sites occupied between AD 400 and 1350. Aerial 3-Dimensional Laser Range Finding (LiDAR) was used to map the fields, construct 10 cm digital elevation models, and examine field slope, aspect, and drainage patterns. Drainage patterns before and after field construction were then modeled to compare natural versus human-modified field topography and hydrology, and to infer the aboriginal aims of field construction. Field function was further examined with soil moisture and chemistry studies to characterize anthropogenic soil signatures, and pollen and flotation analysis to identify cultivars and cultigens. Contrary to expectations, this detailed functional study found little evidence for agave cultivation, which has been the primary cultivar found in other dryland fields of central Arizona. The Queen Creek fields were built prior to the large-scale production of agave in central Arizona. Although agave occurs naturally nearby, these fields were used for a mix of crops, including maize, native cacti, and possibly even cotton and helped sustain a series of intermittently occupied farmsteads and hamlets.*

Keywords: *American Southwest – Hohokam – dryland agriculture – LiDAR – soil chemistry – agave cultivation*

Introduction

Water management and harvesting is an essential element of successful agriculture, especially in arid to semi-arid environments. Often this involves the complicated manipulation and modification of the existing environment. The construction of canals to channel water onto desert lands is perhaps the best known method and the Hohokam of the American Southwest are perhaps best known for the development of the largest and most technologically sophisticated irrigation systems of North America (*Doolittle 1990*, 79-80). Developed as early as between 130 BC and AD 275 in the Salt and Gila River Valleys of central Arizona (*Henderson 1989, 194-196*), these systems in their final form were a complex web of canals, several over 16 km in length that could have watered over 24,000 acres (*Howard - Huckleberry 1991*) and even as much as 9,000 ha (*Schroeder 1943, 380-381*) (Fig. 1). It has been a long-held view that these canal systems were constructed gradually through a process of accretionary growth that sustained the in situ development of a complex network of large villages and the elaborate irrigation-based Hohokam cultural pattern (*Woodbury 1960; Haury 1976; Wilcox - Shenk 1977; Upham - Rice 1980; Neitzel 1987*). Recent research, however, reveals that individual canal alignments exhibit a high degree of instability with numerous instances of abandonment. Canals had a short use-life and were constantly rebuilt, often in response to catastrophic flooding (*Greenwald - Ciolek-Torello 1988; Ackerly - Henderson 1989; Howard 1993*). Henderson (*1989,* 198-199) estimates that the average use-life of canals in one system was roughly 35 years. According to *Doolittle (2002*, 408): "... the entire Salt River Valley for the period extending from AD 0 to 1450 was a dynamic landscape of canals of various sizes and locations undergoing constant renovation and relocation... the valley can be best characterized in terms of the irrigated landscape as a constantly changing mosaic."

Ciolek-Torrello (1998; 2012) argues that the instability of Hohokam canal systems, especially prior to the Classic period, resulted in the expansion of Hohokam agricultural technology and settlements into the smaller river valleys surrounding the Phoenix Basin between the late Pioneer and early Colonial periods (AD 600-900). Small farming settlements were established in the tributaries of the Salt and Gila Rivers, such as the Agua Fria, New River, Cave Creek, and Lower Verde Rivers along the northern edge of the Phoenix Basin and the Queen Creek and Buttes Dam area along its southeastern edge. These areas lacked the large expanses of arable alluvium present along the Salt and Gila Rivers at the center of the Phoenix Basin, but the lower flows of the smaller drainages in these peripheral valleys may have been more easily managed. Furthermore, these valleys were located in more upland areas that provided a great variety of important wild plants that could be exploited and encouraged. Game was also abundant, and these valleys may have been important sources of protein for the large settlements along the Salt and Gila Rivers (*Abbott 2000*). In

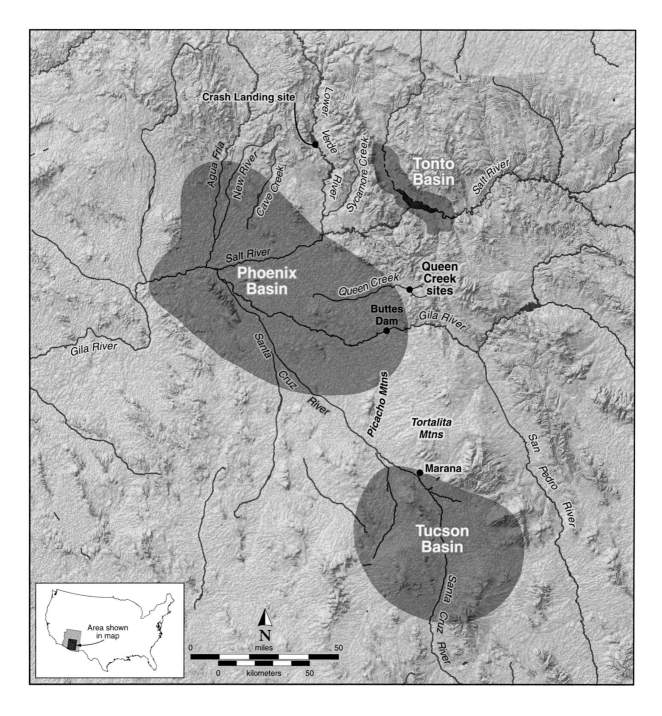

Fig. 1. Map of central and southern Arizona showing project location and other areas mentioned in text.

these smaller upland valleys, the Hohokam supplemented their diet to varying degrees with the agricultural products using a variety of agricultural practices such as floodwater farming, small-scale canal irrigation, and dryland farming.

These less well-known dryland farming systems, which are the subject of this paper, include a variety of farming methods and the man-made features associated with them. These include ancient water-harvesting and water-conservation methods such as runoff and rock-mulch farming, which capture and concentrate intermittent high-density rainfall. These types of systems have been documented throughout the American Southwest (*McGee 1895; Bryan 1929; Stewart 1939; 1940a; 1940b; Hack 1942; Nabhan 1979; 1983; 1984; 1986a; 1986b; Homburg 1994; Pawluk 1995; Sandor et al. 2002; Norton et al. 2003; Homburg - Sandor 2004; Homburg et al. 2004; 2005*) and other settings worldwide (*Parr 1943; Boers - Ben-Asher 1982; Evenari et al. 1982; Bruins 1986, 1990; Bruins et al. 1987; Kowsar 1991; Cohen et al. 1995; Lavee et al. 1997; Niemeijer 1998*).

Dryland agricultural systems include contour rock alignments built along sloping landforms and following natural contours, cross channel alignments, and rock piles (*Rankin - Katzer 1989*). Residential features such as field houses, farmsteads, and hamlets and food processing features such as roasting pits closely associated with these systems were also important components. In the desert regions of central and southern Arizona, dryland farming systems were first developed in the upland regions surrounding the Salt and Gila River Valleys, which are often referred to as the Phoenix Basin. Irrigable alluvium was at a premium along the narrow river valleys in these upland locations, and dryland systems greatly expanded the area that could be cultivated (*Van West - Altschul 1994; 1998*).

In higher elevation areas of the Southwest where rainfall was more abundant, dryland systems may have been used to cultivate maize and other domesticates. In deserts of central and southern Arizona, however, rainfall was usually insufficient for this purpose and high evaporation rates due to high desert temperatures and shallow, rocky soils further reduced soil moisture available for plant use. In these areas, cultivation of native plants such as agave and cacti appears to have taken the place of traditional domesticates in these dryland fields. Based on their study of the Marana community in the northern Tucson Basin, Suzanne and Paul Fish have argued that rock piles in dryland agricultural fields functioned primarily for large-scale cultivation of agave during the Classic period (*Fish et al. 1985a; 1992*). They found support for their inference in the abundance of charred agave remains in roasting pits adjacent to rock pile fields in the foothills of the Tortolita Mountains and in nearby Classic period habitation sites. Significantly this evidence of agave cultivation and use was found outside the modern range of agave (see also *Gasser - Kwiatkowski 1991a; 1991b*). The presence of tabular knives, large flake tools, pulping planes, and sherd scoops at rock pile fields, combined with ethnographic data on agave-processing activities, bolstered their arguments about the magnitude of agave farming in this prehistoric community. Similar rock pile fields have been reported throughout central and southern Arizona near the confluence of the Salt and Verde Rivers (*Canouts 1975*); the Lower Verde Valley (*Homburg 1998*), in Tonto Basin *(Wood and McAllister 1984; Shelley - Ciolek-Torrello 1994)*; on the flanks of the Picacho Mountains (*Halbirt - Ciolek-Torrello 1987*); and along the Gila (*Doelle 1976; Dart 1983; Crown 1984; Vanderpot 1992*), Santa Cruz (*Masse 1979*), Agua Fria, and New Rivers (*Doyel - Elson 1985; Rankin 1989; Rankin - Katzer 1989*). Although many of these fields have been documented, few have been investigated in sufficient detail to determine how they actually functioned.

The concentrations of rock piles that dominated many of these fields were interpreted as mulch gardens that served as individual planters for agave plants and served both to protect the roots of young plantings from disturbance by burrowing animals and to conserve soil moisture. In many areas, agave became a dietary staple as evidenced by high ubiquity values for agave (often exceeding maize values) in macrobotanical samples from houses, middens, and roasting pits of nearby residential sites (*Gasser 1988; Bohrer 1998; Van West - Altschul 1998; Adams 2003; Vanderpot 2009*). Large numbers of tabular tools, which have been closely associated with agave extraction and processing, provide additional evidence of the importance of agave exploitation in the region (*Greenwald 1988; Fish et al. 1992; Van West - Altschul 1998; Vanderpot 2009*). In one study of these tools, agave serum was found on their working surfaces (*Bernard-Shaw 1984*). Hodgson et al. (1989) have identified relict colonies of domesticated varieties of agave that were developed for use in these fields in the Lower Verde Valley and Tonto Basin. Based on such evidence, *Ciolek-Torrello et al. (2009)* and *Vanderpot (2009)* suggest that Hohokam farmers were drawn to the upland valleys of the northern Phoenix Basin, not so much to expand opportunities for floodwater and irrigation farming of maize and other cultigens, but to exploit agave.

The Hohokam first developed dryland agricultural fields in the early Colonial period (AD 750-950), when small clusters of rock piles were built within the boundaries of small villages and hamlets (*Ciolek-Torrello 1998; Ciolek-Torrello et al. 2009*). Extensive evidence of agave use in houses, middens, and roasting pits, as well as large numbers of tabular tools, together with low frequencies of maize and other domesticated plants suggest that these features were used primarily for cultivating agave. Such simple rockpile fields became fully elaborated in the Classic period (AD 1150-1400) as agave became an increasingly important staple in many upland areas and agave cultivation was introduced to the larger, lowland river valleys of the Phoenix and Tucson Basins (*Gasser 1988; Gasser - Kwiatkowski 1991a; 1991b; Fish et al. 1992; Ciolek-Torrello 1998; Kwiatkowski 2003; Vanderpot 2009*). The Crash Landing site was a large dryland agricultural field investigated by Homburg and Ciolek-Torello in the Lower Verde Valley (Fig. 2). This site covered an area of 750 by 350 m and included 11 one- and two-room masonry field houses, long linear rock alignments, and hundreds of rock piles located about a kilometer from the nearest contemporary residential site (*Homburg - Ciolek-Torrello 1998*). The field at Locus 78 depicted in Figure 2 measured 200 by 80 m in area and alone contained 39 individual rock alignments and 245 rock piles. The field houses constructed within and adjacent to this field system contained little evidence of habitation and were probably constructed to provide temporary shelter, while cultivating and monitoring plants, and perhaps for temporary storage of the harvest. Detailed soil fertility and quality studies of the Crash Landing site and other dryland agricultural fields in the Lower Verde area demonstrated how the features functioned to conserve water and nutrients for plant growth in an arid environment with high evaporation rates (*Homburg 1998; Homburg - Sandor 1998*). Their hydrology, however, could not be addressed because it was not possible to map the site micro-topography with the instruments available. Although direct evidence of agave cultivation was not found in these fields, charred agave and tabular tools were abundant in nearby

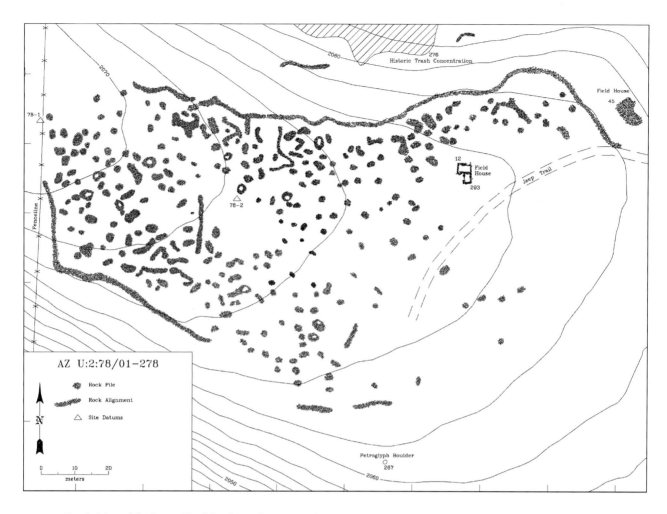

Fig. 2. Map of the Locus 78 of Crash Landing site in the Lower Verde Valley (from Homburg - Ciolek-Torrello 1998).

residential sites and relict colonies of domesticated *Agave murpheyi* were found in the vicinity of one field.

This paper focuses on the study of dryland agricultural systems and related agricultural settlements along the upper Queen Creek drainage, a tributary of the Gila River. Here, SRI investigated 15 prehistoric settlements ranging in age from the Late Archaic (350 BC) to the Late Classic period (AD 1400) for the Arizona Department of Transportation (ADOT) as part of a construction project to widen U.S. Highway 60 (*Wegener - Ciolek-Torello 2011; Wegener et al. 2011*). These sites included small family-sized residential loci (farmsteads), a larger hamlet or village, temporary field houses, limited activity loci, and two large dryland agricultural systems located on the rolling pediment overlooking Queen Creek (Fig. 3). Our objective in this study as outlined in the research design (*Ciolek-Torrello et al. 2005*) was to document these extensive dryland agricultural systems and associated settlements and examine their function. Specifically, what were the components of these systems, how did the individual features function to capture or concentrate water and nutrients, which plants were cultivated in these fields, how did these fields function within the local settlement systems, and, finally, how did such use compare to dryland agricultural systems in other areas of central and southern Arizona?

The Sites and Environmental Setting

The most notable of sites in the study include the Bighorn Wash site, a relatively large site with intermittent occupations ranging from the Late Archaic to the Late Classic period. The earliest occupation is represented by pit houses reflecting intermittent seasonal occupations over a long period of time, followed by more permanent occupation by small farmsteads in the pre-Classic period (AD 750-1150) and a temporary field house in the Late Classic period. The Nicholas Ranch Complex consists of several large dryland agricultural fields and a single large roasting pit that is divided by the existing highway. The Nicholas Ranch Complex was divided into five discrete loci (*Homburg et al. 2011*) (Fig. 4). Locus A was located north of U.S. 60 on the southeast-facing backslope of a hill and Locus B was on the summit and shoulder slope of the hill to the west. Loci C-E are located on hills south of U.S. 60. A large pre-Classic period hamlet or small village is located in the southern part of the site outside of the study area. Carbonate Copy is located at the base of a hill near the Nicholas Ranch Complex (Fig. 5). This site contained evidence of four discrete occupations dating between AD 1 and 1150 with middens, burials, houses, and other pits suggesting seasonal habitation by family-sized groups. Gravelly Horseman consisted of a large,

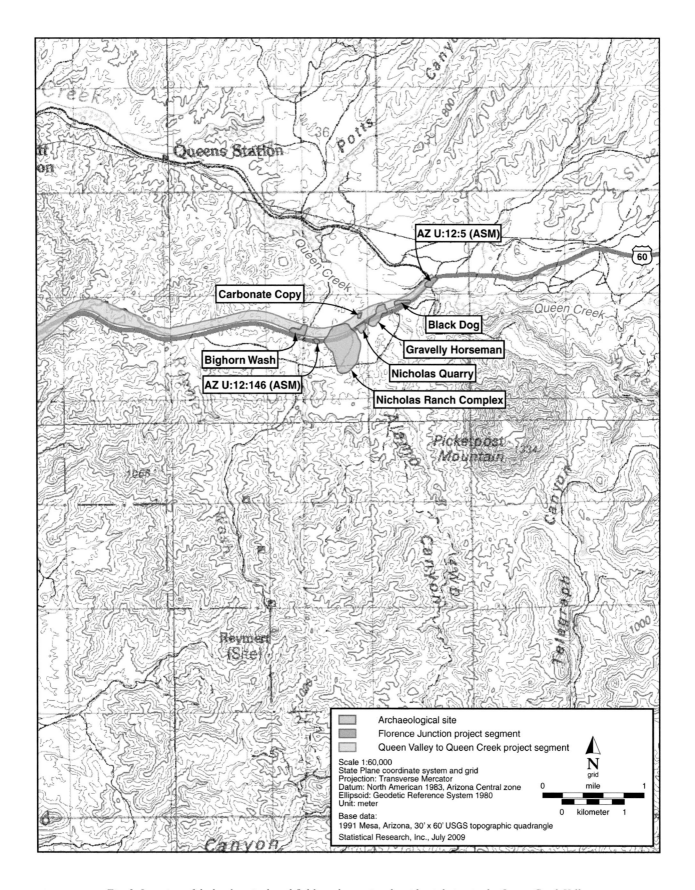

Fig. 3. Location of dryland agricultural fields and associated residential sites in the Queen Creek Valley.

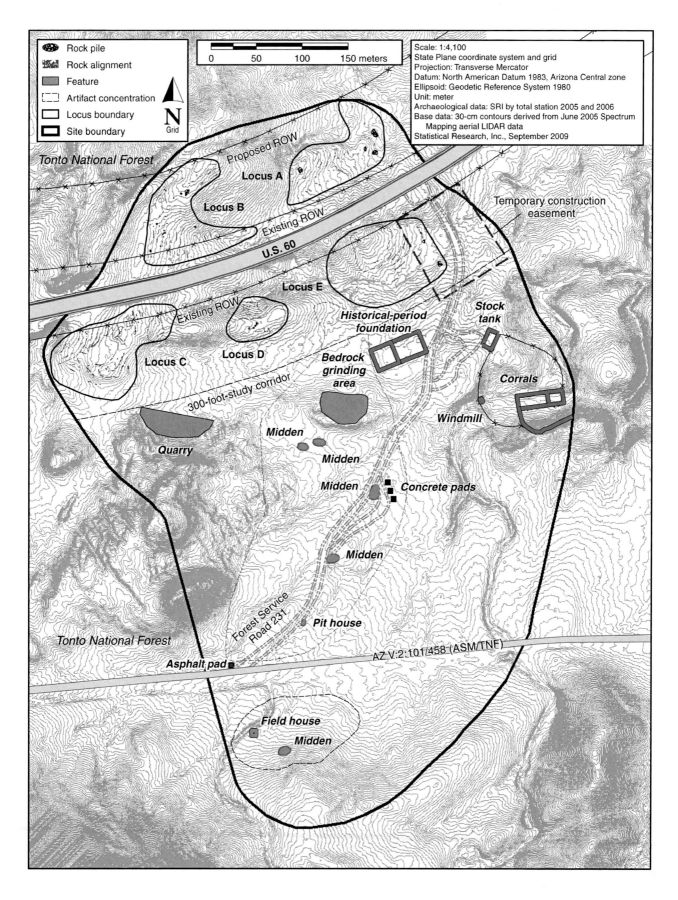

Fig. 4. Map of the Nicholas Ranch Complex (from Wegener - Ciolek-Torello 2011).

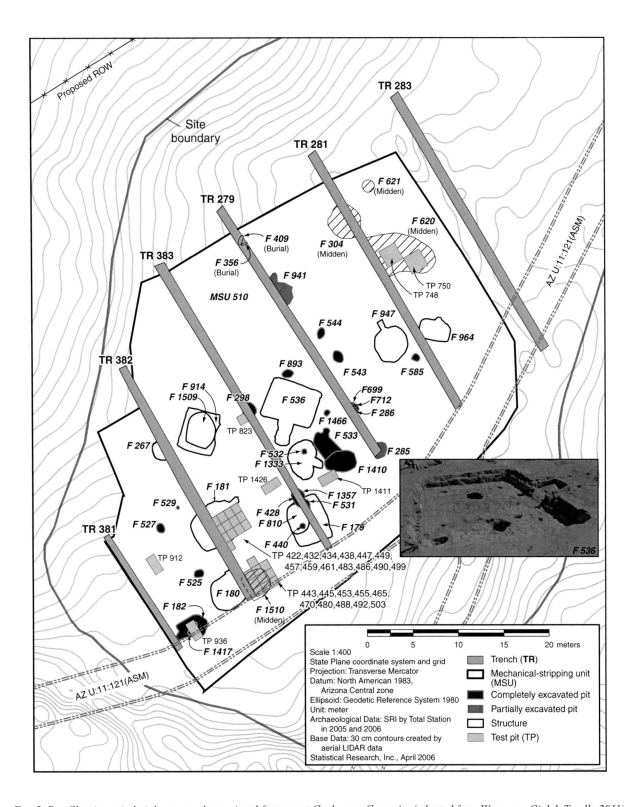

Fig. 5. Pre-Classic period pit houses and associated features at Carbonate Copy site (adapted from Wegener - Ciolek-Torello 2011).

dryland agricultural field (Locus B), located on the south side of U.S. 60 about 300 m east of the Nicholas Ranch Complex, and a residential complex situated on top of a low-lying hill overlooking the confluence of Alamo and Queen Creeks at Locus A, on the north side of the road (Fig. 6). The residential complex includes a cobble-and-post-reinforced adobe pit structure, a deep midden, and other pits that suggest the presence of a farmstead dating

to the end of the pre-Classic period. The Black Dog site consists of three loci separated by the existing highway. A midden, pit houses, and other pits dating to the pre-Classic period indicate the presence of seasonal residences and resource-procurement staging areas. Masonry-walled field houses, a midden, a masonry-walled courtyard or ramada, and other rock features reflect the presence of Classic period field houses (Fig. 7).

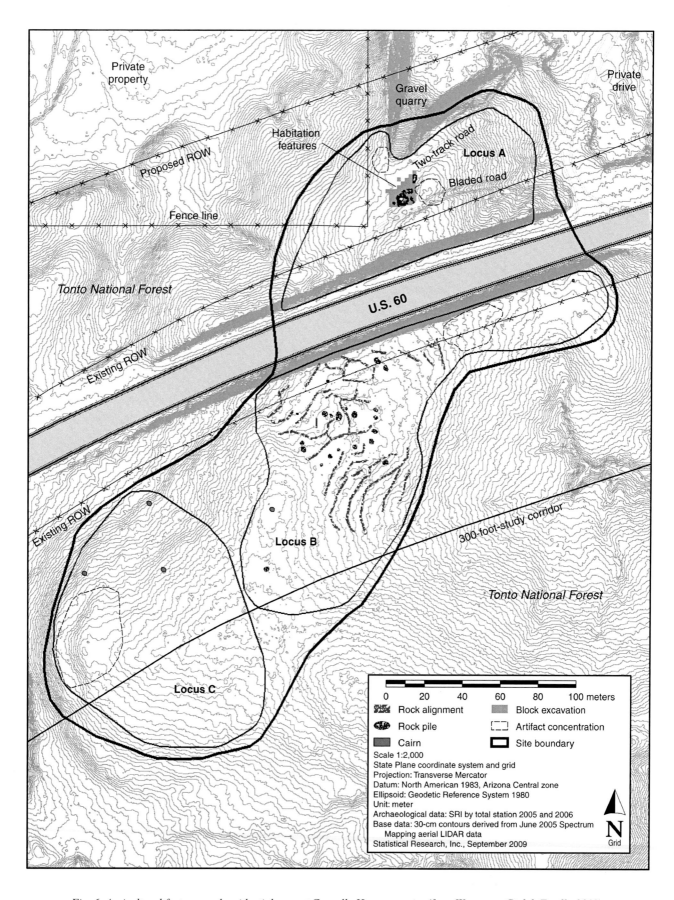

Fig. 6. Agricultural features and residential area at Gravelly Horseman site (from Wegener - Ciolek-Torello 2011).

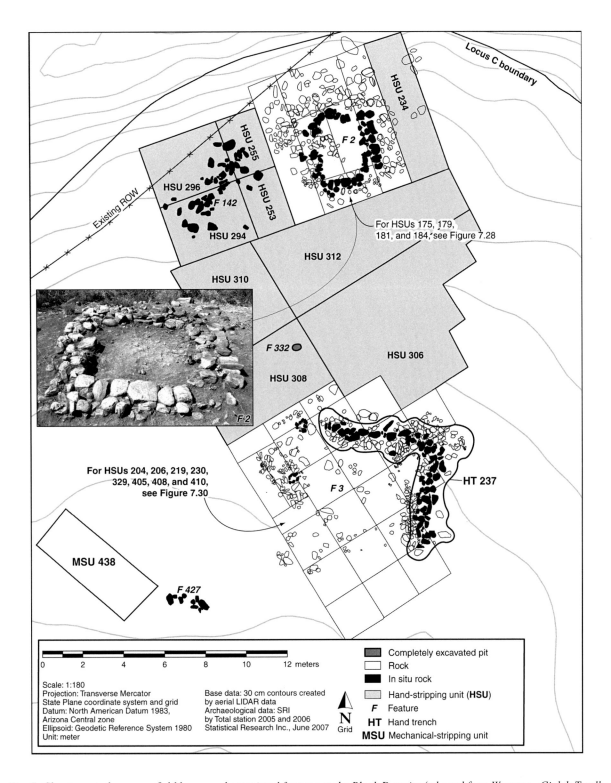

Fig. 7. Classic period masonry field house and associated features at the Black Dog site (adapted from Wegener - Ciolek-Torello 2011).

All of these dryland fields and residential loci were situated on pediments with a thin veneer of sediment above the bedrock overlooking the narrow strip of stream alluvium along Queen Creek. These fields and their associated residential loci are located in the Upland Division of the Sonoran Desertscrub biome, which locally consists of a paloverde-cacti-mixed scrub vegetations series. This unexpectedly rich biotic community contains an overstory of paloverde and ironwood trees and giant saguaro cacti

with an understory of various shrubs and smaller cacti (Fig. 8). Important economic plants include saguaro, prickly pear, and cholla cacti as well as jojoba plants.

The upper Queen Creek Valley, which is located at an elevation of approximately 860 m AMSL, experiences significantly greater rainfall than other upland areas of central and southern Arizona. Orographic lifting of westerly air masses caused by movement over the surrounding

Fig. 8. Sonoran Desertscrub vegetation community in upper Queen Creek Valley, view to Picketpost Mountain.

mountains may account for the relatively high local rainfall pattern. Rainfall records from the nearby Boyce Thompson Arboretum indicate a mean annual precipitation of about 35.5 cm, with one year in four exceeding 50 cm (*Sellers - Hill 1974; Homburg et al. 2011*). Such high rainfall in the semi-arid regions of central and southern Arizona would have made it possible to grow crops like maize with direct rainfall in some years. However, the limited amount of streamside alluvium, thin rocky soils of the pediments, low humidity, and high temperatures (averaging 30° C) during the growing season would have resulted in rapid runoff and high evaporation rates, leaving relatively little available water for plant growth.

Together the six fields comprising the agricultural sites extend over an area of about 4.6 ha with about 1.6 ha covered by agricultural features. In all, 168 rock alignment segments and terraces totaling about 1,700 m in length and 47 rock piles were identified and mapped in these three sites (*Homburg et al. 2011*). At least five different types of features could be identified in these fields. Most of the features were contour alignments, but cross channel alignments were also common. Rock alignments averaged about 11 m in length with a range from 2 to 52 m. Most of the alignments were contour terraces that were built along natural contours, whereas others were bordered terraces that crosscut terraces and functioned to divert water, or cross-channel alignments (check dams) that were built across small channels and swales to slow runoff and erosion (Fig.

9). The rock piles consisted of two types; some may have represented the remains of land clearing to enhance runoff or were stockpiles for future feature construction; whereas others may have been individual planters in mulch gardens used to reduce water transpiration and protect cultivated plant roots (Fig. 10). A light scatter of artifacts, primarily lithic debitage, was dispersed around and between the agricultural features. Many of the flakes could have served as cutting implements used to harvest plants, although they lacked obvious wear indicative of such use. Notably, stone hoes, heavy choppers, and tabular tools associated with agricultural fields in the Southwest were absent. Due to the absence of temporally diagnostic artifacts in direct association with the agricultural features, dating of the fields was based on evidence from the associated residential loci, which indicated possible use from the Late Archaic to late Classic periods. The preponderance of evidence from the residential loci, however, suggests that the most intensive occupation of the area occurred during the Sacaton phase (AD 950-1150) at the end of the pre-Classic period (*Lengyel 2011*).

Methods

Documentation

Our initial objective was to document the extensive dryland agricultural fields in the Queen Creek area. These fields and their associated residential sites were spread along the

Fig. 9. Terraces and other dryland agricultural features at Locus C, Nicholas Ranch Complex, with prickly pear, cholla, and saguaro cactus.

Fig. 10. Agricultural rock pile (from Homburg et al. 2011).

hills and ridges flanking Queen Creek, primarily on lands administered by the U.S. Department of Agriculture, Tonto National Forest. Unfortunately, we could only undertake ground-disturbing activities – that is, excavation – in the narrow 200 ft (61 m) wide corridor adjacent to the existing highway. Thus, our investigatory methods must have minimal impact on the field areas outside of this corridor. We elected to use high-accuracy Light Distance and Ranging (LiDAR) data to create detailed landscape- and site-scale digital elevation models (DEMs) in order to document the agricultural features and to evaluate the topographic effects of rock alignments on surface hydrology (*Homburg et al. 2011; Wienhold 2012*), a procedure that was not possible in our earlier investigation of the Crash Landing Site. The LiDAR scans were obtained by aerial photography over a 2,000 ft (610 m) wide corridor that encompassed all the recorded field areas in the area. To facilitate LiDAR scanning, agricultural features in this corridor were first cleared of a dense understory of cacti and brush. The site areas were inspected for surface artifacts before vegetation clearing and afterwards.

The airborne LiDAR used a laser scanner emitting pulses at 10,000 times per second to determine distance from the instrument to specific targets (*Liu et al. 2005*). A 30 m resolution DEM was downloaded from the 2000 Space Shuttle Endeavor's Shuttle Radar Topography Mission (*Wienhold 2012*, 853). These data sets were tied to the LiDAR data using a global positioning system (GPS) to record the laser scans in three-dimensional space. The raw data were delivered as three-dimensional point clouds with intensity values (*Liu et al. 2005*, 1405). Post-processing involved applying filtering algorithms to remove "noise" such as remaining vegetation and modern cultural features such as the highway and road cutbanks and to create a bare-earth topographic model of the ground surface. The LiDAR data collected had a vertical accuracy of 0.5 m and a horizontal accuracy of 1.5 m. Once the vegetation was filtered out, the topography was interpolated using 10 cm linear kriging to produce high resolution DEMs (Fig. 11).

Further investigation using the ArgGIS 3D Analyst profile function on the LiDAR dataset showed that most of the well-preserved agricultural features only exhibited an elevation change of about 8 cm (*Wienhold 2012*, 853). Field observations, however, indicated that these features actually ranged in height from about 50 cm (the better preserved features) to about 10 cm (eroded features). To correct this inaccuracy, agricultural features were rasterized and given a constant value of 50 cm. Although these features were probably not uniform in height when originally constructed, this procedure produced a better vertical representation in the analysis.

Control datums for each agricultural site were mapped using survey-grade GPS receivers and the locations of all agricultural features within each locus were recorded using a total station. Mapping data for the agricultural rock alignments were collected as polylines and the rock piles were collected as polygons. In addition, agricultural features were mapped by digitizing aerial photographs taken by balloon photography (Fig. 12). Similar recording methods were used to map residential features exposed in the construction corridor.

Large-scale excavations were undertaken in residential sites and features encountered in the construction corridor (*Wegener - Ciolek-Torello 2011*). Pithouses, post-reinforced adobe structures, and masonry field houses were excavated at the residential loci at the Black Dog, Carbonate Copy, Bighorn Wash, and Gravelly Horseman sites along with numerous intramural and extramural pit features, extramural activity areas, and middens. Architectural data, artifacts, and paleobotanical samples recovered from these features provided the primary evidence regarding chronology, settlement function, occupational intensity, seasonality, and subsistence patterns associated with the residents of the area.

Soil Analyses

A sample of agricultural features, such as terraces, rock alignments, and rock piles, were selected for soil sampling to analyze soil properties and to identify any anthropogenic affects of prehistoric agricultural activities (*Homburg et al. 2011*). Soil profiles were documented in test pits placed on representative agricultural features located in the construction corridor. Soil sampling focused on those agricultural features that were the least disturbed, as indicated by rock alignments and rock piles and terraces that lacked rill erosion and extensive sheet-wash erosion. In all, 204 soil samples were collected; these included 191 samples from the surface (0–10 cm depth) of 75 terraces, 65 rock alignments, 10 rock piles, and 41 uncultivated control areas (see *Homburg et al. 2011* for details). The control samples were collected from soils and landscape positions that were similar to those of the agricultural features but lacked evidence of agricultural features. In addition, 12 samples were collected from five soil profiles in test pits and natural exposures. Soil morphological properties (e.g., depth and thickness of soil horizons, color, texture, structure, etc.) were described for all profiles in accordance with the conventions of modern soil survey (*Soil Survey Division Staff 1993, 1999*). Particle-size, bulk density, organic matter, total carbon (C), nitrogen (N), total and available phosphorus (P), pH, and electrical conductivity (EC) were analyzed for all these samples (*Homburg et al. 2011*). Finally, a tension infiltrometer was used to measure unsaturated infiltration rates for 113 sampling locations, including 24 tests at Gravelly Horseman and 89 at the Nicholas Ranch Complex (28 at Loci A and B and 61 at Loci C–E) (Fig. 13). These locations included 45 terraces, 41 rock alignments, 2 rock piles, and 25 control samples. *T*-tests were used to evaluate statistical differences between cultivated and uncultivated soils in different agricultural contexts. Paired *t*-tests were conducted for the rock piles and their controls because there was a basis for pairing, as the controls were collected within 1 m of each respective

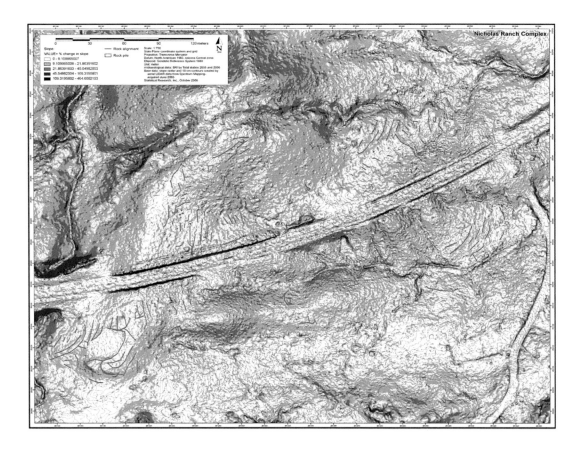

Fig. 11. LiDAR-generated DEM of Locus C, Nicholas Ranch Complex made at 10 cm contour interval and placed on shaded relief surface. Agricultural features mapped by total station are superimposed.

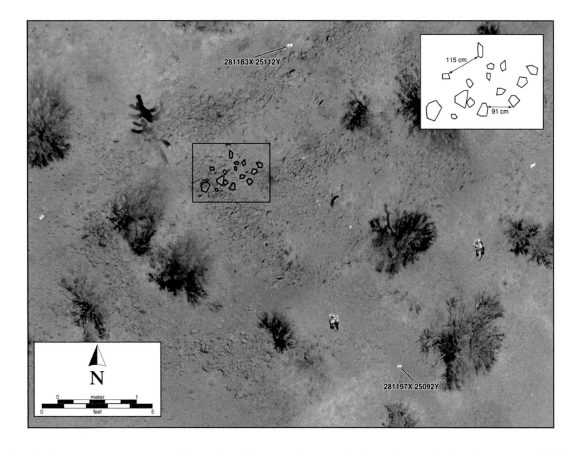

Fig. 12. Photogrammetric mapping of agricultural features using aerial balloon photography (from Homburg et al. 2011).

of the model. In the D-infinity method, flow direction is "encoded as an angle in radians counter-clockwise from east as a continuous quantity between 0 and 2" (*Tarboton 2005*, 8). The flow direction was then computed as the direction of the lowest downward slope of each individual cell or elevation value in the raster. This partitions the flow into two or more downslope directions and is more suitable for dispersal flow on hillslopes (*Neteler - Mitasova 2005*).

The D-infinity function creates a raster map in which each cell records the number of upslope neighbors, including its own contribution, that drain into it (*Tarboton 2005*). This in turn estimates amount of surface flow through a given area by determining the ". . . catchment area, the upslope area per unit contour lengths, taken here as the number of cells times grid cell size" (*Tarboton 2005*, 8). There were no outlet points, or points where drainageways converge, added to the function, so this was applied to each cell in the grid. The modeled results were then computed for all DEMs using both the D8 and D-infinity flow directions. Again, this was due to the focus on rainfall and runoff in this study.

Drainage way shapefiles were defined based on the D8 flow direction grid and a vector network created from the output of the previous function. These shapefiles are created by "tracing down from each source grid" and creating a polyline (*Tarboton 2005*, 10). Due to the use of the D8 flow direction grid, there are instances of the output drainageways running in straight lines downslope, especially on steeper slopes. This was unavoidable because TauDEM does not allow for the option of using the D-infinity for this process. The watersheds, or contributing areas for any point in the landscape, are created from the sub-watersheds draining to each drainageway segment and converted into a polygon (*Tarboton 2005*, 10-11).

Fig. 13. Tension infiltrometer used to measure infiltration rates of soils associated with agricultural features.

rock pile. Statistical analyses were performed using Excel 2003 for all quantitative chemical and physical soil tests.

Hydrological Analysis

In addition to documenting the full extent of the fields and their agricultural features, LIDAR data were used by *Wienhold (2008; 2012)* to analyze the hydrological affects of the construction of agricultural features. *Wienhold (2012, 854-855)* used Terrain Analysis Using Digital Elevation Models (TauDEM) to study surface flow and runoff hydrology in the fields. The details for this procedure are taken from *Homburg et al. (2011, 613)*.

The first step in the analysis involved removing depressions in each DEM, whereby the elevations of depressions were raised to the level of neighboring cells to prevent interference with the routing of flow (*Tarboton 2005*) and to reduce inaccuracies in the resultant model (*Neteler - Mitasova 2005*, 125). According to *Wienhold (2012)*, both the D8 and D-infinity flow directions were calculated for all of the surface rasters. The D8 method computes flow direction from each individual grid cell to one of its neighbors to the nearest 45° based on steepest descent (*Tarboton 2005*). Although this method is fairly obsolete in terms of its use (*Mitasova et al. 1996*), it was necessary to compute because it is required as input in other parts

Paleobotanical Analyses

To identify what plants may have been cultivated in the Queen Creek dryland fields, sediment samples were collected from excavations in houses, middens, and extramural features in the nearby residential sites and the agricultural features in the dryland fields found within the construction corridor. A total of 44 flotation samples and 68 pollen samples were extracted from the sediment samples obtained at the residential sites. In addition, 64 macrobotanical samples were recovered from the features at these sites. A total of 39 pollen samples were extracted from excavation of agricultural features at the Nicholas Ranch and Gravelly Horseman sites. In addition, five flotation samples and three macrobotanical samples were recovered from the single large roasting pit found in the construction corridor adjacent to the agricultural fields at the Nicholas Ranch site.

Results

Together, these various data sets provided valuable insights into the nature of the dryland agricultural systems in the

Queen Creek area and how they may have functioned in the past. Soil studies provided information about general soil fertility and conditions relating to agricultural production, as well as how dryland agricultural features may have functioned to increase fertility and other soil characteristics important to plant growth. By contrast, hydrological studies revealed how these agricultural features may have altered the hydrological characteristics of the field areas and, by inference, how they functioned to channel and conserve water and sediment. Finally, paleobotanical analyses provide insights into what plants may have been cultivated in these dryland fields and what role these fields played in the local subsistence system.

Soil Studies

Both the cultivated and uncultivated soils found in the ancient agricultural systems of Queen Creek were formed in slope alluvium of pediments on hillslopes and in andesitic residuum of summits (or hilltops). Morphological properties of these soils are detailed along with information on the horizon sequences in *Wegener et al. (2011, Appendix T)*, while chemical and physical properties of the soil samples are summarized in *Wegener et al. (2011, Appendix U)*. According to *Homburg et al. (2011, 613)*, these data indicate that these desert soils were generally fertile, with favorable chemical and physical properties for crop productivity, as long as sufficient water was available from direct rainfall and storm runoff for the crop growth. Soil pH is important for soil fertility because it controls the availability of nutrients to plants. Soil pH was neutral for terraces, rock alignments, control samples. No statistical differences were found among these samples. By contrast, the rock-pile soils were slightly acidic with an average pH of 6.3, which is very close to the best pH for maize cultivation (pH = 6.5). Statistically, the difference between the pH of soils underlying rock piles relative to the controls is highly significant (*Homburg et al. 2011, 615*). Overall, however, pH levels in all the cultivated and uncultivated soils sampled at these agricultural sites were well suited to crop production.

Soils from the rock alignments, rock piles, and terraces all had elevated levels for EC, which is a measure of the concentration of soluble salts in soils and is directly related to the availability of soil water for plant uptake. Higher soluble salt content is associated with lower nutrient availability to plants. *Homburg et al. (2011, 616)* attribute these elevated levels to increased water infiltration into the soils of these agricultural features, although the levels were still far too low to affect crop productivity adversely. Organic C and total N levels were also elevated in the rock-alignment and rock-pile soils relative to their controls and to terraces, commonly at levels that were about twice that of the controls and terraces. *Homburg et al. (2011, 616-617)* attribute these differences to increased levels of microbial decomposition of roots, decomposition and incorporation of surficial crop residues and weedy plants, and the armoring effect of the rock-mulch features in minimizing oxidation.

Similar patterns have been found in other soil studies of rock-mulch gardens in central and southern Arizona (*Homburg - Sandor 1998; Homburg et al. 2004*).

Some patterning was also found in the calcium carbonate levels, with terraces and rock alignments having significantly less $CaCO_3$ than the controls, with rock piles being statistically indistinguishable from the controls. *Homburg et al. (2011, 617)* suggest that the greater $CaCO_3$ in the control samples probably reflects the lower amount of water infiltrated in the soil and the greater precipitation of $CaCO_3$ from evaporation on the surface. Although the cultivated and uncultivated soils were both slightly calcareous, the carbonate levels would have an inconsequential effect on agricultural productivity.

Although deficiencies in phosphorous have been found throughout Arizona, available P in soils associated with both agricultural features and control samples far exceeded that necessary for plant cultivation. Rock alignments and terraces, however, had twice the available P as did the controls. *Homburg et al. (2011, 617)* suggest that the high levels of available P may be the result of high amounts of apatite [$Ca5(PO4)3(OH, F, Cl)$] in the soils weathered from the andesitic parent rock underlying the fields. They also suggest that some organic P may have been incorporated into the soil from the addition of manure as a result of historical period cattle grazing in the fields, but such high levels would not explain the strong differences between the soils under rock-alignments and terraces and those from control samples.

Homburg et al. (2011, 617) also found that bulk densities were significantly lower in the rock-alignment and rock-pile soils relative to the controls and terrace soils. They conclude that the soils under rock-mulch features were not compacted and that these features increased water infiltration and soil aeration. *Homburg et al. (2011, 619)* used a tension infiltrometer to model water infiltration at soil conditions that ranged from wet (but not saturated) to dry. They found that unsaturated hydraulic conductivity was significantly higher at the –2 cm tension level for the rock-alignment and rock-pile soils relative to the controls and terraces. They argued that of the three tension levels tested, the –2-cm level is the most significant for crop production in the dryland field systems of central Arizona, because this level measures water infiltration near the saturation point in a way that is analogous to what occurs during events such as during monsoonal storms when storm runoff is concentrated as sheet flow in and around the rock-mulch features. At such times, most water enters the soil at low tensions, just below the saturation point.

Hydrological Analyses

This hydrological analysis is based on work of Michelle Wienhold with the assistance of Dr. James H. Mayer (*Wienhold 2008; 2012;* see also *Homburg et al. 2011, 627*). To gauge the affects of the agricultural features on the hydrology of the field areas two hydrological analyses were conducted, one that involved a representation of the topography of the field areas without agricultural features and another with the agricultural features added. The results before the addition of the features show that the rock alignments were built perpendicular to the natural surface flow (Fig. 14). After the features were added to the DEMs, the surface flow was drastically changed (Fig. 15) and the flow was redirected throughout each of the fields (*Wienhold 2012*, 856). The rock alignments functioned as dams that reduced the slope gradient and slowed and redirected runoff, thereby increased water infiltration into soils (*Homburg et al. 2011*). Further analysis indicated that the shape of the rock alignments affected surface flow in different ways. Water flowed along the rock alignments and based on their shape, was redirected to other areas as it flowed down hill. For example, the northwest oriented rock alignments in Locus C of the Nicholas Ranch Complex functioned to change the direction of flow into a micro-catchment where the majority of rock alignments were built. Most of the rock piles, however, did little to affect surface flow (*Wienhold 2012*, 857). *Wienhold (2012*, Figure 10) prepared a series of graphs to understand better the effect the agricultural features had on surface flow. These graphs compare the before and after values of flow volume, which is a crude measure of the relative volume of surface water that flows through each map cell (Fig. 16). In all but two cases (Nicholas Ranch Complex, Locus C and Gravelly Horseman), the addition of agricultural terraces and rock alignments significantly altered the flow of surface water as more cells had low flow accumulation values after the features were added.

Wienhold (2012, 857) concludes that the functions of prehistoric agricultural features can be ascertained by placing them within a high-resolution modern topographic environment generated by aerial LiDAR. The terrain analyses revealed that rock alignments were placed perpendicular to the surface flow of water. Furthermore, these alignments were placed on 2-10 percent slope gradients that would have made it easier to manage runoff and decrease erosion, and that most of these features were also located on east and southeast facing slopes that reduced evaporation loss from intense afternoon sunlight (*Homburg et al. 2011*, 626).

Paleobotanical Analyses

The record of plant taxa and parts preserved within flotation and macrobotanical samples revealed that subsistence patterns of the people, who occupied the residential sites adjacent to the dryland fields of the Queen Creek area, did not focus on agriculture. Instead, these people relied primarily on cactus fruit and wild plant seeds (*Adams 2011*). *Adams (2011)* found evidence of maize in a limited number of Sedentary and Classic period contexts. She also suggests the possibility that agave plants were being used based on the presence of monocotyledon fibrovascular bundles and tissue fragments in three samples from residential

contexts at the Black Dog and Gravelly Horseman sites. Significantly, however, use of wild plants decreased relative to domesticated plants (maize) and managed plants (agave) by the Sedentary and Classic periods. Today, no native or cultivated varieties of agave occur at or near these Queen Creek dryland fields or residential loci. However, a wild species of agave (possibly *A. chrysantha*) was observed by the senior authors on the slopes of hills about 5 km east of these sites (Fig. 17).

Maize pollen was also sparsely represented in these residential contexts (*Smith 2011*). The absence of agave pollen was not unexpected, as agave pollen is rarely found in archaeological contexts. Agave is an insect-pollinated plant that produces little pollen and the pollen that is produced is commonly very poorly preserved in the soil; for example, no agave pollen was found in composite soil samples collected under relict colonies of *Agave murpheyi* plants found in the lower Verde River Valley (*Bozarth 1997; Homburg 1998*). Like the flotation results, pollen evidence from residential loci suggests a focus on wild plants such as cholla cactus (*Opuntia sp.*), mesquite (*Prosopis sp.*), and especially wild grasses (*Smith 2011*).

A somewhat different picture emerges from paleobotanical samples derived in or near the agricultural features, although the single roasting pit adjacent to the fields at the Nicholas Ranch Complex yielded no evidence of what plant foods may have been processed in it as only mesquite wood charcoal was recovered (*Adams 2011*, 508). The ubiquity measures for maize and cotton pollen were much higher in field contexts compared to nearby residential contexts. For example, the ubiquity measures for Locus A at the Nicholas Ranch Complex were 45 percent for maize and 27 percent for cotton, whereas Locus B yielded ubiquity measures of 25 percent for both taxa (*Smith 2011*, 536). Single samples yielded maize in Loci C and E at Nicholas Ranch and maize was found in two of 12 samples from Gravelly Horseman agricultural features. *Smith (2011*, 536) suggests that the overall level of cultigens pollen at the Nicholas Ranch Complex may in fact be underrepresented.

Discussion

The agricultural features at the Gravelly Horseman and the Nicholas Ranch Complex represent an engineered landscape for the purpose of dryland agriculture using features that functioned as mix of runoff and/or rock-mulch agricultural gardens (*Homburg et al. 2011*, 624). The ancient farmers who built this system were keenly aware of how the local topography affected runoff.

Unlike the degraded conditions of many agricultural soils worldwide, the soils of the dryland fields in the Queen Creek were not degraded and the ancient conservation and management features built in these fields had actually improved soil fertility and productivity. Long-term indicators of soil productivity such as organic matter and nutrient content, bulk density, and soil water

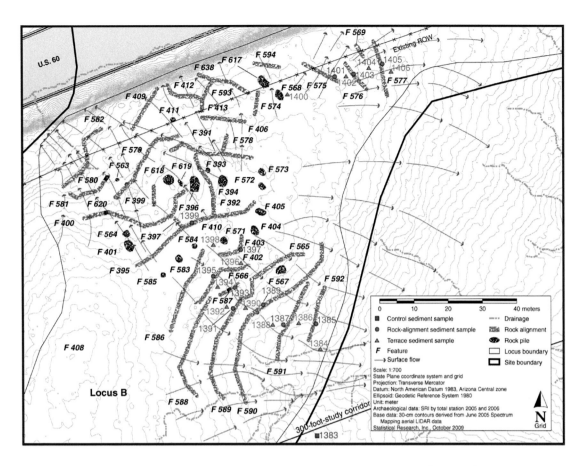

Fig. 14. Natural drainage patterns in agricultural field at Gravelly Horseman site (from Homburg et al. 2011).

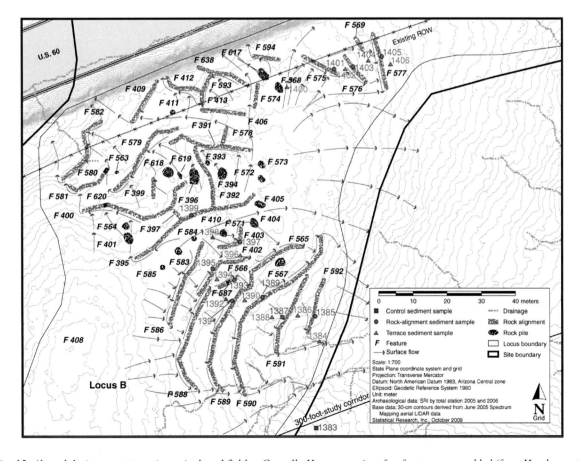

Fig. 15. Altered drainage patterns in agricultural field at Gravelly Horseman site after features area added (from Homburg et al. 2011).

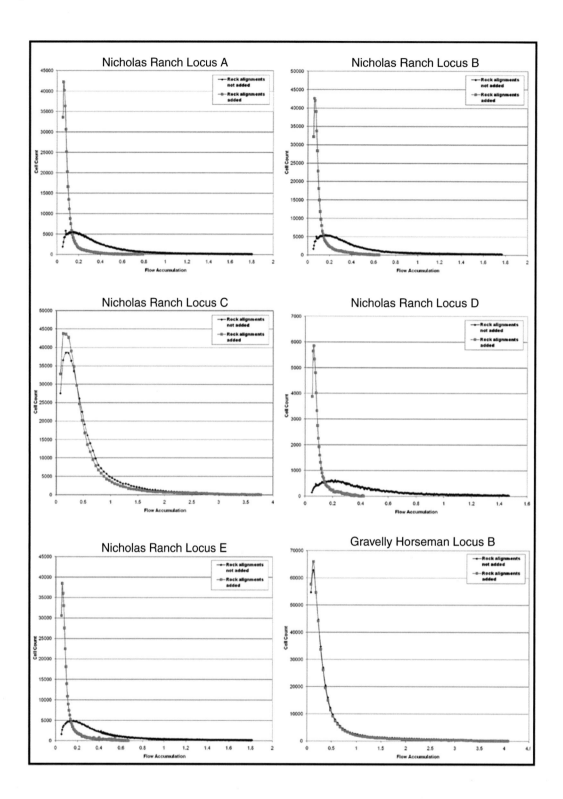

Fig. 16. Flow accumulation values calculated for six fields in the Nicholas Ranch and Gravelly Horseman sites (adapted from Wienhold 2012).

properties indicate that this dryland agricultural system was sustainable, depending on the mix of crops that were cultivated (*Homburg et al. 2011*, 639-640):

> *"Overall, soil properties in this dryland field system were favorable for crop production, an assessment that was especially true for the soils in and immediately adjacent to the rock alignments and rock piles where*

planting must have been concentrated. Relative to the control/terrace soils, the rock-mulch soils of the rock alignments and rock piles had elevated organic matter and nutrient (especially N and P) levels and lower bulk densities that promoted water infiltration during storm events. Salinity levels, although elevated in the rock-mulch features, were far below levels that could have had a detrimental effect on crop production. The

Fig. 17. Wild agave in Queen Creek Valley.

rock-mulch features promoted fertility and moisture retention by armoring the soil and thereby blocking direct sunlight on the soil surface, thus reducing organic matter loss by oxidation and evaporative losses. The rock mulch also served a number of other important agricultural functions. Rock mulch acts to increase water infiltration into the rooting zone, increase heat retention (which protects against frost damage and accelerates seed germination and crop growth), reduce erosion, and protect crops from predation by burrowing animals. The assessment that the rock-mulch soils had elevated productivity is further bolstered by the fact that the plants growing today are concentrated in the rock-mulch soils. This observation indicates that these archaeological features continue to function by promoting denser and more vigorous plant growth for centuries after the field system was abandoned by ancient peoples."

It is unclear, however, what plants were actually cultivated in these fields. It is possible that maize, agave, cactus (e.g., *Opuntia sp.*), or even cotton were cultivated in these fields, possibly as part of a multi-cropping system with different crops grown in different types of agricultural features, on different landscape positions, and perhaps under different climate conditions.

Dryland agricultural fields in these other desert regions of Arizona have been most closely associated with agave

cultivation, especially of domesticated varieties such as *A. murpheyi* and *A. delamateri (Hodgson et al. 1989)*. However, definitive evidence of agave (e.g., pollen from soil samples and macrobotanical remains from nearby roasting pits) were not recovered from any of the Queen Creek field areas and only limited evidence was recovered from nearby residential contexts. Although no direct evidence of agave was identified among the dryland agricultural features, agave is well suited to the thin and rocky soils of the study area and does occur naturally in the vicinity. Notably, however, dryland fields associated with agave cultivation in other areas of Arizona, such as the Crash Landing site, are dominated by rock piles, which are believed to have served as planters protecting individual agave plants or colonies. By contrast, rock piles are in the minority of agricultural features in the Queen Creek dryland fields. Furthermore, the paucity of roasting pits used to process agave, macrobotanical remains of agave, and tabular tools in both the fields and residential areas, suggest that agave cultivation was an insignificant part of the subsistence system if it was cultivated at all. In this respect, the Queen Creek fields stand in stark contrast to other extensive dryland agriculture fields in the desert regions of Arizona.

The high ubiquity values for maize in samples, especially at the Nicholas Ranch Complex, suggest that this domesticate may have been cultivated in these agricultural fields (*Homburg et al. 2011*). Maize cultivation is usually associated with flood water farming and irrigation of streamside terraces in the desert regions of Arizona. As mentioned earlier, rainfall records indicate that rainfall exceeds 50 cm in about one in four years in the upper Queen Creek area. This relatively high precipitation makes maize cultivation a more viable option in the wetter years compared to similar upland regions with dryland agricultural fields, such as the Agua Fria and Lower Verde Valleys in the northern Phoenix Basin and the Tortolita Mountains to the south, especially if the features in these fields acted to collect and conserve runoff and reduce evaporation. *Fish et al. (1985b*, 185) also suggest that maize may have been grown in dryland agricultural features in Tonto Basin along with agricultural weeds, wild buckwheat, and prickly pear cactus. The paleobotanical record from residential features suggests that maize use increased at the expense of wild plant exploitation during the Sedentary and Classic period occupation of the Queen Creek area, precisely the time when we believe the dryland agricultural systems were developed in the area.

Another possibility is that cotton was grown in these fields, even though cotton consumes even greater quantities of water than maize (*Homburg et al. 2011*). Thus, cotton production is normally associated with irrigation agriculture in the Arizona deserts. Cotton, however, also exhibited high ubiquity values among samples taken from Queen Creek dryland agricultural features. Cotton pollen is a large grain that does not typically blow over long distances, so it is unlikely that it was transported by wind from modern cotton fields along the Gila River or other irrigated fields in Arizona (*Homburg et al. 2011,* 641). It is also possible, however, that the cotton pollen found in the Queen Creek dryland agricultural fields was deposited in cattle manure, as cattle are known to be fed on cotton fodder. Otherwise cotton could only have been grown successfully in these fields in the wettest of years (*Homburg et al. 2011*, 641).

Finally, it is possible that native plants such as prickly pear or cholla cactus were cultivated in these dryland fields as *Fish et al. (1985b)* suggested for features in Tonto Basin. Although these wild plants are common in the Queen Creek area today, collection of runoff and reduction of evaporation could have significantly increased their productivity. The dense concentration of prickly pear and cholla cactus found in the fields at the start of our work is strong testimony of this. Furthermore, paleobotanical evidence indicates these cacti were an important part of the local inhabitants' subsistence economy.

In short, evidence for a mix of crops, including maize, native cacti, and possibly even cotton, was identified in the dryland agricultural fields of the Queen Creek area. Agricultural features in these fields had significantly higher soil fertility than the controls, indicating that these features served to enhance production of a variety of crops in these locations (*Homburg et al. 2011*). The rock-mulch features in this dryland agricultural system also served to improve both water infiltration and moisture retention in the shallow rooting zone above bedrock in the hilly pediments of the study area. The critical factor, of course, was that sufficient water was available for plant growth during the growing season. It is likely, however, that rainfall was sufficient on a consistent basis to cultivate domesticated plants such as cotton or maize because of their high rates of water consumption and the high evaporation rates in the area even with the benefit of the runoff collection and mulching effects of the dryland agricultural features. Nevertheless, cultivation of maize and, possibly, cotton, could have been undertaken during wetter years. Crops may have changed from year to year depending on the amount and timing of rainfall with an emphasis on the management of native cacti in drier years. This system, however, was not the primary basis of the local economy but likely served to supplement food obtained by more productive systems, such as floodwater farming and irrigation along the streamside terraces of Queen Creek. At best, the dryland fields were only part of a mixed economy that focused on wild-plant collection, hunting, agriculture, and the management of selected wild plants. Furthermore, it is clear from the paleobotanical record that wild plant foods were always more important to the residents of the area than were domesticated plant products. Finally, excavations at the nearby residential loci indicate that this mixed economy initially supported only small, family-sized seasonal settlements. Development of the dryland fields in the Sedentary period may have increased food productivity, which in turn made possible the construction of more intensive, but still only intermittently occupied

farmsteads and hamlets. By the Classic period, the absence of settlements more substantial than temporarily occupied field houses suggest that the fields continued to be used by farmers who resided in more distant settlements and only returned to these fields to plant and harvest their crops.

Conclusions

Aerial LiDAR provided a rapid, nondestructive, and cost-effective means to prepare precise topographic models of the extensive dryland agricultural fields of the Queen Creek Valley. The highly detailed topographic maps provided by aerial LiDAR combined with balloon aerial photogrammetry and conventional total station mapping of agricultural features enabled us to conduct a hydrological analysis that examined how agricultural features affected drainage patterns within the fields. Soil studies indicated that the ancient conservation and management practices used in these fields improved the capture and retention of monsoonal sheet flow, and that these fields were sustainable, depending on the mix of plantings. However, these fields were probably used for cultivation of domestic crops only periodically when rainfall was at a peak. Paleobotanical analysis indicated a persistent reliance on native cacti, especially cholla, and a host of native weedy annuals. Maize and cotton cultivation was secondary. Unlike the other dryland agricultural fields of central and southern Arizona, agave cultivation does not appear to have been an important factor in the construction and use of these fields.

Although these various analyses provide a detailed picture of the function of these agricultural fields, a more comprehensive understanding of their role in local settlement systems emerges when data from these fields are placed within the context of analytic data from associated residential sites and comparison with dryland agricultural practices in other areas of central and southern Arizona.

Chronological evidence regarding the construction and use of these fields is not firm, but it is likely that they were first constructed in the sedentary period when occupation of this portion of the Queen Creek area was most intense. As such, these fields most likely predate the construction of extensive dryland fields associated with agave production in other areas of central and southern Arizona. Despite the large scale of the Queen Creek dryland agricultural fields, these fields probably only supplemented production from traditional agricultural practices along the narrow streamside terraces of Queen Creek and activities associated with gathering of native wild plants. During the Sedentary period, this system supported only small family-sized farmsteads, probably on a short-term and intermittent basis. By the Classic period, residence appears to have shifted to more distant areas of the Queen Creek Valley such as the Superior Ruin, and field houses were established near the fields for temporary occupation. By the Classic period, elsewhere in the desert regions of central and southern Arizona, Hohokam farmers had moved to large-scale production of agave. They constructed extensive dryland agricultural fields in the low desert regions well outside the natural range of this plant taxon. The question remains why the Classic period residents of the upper Queen Creek area did not adapt their fields to agave production despite the presence of native agave species in the area or why similar technology was not used more often in similar upland areas of the region to cultivate domestic crops and encourage wild plants. Perhaps more careful examination of plant remains associated with these types of fields may reveal evidence of use for growing plants other than agave.

Acknowledgments

The authors wish to acknowledge the ADOT, Historic Preservation Program for giving us the opportunity to study these fields and for funding the research. We also wish to thank the Tonto National Forest for providing access to the field areas outside of the highway right-of-way and, especially, Michael Sullivan, archaeologist and U.S. Forest Service/ADOT Heritage Resource Liaison at the Tonto National Forest, without whose enthusiasm and support documentation and analysis of these fields would never have transpired. Finally, we wish to thank Statistical Research for supporting the authors in the preparation of the original presentation at the European Association of Archaeologists meeting in Helsinki that led to this paper and for the preparation of this paper itself.

References

Abbott, D. 2000: Ceramics and Community Organization among the Hohokam. Tucson: University of Arizona Press.

Ackerly, N. – Henderson, T.K. eds 1989: Prehistoric Agricultural Activities on the Lehi-Mesa Terrace: Perspectives on Hohokam Irrigation Cycles. Flagstaff: Northland Research.

Adams, K. 2003: Plant remains. In: R. Ciolek-Torrello - E. Klucas - R. Vanderpot eds, Analyses of Prehistoric Remains, From the Desert to the Mountains: Archaeology of the Transition Zone: The State Route 87–Sycamore Creek Project, vol. 2. Technical Series 73. Tucson: Statistical Research, 223-246.

Adams, K. 2011: Plant use along U.S. 60, Queen Valley to Queen Creek Project segment: The flotation and macrobotanical records. In: R.M. Wegener - M.P. Heilen - R. Ciolek-Torrello - J.D. Hall eds, Analyses of Prehistoric Materials in the Queen Valley to Queen Creek Area. Early Agricultural, Formative, and Historical-period Use of the Upper Queen Creek Area: The U.S. 60 Archaeological Project, vol. 4. Technical Series 92. Tucson: Statistical Research, 479-517.

Bernard-Shaw, M. 1984: The stone tool assemblage of the Salt-Gila Aqueduct Project sites. In: L. Teague - P. Crown ed., Specialized Activity Sites, Hohokam Archaeology along the Salt-Gila Aqueduct Central Arizona Project, vol. 3. Archaeological Series 150, vol. 3. Cultural Resource Management Division, Arizona State Museum. Tucson: University of Arizona, 337-443.

Boers, T.M. – Ben-Asher, J. 1982: A review of rainwater harvesting. Agricultural Water Management 5, 145-158.

Bohrer, V. 1998: Pieces from the landscape: Flotation analysis of plant remains from sites in the vicinity of Kitty Joe Creek. In: G. Woodall - D. Barz - M. Neeley eds, Rocks, Roasters, and Ridgetops: Data Recovery Across the Pioneer Road Landscape, State Route 87—Segment F, Maricopa and Gila Counties, Arizona. Project Report No. 94-77B. Tempe: Archaeological Research Services, 295-312.

Bozarth, S. 1997: Pollen and opal phytolith evidence of prehistoric agriculture and wild plant utilization in the Lower Verde River Valley, Arizona. Unpublished Ph.D. dissertation, Department of Geography. Lawrence: University of Kansas.

Bruins, H. 1986: Desert Environment and Agriculture in the Central Negev and Kadesh-Barnea during Historical Times. Nijkerk, the Netherlands: MIDBAR Foundation.

Bruins, H. 1990: Ancient agricultural terraces at Nahal Mitnan. Atiqot 10, 10-28.

Bruins, H. – Evenari, M. – Rogel, A. 1987: Run-off farming anagement and climate. In: L. Berkofsky - M. Wurtele eds, Progress in Desert Research, Totawa, New Jersey Rowman and Littlefield, 3-14.

Bryan, K. 1929: Flood-water farming. Geographical Review 19, 444-456.

Canouts, V. ed. 1975: An Archaeological Survey of the Orme Reservoir. Archaeological Series No. 93. Arizona State Museum, Tucson, University of Arizona.

Ciolek-Torrello, R. 1998: Prehistoric settlement and demography in the Lower Verde Region. In: S. Whittlesey - R. Ciolek-Torrello - J. Altschul eds, Overview, Synthesis and Conclusions, Vanishing River: Landscapes and Lives of the Lower Verde Valley, The Lower Verde Archaeological Project. Tucson, SRI Press, 531-595.

Ciolek-Torrello, R. 2012: Hohokam household organization, sedentism, and irrigation in the Sonoran Desert, Arizona. In: J. Douglass - N. Gonlin eds, Ancient Households of the Americas: Conceptualizing what Households Do. Boulder: University Press of Colorado, 221-268.

Ciolek-Torrello, R. – Klucas, E. – Wegener, R. – O'Mack, S. – Deaver, W. 2005: Archaeological Investigations along U.S. 60: Treatment Plan for Florence Junction to Superior, and Data Recovery Plan for Queen Valley to Queen Creek Bridge, Pinal County, Arizona. Technical Report 02-47. Tucson: Statistical Research.

Ciolek-Torrello, R. – Klucas, E. – Vanderpot, R. eds, 2009: Conclusions and syntheses. From the Desert to the Mountains: Archaeology of the Transition Zone: The State Route 87–Sycamore Creek Project, vol. 3. Technical Series 73. Tucson: Statistical Research.

Cohen, I.S. – Lopes, V. – Slack, D.C. – Yanez, C.H. 1995: Assessing Risk for Water Harvesting Systems in Arid Environments. Journal of Soil and Water Conservation 50, 446-449.

Crown, P. 1984: Prehistoric agricultural technology in the Salt-Gila Basin. In: L.S. Teague - P.L. Crown eds, Hohokam Archaeology along the Salt-Gila

Aqueduct Central Arizona Project, Vol. 7: Environment and Subsistence, Archaeological Series No. 150. Arizona State Museum. Tucson: University of Arizona, 207-260.

Dart, A. 1983: Agricultural features. In: L. Teague - P. Crown eds, Specialized Activity Sites. Hohokam Archaeology along the Salt-Gila Aqueduct Central Arizona Project, vol. 3. Archaeological Series No. 150, vol. 3. Cultural Resource Management Division, Arizona State Museum. Tucson: University of Arizona, 345-573.

Doelle, W. 1976: Desert Resources and Hohokam Subsistence: The CONOCO Florence Project. Archaeological Series No. 103. Cultural Resource Management Division, Arizona State Museum. Tucson: University of Arizona.

Doolittle, W. 1990: Canal Irrigation in Prehistoric Mexico. Austin: University of Texas Press.

Doolittle, W. 2002: Cultivated Landscapes of Native North America. Oxford: Oxford University Press.

Doyel, D. - Elson, M. eds 1985: Hohokam Settlement and Economic Systems in the Central New River Drainage, Arizona. Publications in Archaeology No. 4. Phoenix: Soil Systems.

Evenari, M. - Shanan, L. - Tadmor, N. 1982: The Negev: The Challenge of a Desert. 2nd ed. Cambridge, Massachusetts: Harvard University Press.

Fish, S. - Fish, P. - Miksicek, C. - Madsen, J. 1985a: Prehistoric Agave Cultivation in Southern Arizona. Desert Plants 7(2), 107-112.

Fish, S. - Gasser, R, - Swarthout, J. 1985b: Site function and subsistence patterns. In: G. Rice ed., Studies in the Hohokam and Salado of the Tonto Basin. Report No. 63. Office of Cultural Resource Management, Department of Anthropology. Tempe: Arizona State University, 175-190.

Fish, S. - Fish, P. - Madsen, J. 1992: The Marana Community in the Hohokam World. Anthropological Papers No. 56. Tucson: University of Arizona Press.

Gasser, R. 1988: Flotation studies. In: D. Weaver ed., Environment and Subsistence. The Tucson Aqueduct Project: Hohokam Settlement Along the Slopes of the Picacho Mountains. Research Paper 35, vol. 5. Flagstaff: Museum of Northern Arizona, 143-235.

Gasser, R. - Kwiatkowski, S. 1991a: Regional signatures of Hohokam plant use. Kiva 56, 207-226.

Gasser, R. - Kwiatkowski, S. 1991b: Food for thought: recognizing patterns in Hohokam subsistence. In: George J. Gumerman ed., Exploring the Hohokam: Prehistoric Desert Peoples of the American Southwest, Amerind Foundation New World Studies No. 1. Albuquerque: University of New Mexico Press, 417-459.

Greenwald, D.H. - Ciolek-Torrello, R. eds 1988: Archaeological investigations at the Dutch Canal Ruin, Phoenix, Arizona: Archaeology and History along the Papago Freeway Corridor. Research Paper No. 38. Flagstaff: Museum of Northern Arizona.

Greenwald, D.M. 1988: Ground stone. In: M. Callahan ed., Material Culture. The Tucson Aqueduct Project: Hohokam Settlement Along the Slopes of the Picacho Mountains. Research Paper 35, vol. 4. Flagstaff: Museum of Northern Arizona, 127-220.

Hack, J. 1942: The Changing Physical Environment of the Hopi Indians of Arizona. Papers, Vol. 35, No. 1. Peabody Museum of Archaeology and Ethnology. Cambridge, Massachusetts: Harvard University.

Halbirt, C. - Ciolek-Torrello, R. 1987: The Rock Terrace site, NA18,017. In: R. Ciolek-Torrello ed., The Picacho Area Sites. The Tucson Aqueduct Project: Hohokam Settlement Along the Slopes of the Picacho Mountains. Research Paper 35, vol. 3. Flagstaff: Museum of Northern Arizona, 217-254.

Haury, E. 1976: The Hohokam, Desert Farmers and Craftsmen: Excavations at Snaketown, 1964–1965. Tucson: University of Arizona Press.

Henderson, T.K. 1989: Prehistoric Agricultural Activities on the Lehi-Mesa Terrace: Excavations at La Cuenca Del Sedimento. Report prepared for Arizona Department of Transportation Contract 86-102. Flagstaff: Northland Research, Inc.

Hodgson, W. - Nabhan, G. - Ecker, L. 1989: Prehistoric Fields in Central Arizona: Conserving Rediscovered Agave Cultivars. Agave 3(3), 9-11. Phoenix: Desert Botanical Gardens.

Homburg, J. 1994: Soil fertility in the Tonto Basin. In: R. Ciolek-Torrello - J. Welch eds, Changing Land Use in the Tonto Basin. The Roosevelt Rural Sites Study, vol. 3. Technical Series 28. Tucson: Statistical Research, 253-295.

Homburg, J. 1998: Prehistoric dryland agricultural fields of the Lower Verde. In: J. Homburg - R. Ciolek-Torrello eds, Agricultural, Subsistence, and Environmental Studies. Vanishing River: Landscapes and Lives of the Lower Verde Valley: The Lower Verde Archaeological Project, vol. 2. CD-ROM. Tucson: SRI Press, 103-126.

Homburg, J. - Ciolek-Torrello, R. 1998: The Crash Landing Complex: agricultural sites and field houses. In: J. Homburg - R. Ciolek-Torrello eds, Agricultural, Subsistence, and Environmental Studies. Vanishing River: Landscapes and Lives of the Lower Verde Valley: The Lower Verde Archaeological Project, vol. 2. CD-ROM. Tucson: SRI Press, 57-83.

Homburg, J. - Sandor, J. 1998: An agronomic study of two classic period agricultural fields in the Horseshoe Basin. In: J. Homburg - R. Ciolek-Torrello eds, Agricultural, Subsistence, and Environmental Studies. Vanishing River: Landscapes and Lives of the Lower Verde Valley: The Lower Verde Archaeological Project, vol. 2. CD-ROM. Tucson: SRI Press, 127-148.

Homburg, J. - Sandor, J. 2004: Ancient agricultural soils of a gridded field complex in the Safford Basin. In: B. Houser - P. Pearthree - J. Homburg - L. Thrasher eds, Quaternary Stratigraphy and Tectonics, and Late Prehistoric Agriculture of the Safford Basin (Gila and San Simon River Valleys), Graham County, Arizona. Open File Report 2004-1062. Reston, Virginia: U.S. Geological Survey, 52-68.

Homburg, J. - Sandor, J. - Lightfoot, D. 2004: Soil investigations. In: W. Doolittle - J. Neely eds, The Safford Valley Grids: Prehistoric Cultivation in the Southern Arizona Desert. Anthropological Papers No. 70. Tucson: University of Arizona Press, 62-78.

Homburg, J. – Sandor, J. – Norton, J. 2005: Anthropogenic influences on Zuni agricultural soils. Geoarchaeology: An International Journal 20(7), 661-693.

Homburg, J.A. – Wienhold, M.L. – Windingstad, J. 2011: Anthropogenic effects on soil productivity of a dryland agricultural system. In: R.M. Wegener - M.P. Heilen - R. Ciolek-Torello - J.D. Hall eds, Analyses of Prehistoric Materials in the Queen Valley to Queen Creek Area. Early Agricultural, Formative, and Historical-period Use of the Upper Queen Creek Area: The U.S. 60 Archaeological Project, vol. 4. Technical Series 92. Tucson: Statistical Research, 593-641.

Howard, J. 1993: A paleohydraulic approach to examining agricultural intensification in Hohokam irrigation systems. Research in Economic Anthropology, Supplement 7, 263-324. Greenwich, Connecticut: JAI Press.

Howard, J. – Huckleberry, G. eds 1991: The Operation and Evolution of an Irrigation System: The East Papago Canal Study. Soil Systems Publications in Archaeology no. 18. Phoenix.

Kowsar, A. 1991: Floodwater spreading for desertification control: An integrated approach. An Iranian Contribution to the Implementation of the Plan of Action to Combat Desertification. Desertification Bulletin 19, 3-18.

Kwiatkowski, S. 2003: Evidence for subsistence problems. In: D. Abbott ed., Centuries of Decline During the Hohokam Classic Period at Pueblo Grande. Tucson: University of Arizona Press, 48-69.

Lavee, H. – Poesen, J. – Yair, A. 1997: Evidence of high efficiency water-harvesting by ancient farmers in the Negev Desert. Journal of Arid Environments 35, 341-348.

Lengyel, S. 2011: Chronometric dating and site chronologies. In: R.M. Wegener - M.P. Heilen - R. Ciolek-Torello - J.D. Hall eds, Analyses of Prehistoric Materials in the Queen Valley to Queen Creek Area. Early Agricultural, Formative, and Historical-period Use of the Upper Queen Creek Area: The U.S. 60 Archaeological Project, vol. 4. Technical Series 92. Tucson: Statistical Research, 9-51.

Liu, Z. – Martina, M.L.V. – Todini, E. 2005: Flood forecasting using a fully distributed model: Application of the TOPKAPI Model to the Upper Xixian Catchment. Hydrology and Earth Systems Sciences 9, 347-364.

Masse, W.B. 1979: An intensive survey of prehistoric dry farming systems near Tumomoc Hill in Tucson. Kiva 45, 141-186.

McGee, W.J. 1895: Beginnings of agriculture. American Anthropologist 8, 350-375.

Mitasova, H. – Hofierka, J. – Zlocha, M. – Iverson, L.R. 1996: Modelling topographic potential for erosion and deposition using GIS. International Journal of Geographical Information Systems 10(5), 629-641.

Nabhan, G. 1979: The ecology of floodwater farming in arid Southwestern America. Agro-Ecosystems 5, 245-255.

Nabhan, G. 1983: Papago fields: Arid Lands Ethnobotany and Agricultural Ecology. Ph.D. dissertation, University of Arizona, Tucson. Ann Arbor, Michigan: University Microfilms.

Nabhan, G. 1984: Soil fertility renewal and water harvesting in Sonoran Desert agriculture: the Papago example. Arid Lands Newsletter 20, 21-28.

Nabhan, G. 1986a: Ak-Chin "arroyo mouth" and the environmental setting of the Papago Indian fields in the Sonoran Desert. Applied Geography 6, 61-75.

Nabhan, G. 1986b: Papago Indian desert agriculture and water control in the Sonoran Desert, 1697–1934. Applied Geography 6, 43-59.

Neitzel, J. 1987: The sociopolitical implications of canal irrigation: A Reconsideration of the Hohokam. In: S.W. Gaines ed., Coasts, Plains and Deserts: Essays in Honor of Reynold J. Ruppé. Anthropological Research Paper No. 38. Tempe: Arizona State University, 205-212.

Neteler, M. – Mitasova, H. 2005: Open Source GIS-A GRASS GIS Approach. Boston: Kluwer Academic.

Niemeijer, D. 1998: Soil nutrient harvesting in indigenous teras water harvesting in eastern Sudan. Land Degradation and Development 8, 323-330.

Norton, J. – Sandor, J. – White, C.S. 2003: Hillslope soils and organic matter dynamics within a native American agroecosystem on the Colorado Plateau. Soil Science Society of America Journal 67, 225-234.

Parr, C.H. 1943: Flood water farming. Indian Farming 9, 510-515.

Pawluk, R. 1995: Indigenous Knowledge of Soils and Agriculture at Zuni Pueblo, New Mexico. Unpublished Master's thesis, Department of Agronomy, Iowa State University, Ames.

Rankin, A. 1989: Agricultural Features. In: M. Green ed., Settlement, Subsistence, and Specialization in the Northern Periphery. The Waddell Project, vol. 2. Cultural Resources Report No. 65. Tempe: Archaeological Consulting Services, 981-1020.

Rankin, A. – Katzer, K. 1989: Agricultural systems in the ACS Waddell Project Area. In: M. Green ed., Settlement, Subsistence, and Specialization in the Northern Periphery. The Waddell Project, vol. 2. Cultural Resources Report No. 65. Tempe: Archaeological Consulting Services, 981-1020.

Sandor, J. – Norton, J. – Pawluk, R. – Homburg, J. – Muenchrath, D.A. – White, C.S. – Williams, S.E. – Havner, C.I. – Stahl P.D. 2002: Soil knowledge embodied in a Native American runoff agroecosystem. Transactions of the 17th World Congress of Soil Science. Bangkok: Congress of Soil Science.

Schroeder, A. 1943: Prehistoric canals in the Salt River Valley, Arizona. American Antiquity 8, 380-386.

Sellers, W. – Hill, R. 1974: Arizona Climate, 1931-1972. Tucson: University of Arizona Press.

Shelley, S. – Ciolek-Torrello, R. 1994: Porter Springs Recreation Area. In: R. Ciolek-Torrello - S. Shelley - S. Benaron eds, The Roosevelt Rural Sites Study, Vol. 2: Prehistoric Rural Settlements in the Tonto Basin, Part 1. Technical Series No. 28. Tucson: Statistical Research, 99-221.

Smith, S.J., 2011: Pollen analysis from settlements and fields: the U.S. Highway 60 Queen valley to Queen

Creek Project segment. Technical Series 92. In: R.M. Wegener - M.P. Heilen - R. Ciolek-Torello - J.D. Hall eds, Analyses of Prehistoric Materials in the Queen Valley to Queen Creek Area. Early Agricultural, Formative, and Historical-period Use of the Upper Queen Creek Area: The U.S. 60 Archaeological Project, vol. 4. Tucson: Statistical Research, 514-548.

Soil Survey Division Staff 1993: Soil Survey Manual. Agriculture Handbook No. 18. USDA Natural Resources Conservation Service. Washington, D.C.: U.S. Government Printing Office.

Soil Survey Division Staff 1999: Soil Taxonomy: A Basic System of Soil Classification for Making and Interpreting Soil Surveys. Agriculture Handbook No. 436. USDA Natural Resources Conservation Service. Washington, D.C.: U.S. Government Printing Office.

Stewart, G. 1939: Conservation practices in primitive agriculture of the Southwest. Soil Conservation 5, 112-115, 131.

Stewart, G. 1940a: Present-day flood water irrigation. Conservation in Pueblo Agriculture, part 2. The Scientific Monthly 51, 329-340.

Stewart, G. 1940b: Primitive practices: conservation in Pueblo agriculture, part 1. The Scientific Monthly 51, 201-220.

Tarboton, D.G. 2005: Review of Proposed CUAHSI Hydrologic Information System Hydrologic Observations Data Model. Logan: Utah State University.

Upham, S. – Rice, G. 1980: Up the canal without a pattern: modeling Hohokam interaction and exchange. In: D.E. Doyel - F. Plog eds, Current Issues in Hohokam Prehistory: Proceedings of a Symposium. Anthropological Research Papers No. 23. Tempe: Arizona State University, 78-105.

Vanderpot, R. 1992: Rockpile Areas and Other Specialized Activity Sites on the Gila River Terrace: An Appraisal of Hohokam Auxiliary Agricultural Strategies near Florence, Arizona. Technical Series 32. Tucson: Statistical Research.

Vanderpot, R., 2009: Land Use and Subsistence. From the Desert to the Mountains: Archaeology of the Transition Zone: The State Route 87–Sycamore Creek Project, vol. 3. Technical Series 73. Tucson: Statistical Research, 135-168.

Van West, C. – Altschul, J. 1994: Agricultural productivity and carrying capacity in the Tonto Basin. In: R. Ciolek-Torrello - J. Welch eds, Changing Land Use in the Tonto Basin. The Roosevelt Rural Sites Study, vol. 3. Technical Series 28. Tucson: Statistical Research, 361-435.

Van West, C. – Altschul, J. 1998: Environmental variability and agricultural economics along the Lower Verde River, A.D. 750–1450. In: S. Whittlesey - R. Ciolek-Torrello - J. Altschul eds, Overview, Synthesis, and Conclusions. Vanishing River: Landscapes and Lives of the Lower Verde Valley: The Lower Verde Archaeological Project. CD-ROM. Tucson: SRI Press, 337-392.

Wegener, R. – Ciolek-Torello, R. 2011: Queen Valley to Queen Creek Prehistoric Archaeology. The U.S. 60 Archaeological Project: Early Agricultural, Formative, and Historical-Period Use of the Upper Queen Creek Region, Vol. 2. Technical Series 92. Tucson: Statistical Research, Inc.

Wegener, R. – Heilen, M. – Ciolek-Torello, R. – Hall, J. 2011: Queen Valley to Queen Creek Prehistoric Analyses. The U.S. 60 Archaeological Project: Early Agricultural, Formative, and Historical-Period Use of the Upper Queen Creek Region, Vol. 4. Technical Series 92. Tucson: Statistical Research, Inc.

Wienhold, M. L., 2008: Pre-hispanic land use and settlement in Queen Creek valley, Arizona: hydrological, erosion, and predictive modelling. Unpublished Master's dissertation. University College London.

Wienhold, M.L. 2012: Prehistoric land use and hydrology: a multi-scalar spatial analysis in central Arizona. Journal of Archaeological Science 40, 850-859.

Wilcox, D. – Shenk, L. 1977: The Architecture of the Casa Grande and its Interpretation. Archaeological Series No. 115. Arizona State Museum. Tucson: University of Arizona.

Wood, J.S. – McAllister, M.E. 1984: Second foundation: settlement patterns and agriculture in the Northeastern Hohokam Periphery, Central Arizona. In: S. Fish - P. Fish eds, Prehistoric Agricultural Strategies in the Southwest. Anthropological Research Papers No. 33. Tempe Arizona State University, 271-289.

Woodbury, R. 1960: A reappraisal of Hohokam irrigation. American Anthropologist 63, 550-560.

Aerial Archaeology – a Partner in Archaeological Heritage Management
An Example from Belgium

Marc Lodewijckx, René Pelegrin, Tom Debruyne and Claire Goffioul

Abstract: *Although aerial archaeology in Belgium is still most commonly used as a survey instrument, its role is becoming increasingly more significant and its application more versatile, especially within the framework of heritage management. In mainly rural environments, aerial archaeology can be a highly effective tool not only for making a synopsis of the archaeological sites and off site features and their complex spatial and chronological associations but also for a number of problems raised in the framework of a good preservation and efficient management of the archaeological remains in delicate environments which are under constant pressure because of the competing claims made by the many other actors for more land and space for various activities and new functions.*

Keywords: *aerial archaeology – heritage management – Belgium*

Short history of the research

Aerial archaeology in Belgium goes back to the 1950s and 1960s when Professor Joseph Mertens first used aerial photographs taken by the Ministries of Defence and Public Works to reconstruct the main elements of the Roman habitation of the loess region of central Belgium. He focused primarily on the Roman roads and actual plot structures of the Roman villa estates that appear to have been plentiful in these fertile areas (*Mertens 1957*). After the Second World War, the Ministry of Defence continued to use aerial photography, especially for the creation of military maps but this information was also made available to the public by the Military Geographical Institute who produced topographic 1:10,000 scale monochrome maps and 1:25,000 scale multi-colour maps. The aerial photographs taken by the Ministry of Public Works were primarily for the planning of new infrastructure and, because of the high altitude, were less suitable for detecting small-scale archaeological remains. Nevertheless, from the air, a regular pattern of field boundaries became visible (Fig. 1) and although the chronological interpretation of all these elements remained problematic, the discovery of these old configurations was nevertheless a breakthrough in archaeological research in Belgium (*Mertens 1964*). The Ministry of Defence's willingness to organise special photo flights to focus on archaeological features (if this was appropriate in the pilot's training scheme) provided a particularly useful opportunity for archaeological research. It quickly became clear that aerial archaeology was a strong instrument in the research of archaeological remains, especially for larger structures in an open landscape (Fig. 2). However, the settings and conditions which are required to enable the regular use of aerial archaeology are not available to archaeologists, who are expected to work with a limited budget and within the framework of an excavation or other specific conditions on the ground.

It was also in the 1960s that Charles Léva, industrial and amateur archaeologist, began to make archaeological survey flights at his own expense, mainly over the fertile loess area in central Belgium, in a predominantly agricultural area (*Bréart et al. 1999*). He focused primarily on the Roman infrastructure, land development patterns, roads, villa estates, dismantled tumuli, burial sites and any traces of military presence, including the mysterious camps that Caesar set up during the period of conquest that, so far, seemed to have escaped any attention. Charles Léva was a friendly, jovial man with a particular mistrust of the professional archaeologists who had yet to verify, on the ground, the huge number of interesting discoveries that he had made from the air. After his death in 2001, his vast archive of photos, many of high archaeological value, went to the Heritage Service of the Walloon Region and are now available for further investigation.

In the 1970s, Jacques Semey, a former military pilot, contacted the Archaeological Department of Ghent University because he was convinced that many of the anomalies he had observed in the landscape during his flights were indications of archaeological remains. Archaeologists soon confirmed his convictions and integrated the practice of examining features on aerial photographs with their normal ground surveys. Because of the scarcity of Roman remains, their field research focused specifically on the Bronze Age burial mounds in East and West Flanders. Jacques Semey no longer conducts aerial archaeology but his archive, now held by Ghent University, contains more

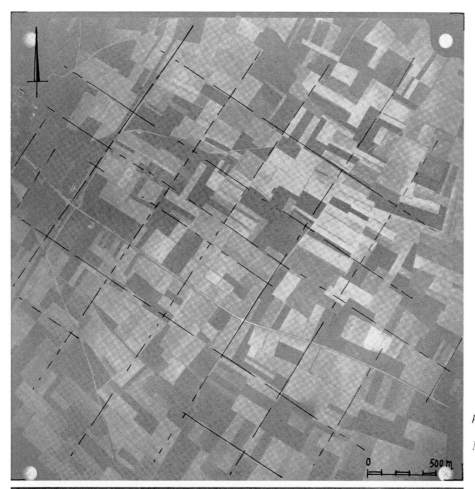

Fig. 1. A regular pattern of old field boundaries is indicated by Prof. Joseph Mertens on these high-altitude pictures of the region near Landen. Original picture: Ministry of Public Works (Mertens 1964, fig. 15).

Fig. 2. The Roman road from Tienen to Tongeren (ahead) at Brustem. The Roman tumulus nearby is still well preserved. Original picture: Ministry of Defence (Mertens 1964, fig. 6).

Fig. 3. A picture of our first trial trench at Wange (Landen) in 1979 taken by the Ministry of Defence. The wing, with camouflage painting, of the Fouga CM.170R Magister is visible in the right corner of the picture.

than 60,000 slides which are still an interesting source for further research, not only for prehistoric vestiges but also for more recent relics, like the trenches of World War I in Flanders Fields (*Bourgeois - Meganck 2005*).

After Professor Joseph Mertens retired from Leuven University in 1986, we continued to use aerial archaeology, but on a smaller scale. Occasionally we were able to persuade the military (Fig. 3) or Charles Léva (Fig. 4) to fly for a specific purpose: to take photographs of our excavations or check out the archaeological sites that we had detected during field surveys. Although of excellent quality, these pictures made only a small contribution to the research projects which were carried out during this period.

In 1997, the universities of Ghent and Leuven were both awarded a joint research project, entitled 'Digital data for the Flemish past: towards an integrated archaeological archive'. The project, which aimed to develop a digital database of archaeological sites in Flanders, was part of the objectives set by the *Impulsprogramma Humane Wetenschappen* of the Ministry of the Flemish Community, Department of Science, Media and Innovation and ran for three years (1997 - 1999). It was agreed that Ghent would make an inventory of the archaeological sites in the provinces of West and East Flanders and that Leuven would be responsible for producing an archaeological inventory of the provinces of Antwerp, Limburg and Flemish Brabant. With the positive results of the aerial archaeology at

Ghent University in mind, we looked for opportunities to start air reconnaissance to swiftly enhance the number of archaeological sites in the region for which we were responsible. That same year, René Pelegrin, a pilot at Aero Kiewit, contacted us in connection with a number of features that he had perceived from the air in different areas. It was instantly clear that he was the right person to coordinate aerial archaeology at Leuven University. The commitment of our university to aerial archaeology increased during the following years, as more competent pilots joined the group and we were able to carry out more flights. Thanks to the valuable support of Jacques Semey, we were able to build up the necessary experience at relatively short notice so that at a very early stage survey flights could be carried out as efficiently as possible (*Bourgeois et al. 2002*).

The ultimate goal of the joint research project was to develop a uniform database of archaeological sites in Flanders. This was urgently needed, not only as a tool for further scientific research but, more importantly, to manage the archaeological heritage in Flanders in a more efficient way. The database was implemented in Access and linked to a GIS component in ArcView which contained a set of digitised maps, including topographic maps, soil maps, cadastral maps and orthogonal aerial photographs, which were made available to us by the GIS Support Centre of the Flemish Community (Fig. 5). The database was called HAVIK, which stands for *Heel Archeologisch Vlaanderen in Kaart [All of Archaeological Flanders Mapped]*. In

Fig. 4. A picture of our first excavation at Overhespen in 1983, taken by Charles Léva.

the course of the development, all available data relating to archaeological sites in Flanders were processed into the database. This information came from all kinds of publications: from licensing and doctoral dissertations, surveys and personal information, from both professional and amateur archaeologists. Within the framework of this project, our colleagues from Ghent University primarily focused on the survey and inventory of the archaeological sites that are visible on the many slides of the archives of Jacky Semey.

The fruitful collaboration with Ghent University continued after 31 December 1999 thanks to a new project grant-aided by the Max-Wildiers Fund (2000 - 2003) which, in addition to helping us to actually implement and develop the database, specifically targeted the application of the aerial surveys. Based on our previous results, it had become clear to the government that aerial surveys were one of the most efficient ways of detecting new archaeological sites (*Roovers et al. 2001*). The HAVIK database served as a prototype for the CAI database, the Central Archaeological Inventory of the Flemish government, and after the completion of the Max-Wildiers project, the data from the HAVIK database from both universities were incorporated into the CAI. Since then, the CAI has been the standard database of Flemish archaeology. To continue aerial surveys in the common interest, we received a grant from the Flemish Government which supported the work from

2002 to 2004. Other archaeologists were incorporated in the survey flights at regular intervals so we could transmit our expertise. The allowance for aerial archaeology ceased after 2004 because of various reorganisations and cutbacks and we had to look for other opportunities to finance our survey flights.

In 2004, during our surveys in southern parts of Flanders, we unintentionally discovered some new sites in the territory of Wallonia because the linguistic border is, of course, not perceptible from the air and the landscape and archaeological features on both sides of the border are very alike. This immediately aroused the interest of a number of Walloon archaeologists and very soon a more intense collaboration between Leuven University and the *Service de l'Archéologie de la Région Wallonne* was proposed. The archaeologist Claire Goffioul was appointed liaison officer and directed us to interesting areas where success was ensured (Fig. 6). From 2006 to 2008, our team conducted a number of survey flights above the Walloon loess area (Hesbaye), the Meuse valley, the Condroz and the Ardennes. Almost immediately this bore fruit and many new archaeological features emerged. This provided real incentives for new investigations to be made on the ground and a much better understanding of the relationships between various off-site features and finds was created enabling them to be merged into one complex site (*Goffioul et al. 2010*). In 2008, because of cutbacks and shifting

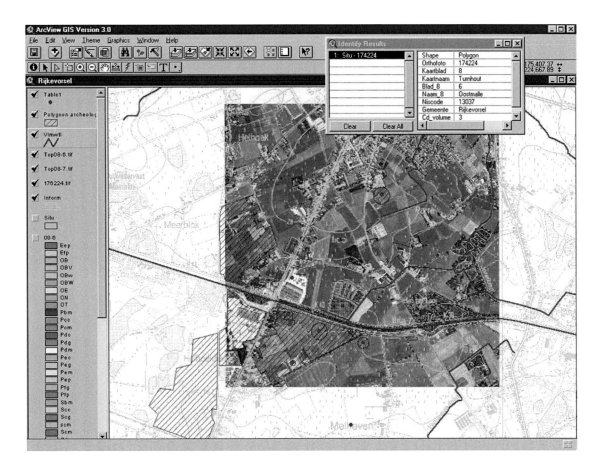

Fig. 5. A slide from the original database HAVIK, showing the GIS component with the topographic map and the hydrographic data highlighted, partly covered by the orthogonal aerial photograph near Rijkevorsel (Campine). A number of circular features which need further investigation are indicated in red on the map.

Fig. 6. A ditch, probably surrounding an LBK settlement in Wallonia. Photo taken by René Pelegrin.

Fig. 7. A marvelous composition of square features near Tienen (a PORTIVA area). As there are no obvious archaeological findings on the ground, the date of this site is not clear. Photo taken by René Pelegrin.

priorities, the funding from the Walloon Region was no longer guaranteed and once again we had to look for other institutions or authorities which might be interested in the contribution that aerial archaeology can make.

After a number of temporary deals and agreements expired, a long-term collaboration was established with the Inter-Municipal Archaeological Service PORTIVA which supports a number of municipalities in the province of Flemish Brabant and is responsible for the archaeological monitoring of construction and infrastructure works in the municipalities of Tienen, Hoegaarden, Linter, Glabbeek and Bierbeek. The archaeologist in charge is Tom Debruyne, a former student of Leuven University, who is competent in local archaeology. The area covered is large enough to fly throughout the entire year (Fig. 7). The region contains different types of landscape (e.g. Hageland and Hesbaye) and there are, therefore, an interesting variety of archaeological features (*Lodewijckx et al. 2011*).

Methodology

Our home base is Kiewit airfield near Hasselt in the province of Limburg. Flights are organised all year round in a four-seater, single-engine, high-wing Cessna 172 *Superhawk*, with two pilots for safety reasons. This aeroplane is equipped with digital on-board instruments and a highly sophisticated GPS, which guarantees that the exact location of the observed and photographed features is found. Photographs are taken by hand, first as slides with an analogue camera Canon EOS 50E QD, then with an experimental digital camera Nikon D100 or D60 and for many years we have also used a digital Canon EOS 500D. The instruments are set to high resolution for maximum sharpness of details. The flight data are registered in Google Maps and all the images, flight information and exact locations are immediately transferred to the PORTIVA service which provides instantaneous monitoring and recording of the data and then inputs this into the CAI database, the Central Archaeological Inventory of the Flemish government. This way, new discoveries are automatically made available to all the archaeologists in charge of research and heritage management in Flanders, be this at local or regional level. The digital images are stored at various locations in specialised databases where they can be accessed and checked and subsequently used in future applications.

When the photographic and the topographic data are stored, a suggestion as to how the recorded feature might be archaeologically interpreted is also included in the database. In most cases this is only an initial clarification and perception of the features that are visible in the aerial picture, based on our earlier experience of identifying

Fig. 8. From the air, the abandoned meanders in the river Demer, west of Zichem, are easily observable. Photo taken by René Pelegrin.

features and their follow-up on the ground by field walking and auguring. In the past years the work of archaeologists, particularly those who are responsible for heritage management, has become more extensive. The application of a wider range of new methods like electric and magnetic surveys, ground radar, special auguring techniques, together with the more traditional methods such as field walking, mapping old findings and trial trenches, has led to the development of new insights into the use and organisation of the landscape in different periods. Evaluation maps give a regional overview of the various known archaeological structures from a particular period. This way, hiatuses in our knowledge can be recognised more easily and more specific research, often through additional aerial survey flights, can be organised successfully. This archaeological database is available to archaeological curators at different levels who can use the information from the aerial surveys to take appropriate measures for the preservation of archaeological remains in situ.

Archaeologists from other services are now aware that aerial surveys represent a specific approach to archaeological discovery; an approach which requires a particular skill set and a deal of specialised knowledge. Requests from colleagues to check specific sites are frequent, so we will never be out of work. However, even though the demand is there, funding continues to be a real issue. A number of sponsors prefer their budgets for archaeology to be spent on genuine 'on the ground' fieldwork and are of the opinion that aerial surveys are not reliable and cannot be guaranteed to provide the required result. Indeed, weather conditions, especially long-term weather conditions, are the most important determining factors affecting the success or failure of the discovery of new archaeological sites. Over the past few years, the spells of dry weather have been too short for a large number of archaeological features to appear. In general, the ideal weather conditions for archaeological surveys have been rare during the past decade. Continuous flights in the same region are, however, very helpful in compiling a more complete picture of all the archaeological features in a particular area (Fig. 8).

Archaeological features show up as soilmarks or cropmarks, depending on the season. Snowmarks are rare but have been observed. The nature of the subsoil and the kind of crops grown also exert an influence on the success or failure of aerial reconnaissance. The features observed in the landscape consist mainly of patches and lines and their archaeological significance is often difficult to interpret, but over the past years we have acquired more experience, and more self-confidence, in interpreting the archaeological features on the ground (*Lodewijckx - Pelegrin 2011b*).

We first concentrated our attention on the less prospected

area of the Campine/Kempen, a sandy region in the north of the provinces of Antwerp and Limburg, but the landscape did not reveal many archaeological features so we then focused on the loess region of the Hesbaye and the neighbouring areas, such as the Hageland and the Meuse valley.

Campine

Bearing in mind the remarkable results that our Ghent colleagues had in the silty loam area of the provinces of West and East Flanders, we originally started our aerial surveys in the adjacent area of the Campine (Flemish: *Kempen*), a natural region in north-eastern Flanders and parts of the south-western Netherlands. This region is located on the right hand side of the River Scheldt and the soil is much sandier than the region surveyed by our Ghent colleagues. Because of the poor quality of the soil, the Campine was sparsely populated and consisted mainly of meres, areas of sandy heath and wetlands. Because of its open character, the Campine was apparently very attractive to hunters and gatherers in the Late Palaeolithic and Mesolithic periods. Excavations, especially on the Dutch territory, revealed that the habitation history had continued throughout the Bronze and Iron Age. Vestiges from the Roman period are scarce and consist of rather small farmsteads and a few cremation burials. The population starts to grow again in the early middle Ages and continues through the later periods although the region remained a poor and deprived area. When coalmines opened in Limburg and Wallonia, large parts of the heathlands were transformed into woodland with mainly pine that grows easily and could be used in the underground tunnelling of the coalmines. At the end of the 20th century, all the coalmines were closed and, because of its proximity to the expanding port of Antwerp, the region became more and more industrialised. In addition, some large areas were preserved for recreational purposes and others to provide housing for the constant urban sprawl.

For this reason, it was important to start conducting archaeological surveys in the area; airborne surveys as well as those on the ground. The archaeological information collected to date is rather limited, generally because of the low level of interest shown in the region in archaeological history, and specifically because of the rather poor discoveries made in the past. In addition there are also a number of specific situations which prevent the easy discovery of new archaeological sites. One of these is the former animal housing system, which is based on the repeated spreading of straw in indoor stalls; this is then used to fertilise the neighbouring fields and large areas became covered with a thick layer of dark earth, which shelters older dwellings and makes detecting zones of any archaeological importance a rather challenging business. We began surveying the area in 1997 and, although the presence of several burials dating from the late Neolithic period until the early Iron Age was confirmed, we failed to find any indications of new burial mounds in the area. However, the number of burial mounds is much lower,

especially for the early Bronze Age, when compared to the area surveyed by Ghent University, although the spread of these mounds appears to be sparser towards the Campine area. Nevertheless, despite the difficulties with the actual landscape and land use, a number of features were discovered that warranted further research.

In 2003, Leuven University was given a grant by the Research Foundation Flanders to execute a more detailed research of the northern part of Campine, focusing especially on the Bronze and Iron Age occupations. An evaluation was carried out at a selection of about 30 sites, based on new indications which were brought to light by our survey flights, sometimes in combination with old discoveries. The preservation of potential archaeological remains was examined by field walking, auguring and, in a limited number of cases, by a more detailed topographic survey of the site. In general, the results were rather discouraging providing only modest amounts of archaeological material and few useful indications that could be employed to reconstruct the original use of the landscape by previous communities. Earlier random finds and small-scale research projects completed in the 19th and early 20th centuries have revealed interesting indications and archaeological findings but, since then, the landscape appears to have changed immensely, especially by more intensive agricultural activities (*Lodewijckx et al. 2006*). The traditional modest fields and pastures have become much larger and many sites appeared to have been completely flattened by heavy equipment and special techniques so that more proficient crops can be grown and a better harvest yielded. In most areas, the traditional rural landscape with small-scale characteristics has disappeared completely and with it the scarce traces of past human activity, such as Celtic fields and burial mounds, have vanished. Nevertheless, the efforts to detect, investigate and protect the remaining archaeological vestiges have since been multiplied, often financed by contractors and/or local authorities. We hope, therefore, that enough information has been preserved to reconstruct the archaeological history of this interesting region (Fig. 9).

Hageland

The Hageland, located further south of the sandy Campine area, was a former coastal area and it is this former position that has shaped the features found today. A series of former offshore banks can still be identified as a ridge of ironstone hills running from east to west. The region displays a variety of soils and landscapes which have had their effect on the use of the individual land plots. Larger cities, like Leuven, Tienen, Diest, Aarschot and Zoutleeuw, are situated along the periphery of the Hageland. Settlements consist of a miscellaneous pattern of small villages and isolated farmsteads. Parcels are genuinely small and covered with a variety of plants and crops, largely depending on the fertility of the soil in question. Vineyards still flourish on slopes facing south, just as they did centuries ago. The history of this region is not well known and is largely

Fig. 9. A view from the Campine near Zondereigen. Photo taken by René Pelegrin.

interspersed with mythological tales and legends. As a consequence of the small surface area of the individual plots and because of the permanent cover on most of them, aerial archaeology is not very rewarding as a survey instrument. Nevertheless our efforts were rewarded by the discovery of a few new sites, such as the double ditch enclosure around the promontory Michelsberg fort at Assent. Stray finds and a number of rather small excavations had identified the site as a settlement of the middle Neolithic Michelsberg culture (*Vermeersch 1972*), but, until our survey, no-one had yet noticed the typical double ditch enclosure that surrounded the original settlement. One day a double ditch suddenly became visible from the air on one parcel and the following year, when the crops were altered, it appeared on the adjacent parcel as well. This led to a reconstruction of the extension of the enclosure (*Lodewijckx et al. 2005b*). Recently, a few trenches were made through the ditches by the Archaeological company RAAP to confirm the dating and to document the ditches. The site has now been legally protected.

Another fascinating site in the Hageland is the moated castle of Horst at Sint-Pieters-Rode which is now situated in a large pond in the valley of the Wingebeek (Fig. 10). Its most notable component is the central keep that dates back to the 15th century (*Doperé - Ubregts 1991*). The more recent part of the castle was constructed as a Renaissance

luxury palace, mainly used for hunting parties. Although practically in ruins and with many components missing or damaged, the castle has remained largely untouched since the middle of the 17th century and is considered to be one of the jewels of the Hageland. In 2001 and 2002 we executed some small excavations in the basements of the castle and in the courtyard, to try and fill in these missing links in the construction history of the castle (*Lodewijckx - François 2002; François - Lodewijckx 2003*). On the basis of these foregoing studies, detailed plans for a thorough restoration of the site were worked out which are now being completed on a phase by phase basis. We expect the castle and the surrounding landscape to regain its former glory in the very near future.

A less cheerful story and a site of great concern is the isolated keep of the Maagdentoren at Zichem which is the only remains left of a stronghold near the River Demer (*Doperé - Ubregts 1991*). It has been legally protected from the 1930s but grants have usually been spent on other, more urgent, restorations elsewhere. For decades the maintenance of this impressive but vulnerable monument was neglected, mainly because of its isolated location and lack of any particular function. On a Sunday morning, on 1 June 2006, the Maagdentoren partly collapsed without there being any witnesses or casualties (Fig. 11). It is likely that its foundations were weakened and destabilised because

Fig. 10. The castle of Horst at Sint-Pietersrode (Hageland). Photo taken by René Pelegrin.

Fig. 11. The Maagdentoren at Zichem, a few days after a section of the walls collapsed (1 June 2006). Photo taken by René Pelegrin.

Fig. 12. Snowmarks indicate the remains of the bastions of the former citadel at Zoutleeuw. Photo taken by René Pelegrin.

of the previous winter flooding of the River Demer. We were asked to take aerial pictures of this new situation in order to complete an upcoming dossier. So far, a number of conservation measures have been taken and executed to prevent the tower from crumbling completely. As it is impossible to reconstruct the breach properly, several inventive restoration plans have been drawn up but, despite its importance to the history of the area, the future of this remarkable monument remains unclear.

For many years we executed surveys and excavations in the historic city of Zoutleeuw, situated in the southeastern part of the Hageland (*Lodewijckx et al. 2005a*). Although rather small, Zoutleeuw became one of the seven fortified towns of the Duchy of Brabant. It owed its wealth to its port and its location on the road leading from Bruges to Brussels, Leuven, Tienen and the cities of the German Hanseatic League. The affluent heritage of the historic buildings and ecclesiastical art provide conspicuous evidence of the former wealth of the city. Literary sources reveal that Zoutleeuw was already fortified before 1133. In the 14th century, the population increased to such a great extent that enlargement of the municipal territory became necessary and so a second wall was built between 1330 and 1350. In the 17th century, the city was heavily fortified by Spanish troops. In 1671, the upper and oldest hamlet of the city was confiscated to build a square bastioned citadel, surrounded by a wide ditch. Around 1700, a plan was drawn up to rebuild the square citadel and convert it

into a large pentagon. These plans were only partly realised in 1705 when it was recaptured by an Anglo-Dutch army commanded by the Duke of Marlborough. In the 19th century a railway was constructed through the remains of the citadel and the construction of additional roads, football fields and further infrastructure have affected the strongholds (Fig. 12). Our aerial surveys and archaeological research on the ground have contributed significantly to a better understanding and a more effective management of the archaeological values of this picturesque historic city.

Hesbaye

Undoubtedly the most fascinating area for aerial archaeology is the loess belt in central Belgium. The Roman towns of Tongeren and Tienen are situated in the eastern part, which is called Hesbaye (Flemish: *Haspengouw*). In this region, the villages are small and concentrated in the valleys, bordering the rivers. Because of the continual scaling up of agricultural activities, the plots are very large and remain under continuous cultivation. The fertility of the soil is high so pastures and wooded areas are rare. By combining soilmarks in the autumn and winter periods and cropmarks in the spring and summer, aerial archaeology can be accomplished all year round. However, because of the outstanding quality of the arable soil and the low stress sensitivity of the crops, survey flights are not always successful as archaeological features usually only appear under rather extreme weather conditions, such as after long spells of dry weather (*Lodewijckx - Pelegrin 2011b*).

Although we have executed ground surveys and excavations in the area for many years, we are very pleased to be able to work with new services that have been created for the management of the archaeological heritage in this rich area. We have worked with both the Department of Archaeology of the Ministry of the Walloon Region, represented by Claire Goffioul for the Walloon part of the Hesbaye, and the inter-municipal service PORTIVA, represented by Tom Debruyne, for the western area in Flanders. The strong collaboration with the Department of Archaeology of the Ministry of the Walloon Region was, however, only temporary because of the budget cuts referred to earlier. Nevertheless, we keep in contact and if we occasionally cross the regional border between Flanders and Wallonia and find new archaeological indications, we contact them immediately and inform them about these findings. We now have a strong partnership with the inter-municipal service PORTIVA, not only in relation to this part of the Hesbaye but also for the area in the Hageland which falls under its jurisdiction.

The Hesbaye region is a very fertile area where, for many millennia, a substantial number of different communities of people have lived. The oldest findings go back as far as the Middle Paleolithic and, from the Mesolithic period onwards, the region was already densely populated (*Lodewijckx 1995*). In this regard, the fine-grained quartzite outcrop at Wommersom, located east of Tienen, was undoubtedly an important factor in attracting people to the area. We ourselves have excavated various settlements of the LBK (*Linearbandkeramik*) people in the northern part of the Hesbaye, e.g. sites at Wange and Overhespen, situated not far from the quartzite outcrop at Wommersom (*Lodewijckx 1990*). These dwellings go back as far as 5,300 BC and represent the first farming communities in the region. The immigrants had clear links with the local communities and also contact with other Neolithic cultures which came from the south along the Atlantic coast. These LBK settlements are very small and cannot easily be detected by aerial archeology (*Lodewijckx - Bakels 2000*).

The human occupation of the region continued throughout the centuries and, especially from the Roman period onwards, the remains and findings become very abundant and, at the same time, much more extensive. Aerial archaeology is a superb instrument for generating an overview of the extension of these villa estates and their off-site activities (*Opsteyn - Lodewijckx 2001*). However, because of the lack of good-quality building stone, the majority of abandoned Roman constructions appear to have been dismantled in later times, e.g. for the construction of early churches, and are, therefore, hard to discover. However, many interesting features from the Roman past are visible from the air. Straight Roman roads opened up the province and gave way to long-term economic prosperity. Roads from and towards the main city of Tongeren, in

particular, are clearly identifiable because their surfaces were covered with a layer of pebbles or hard rock and because they retained their role as major arteries until long after the Middle Ages. For their large-scale agricultural venture, the Romans divided the fertile landscape of the Hesbaye into generously proportioned plots and on each parcel a traditional farmhouse was established. The dwellings were usually sited at carefully chosen locations on the allotments and often had a marvellous panoramic view over the valley. The owners of the generously proportioned estates were buried in large coffins underneath vast mounds (*tumulus*) erected alongside the roads and clearly visible in the landscape. The exquisite grave goods contained in these tombs consisted of an abundance of samian ware, beautiful glass vessels, metal canisters and personal objects of remarkable extravagance, representing the wealth and social standing of these refined Roman citizens. As many as 100 of these burial mounds are still preserved, sometimes in groups of two to four tombs in a row along the roadside; many tombs are still as high as 10 to 15 m and, although they are often eroded and in a poor state of preservation, because of their towering position with windswept trees on top, they are still majestic marks in the frequently completely bare landscape. Many others have been levelled to give way to additional fields. Most of them appear to have been originally provided with a circular wall at the base and, although the stones have later been removed, the foundation trench often shows up as a circular mark in the field (*Lodewijckx - Pelegrin 2011b*).

Few Roman villa estates are still visible from the air because of the reuse of their building material in later centuries. And, although they barely appear during survey flights, on the basis of repeated ground surveys, we can assert that many small-scale farmsteads were also present in the landscape during the Roman period. So far, it is not clear whether they subsisted within the framework of a larger villa estate or whether they were specialised in the cultivation of specific crops or in breeding a particular animal species, like sheep, goats, cattle or horses. In contrast to the villa owners, these farmers are unlikely to have had the resources to build their own stone dwellings and, in most cases, there is very little left of the original constructions. It is probable that the Romans smartened up their landscape with all sorts of constructions, such as mansions, cemeteries, small shrines and other monuments.

Unfortunately, one of the major problems we are confronted with in this area is the extensive erosion of the loess soils which is caused by anthropogenic factors. This erosion has been caused almost entirely by intensive farming activities and the old practice of leaving the land bare in wintertime. Consequently, heavy rainfall on the hilltops and on the upper parts of slopes in particular, truncates soil profiles, covers lower surfaces in sinks, and deposits the washed-off material on the valley floors. Bearing in mind an erosion rate of 1mm per year, the loss of land after 2,000 years rises to no less than 2 m. During the last decades, in particular, the increase in large-scale agricultural operations has

Fig. 13. A view of the industrial landscape near Liège in the Meuse valley. Photo taken by René Pelegrin.

intensified this erosion process. Field surveys and detailed auguring indicate that the original landscape had a varied and heterogeneous relief which has been transformed into a uniform and largely flattened relief by centuries of unrelenting agricultural activity. Many archaeological sites have almost completely disappeared because of the persistent erosion of the topsoil layers. These days, to safeguard the productiveness of these valuable soils, more attention is paid to preventing or reducing this erosion. However, our surveys show the consistent negative impact of these erosion processes on the preservation of archaeological sites.

Meuse valley and Ardennes

A few years ago, at the request of the Department of Archaeology of the Ministry of the Walloon Region, a number of flights were executed above the Meuse valley and the Ardennes. The landscape here is totally different from the former and the Meuse valley in particular, comprises an enormous number of industrial estates, some operating and some abandoned or already (partly) dismantled. These flights gave an exciting overview of a vast industrial area that has provided prosperity to the region for many decades, from the former mining installations, the production plants for semi-finished products and, more usually on the boundaries, the factories for the finished merchandise (Fig. 13). In the midst of these installations, one can detect the

remains of the original villages along the Meuse, abandoned castles and impressive fortresses from previous centuries and the more recent facilities for tourists which are usually found in more pleasurable environments.

The Ardennes is a region of extensive forests, rolling hills and ridges. The rough terrain limits the opportunities for agriculture although, in cleared areas, arable and dairy farming forms the backbone of economic life. The scenic beauty of the region and its wide variety of outdoor activities, including hunting, cycling, walking and canoeing, make it a popular tourist destination. Thus, our survey flights in this area remained restricted and were limited to either making an initial check of the archaeological potential of the region or documenting the already acknowledged archaeological sites. Although the time spent on survey flights was rather limited, we hope to reach a new agreement in future so that we can continue to pursue our valuable work in an advantageous partnership.

Some reflections

The case studies included above are representative of the conditions under which archaeology operates in Belgium today. Pressure on the rural environment is increasingly evident, because of a number of different causes such as the quest for increased productivity, the need for more industrial estates and residential areas and ecological

Fig. 14. Erosion processes are a serious threat to the preservation of archaeological remains in the subsoil, especially in the Hesbaye loess zone. Photo taken by René Pelegrin.

sustainability. Undoubtedly, many archaeological sites have been destroyed by these kinds of activities. But events such as these have raised a genuine awareness and, in some cases, created more opportunities for archaeologists to take the necessary action, starting with an attempt to boost our knowledge of the phenomena that play such an important role in the history and preservation of rural archaeological sites. What we are attempting to do is proceed from amassing scientific knowledge of archaeological sites and historic landscapes towards devising their legal protection. In recent years a better understanding of the complexity of the historic landscape has led to a better management of the various elements that are involved; but much more progress needs to be made in future. We must find new methods of managing archaeological and cultural heritage in agricultural and forested areas. Apart from the maintenance and improvement of the environmental conditions of farming operations, the main objective of the new managerial methods has to be the conservation of archaeological elements in the historic landscape as a whole (Fig. 14). Problems caused by the increased mechanisation of agriculture and forestry, new kinds of crops, the use of agro-chemical products etc. has to be compensated for by new measures which implement more archaeological activity and offer better methods of heritage management in a rural environment (*Lodewijckx 2002*).

Although conditions for the proper management of the heritage in a rural environment need to be improved in future, we are happy to note that the management of archaeological sites is now being given priority and that a variety of new measures and tasks are being devised to prevent information from classified sites and as yet undiscovered sites from being lost. In the past, the main interest was focused on building heritage but we are pleased to see that nowadays more attention is paid to the management of larger areas, not only for the benefit of the individual remains but to make a link between the various interests of economic activities, the enlargement of residential areas and the preservation of biologically important areas and historical landscapes. In this perspective, awareness is growing of the fact that, within these landscapes, it is not only the individual sites that are important but it is the relationship between all the preserved elements of people's lives and their use of the environment within this landscape which is equally important if we are to understand and learn about life and land use in previous times.

Within this general evolution, the role of aerial archaeology has also changed. In the past, the main purpose of aerial archaeology was to detect new sites or document excavations and other events on certain important sites.

*Fig. 15. Farmers provide a strip of grass along the boundaries of their fields in an attempt to stop the erosion of the fertile topsoil.
Photo taken by René Pelegrin.*

Although that is still a part of the demands from the archaeological field, the main purpose of aerial archaeology has become the detection of less important features and off-site elements within the landscape in order to understand and assess all the elements from the past and their worthiness to be registered, documented and preserved for the future and in the common interest.

Another important issue is public support for the actions taken by the government to achieve better heritage management. On the one hand, measures put in place for the benefit of heritage sites can conflict with the individual or communal use of land and property, especially when individual sovereignty is threatened by constricting and controlling rules and regulations from the authorities (Fig. 15). It is often in these circumstances that crucial management methods are challenged by the general public. On the other hand, society as a whole can largely profit from the good management of historical and archaeological sites. Although a good balance is often hard to find, a broad-spectrum improvement of heritage management is a necessity for the well-being of a community. Heritage management here in Belgium, as it is in other countries, is becoming more important and an increasing concern of regional and local authorities.

This evolution has meant that the role of aerial archaeology has shifted from a purely scientific one to one which is more socially embedded within the management of heritage as a whole. That is why we are now focusing less on the detection of individual sites and why, together with other actors in landscape management and government authorities at different levels, we are trying to make a contribution to a better understanding of the still visible, and also the invisible (or less easily visible), elements within the composition of a landscape. We hope that aerial archaeology will be welcomed as a full partner in the planning process and management of historic landscapes right across Europe (*Lodewijckx - Pelegrin 2011a*).

References

Bourgeois, J. - Meganck, M. eds. 2005: Aerial Photography and Archaeology 2003. A Century of Information, Papers presented during the conference held at Ghent University, December 10th-12th, 2003. Archaeological Reports Ghent University (ARGU) 4, Ghent: University Press.

Bourgeois, J. - Roovers, I. - Meganck, M. - Semey, J. - Pelegrin, R. - Lodewijckx, M. 2002: Flemish Aerial Archaeology in the Last 20 Years: Past and Future Perspectives. In: R.H. Bewley - W. Raczokowski eds, Aerial Archaeology, Developing Future Practice. Proceedings of the NATO Advanced Research Workshop on Aerial Archaeology – Developing Future Practice, Leszno (Pl), 15-17 November 2000, Swindon, 76-83.

Bréart, B. - Nowicki, F. - Léva, Ch. eds 1999: Archéologie aérienne. Actes du Colloque international tenu à Amiens (France) du 15 au 18 octobre 1992. Revue archéologique de Picardie 17, Amiens.

Doperé, F. - Ubregts, W. 1991: De donjon in Vlaanderen. Architectuur en wooncultuur. Acta Archaeologica Lovaniensia, Monographiae 3. Leuven: University Press.

François, B. - Lodewijckx, M. 2003: Verdergezet onderzoek in het kasteel van Horst te Sint-Pieters-Rode (Vl.-Br.). Archaeologia Mediaevalis 26, 42-44.

Goffioul, C. - Pelegrin, R. - Corthouts, L. - Lodewijckx, M. - Léotard, J.-M. 2010: Aerial Surveys in the Belgian Province of Liège. Abstracts Book of the International Aerial Archaeology Conference, Bucharest, Romania, 15-18 September 2010, 13.

Lodewijckx, M. 1990: Les deux sites rubanés de Wange et d'Overhespen (Belgique, prov. Brabant). In: D. Cahen - M. Otte eds, Rubané et Cardial. Actes du Colloque international de Liège, novembre 1988. Etudes et Recherches archéologiques de l'Université de Liège (E.R.A.U.L.) 39. Liège: University Press, 105-116.

Lodewijckx, M. 1995: Essay on the Issue of Continuity Applied to the Northern Hesbaye Region (Central Belgium). In: M. Lodewijckx (ed.), Archaeological and Historical Aspects of West European Societies. Acta Archaeologica Lovaniensia, Monographiae 8. Leuven: University Press, 207-220.

Lodewijckx, M. 2002: Flanders (Belgium): a Changing Archaeological Policy in a Changing Landscape. Book of Abstracts of the 8th Annual Meeting of the European Association of Archaeologists, Thessaloniki (Gr), 24-29 September 2002, 119.

Lodewijckx, M. - Bakels, C. 2000: The Interaction between Early Farmers (Linearbandkeramik) and Indigenous People in Central Belgium. In: J.C. Henderson ed., The Prehistory and Early History of Atlantic Europe. British Archaeological Reports, International Series 861. Oxford: Archaeopress, 33-46.

Lodewijckx, M. - François, B. 2002: Beperkt onderzoek in het kasteel van Horst te Sint-Pieters-Rode (Vl.-Br.). Archaeologia Mediaevalis 25, 27-30.

Lodewijckx, M. - Pelegrin, R. eds 2011a: A View from the Air, Aerial Archaeology and Remote Sensing Techniques: Results and Opportunities. British Archaeological Reports, International series 2288. Oxford: Archaeopress.

Lodewijckx, M. - Pelegrin, R. 2011b: The Roman Landscape of Central Belgium. In: M. Lodewijckx - R. Pelegrin eds, A View from the Air, Aerial Archaeology and Remote Sensing Techniques: Results and Opportunities. British Archaeological Reports, International series 2288, Oxford: Archaeopress, 143-150.

Lodewijckx, M. - Kumps, F. - Opsteyn, L. - Scheers, S. - Wouters, L. 2005: Riverbed Explorations in the Historic Town of Zoutleeuw (Central Belgium). In: H. Stoepker ed., Archaeological Heritage Management in Riverine Landscapes. Rapportage Archeologische Monumentenzorg (RAM) 126, Amsterdam, 55-74.

Lodewijckx, M. - Vanmontfort, B. - Pelegrin, R. 2005: Een midden-neolitisch aardwerk op de Hermansheuvel te Assent (Vlaams-Brabant). Notae Praehistoricae 25, 175-177.

Lodewijckx, M. - Pelegrin, R. - Verfaillie, K. 2006: Evaluatie van de Brons- en IJzertijdsporen in de Noorderkempen. Lunula Archaeologia Protohistorica XIV, 5-7.

Lodewijckx, M. - Pelegrin, R. - Corthouts, L. - Debruyne, T. 2011: New Opportunities for Aerial Archaeology in Belgium. Abstracts Book of the 17th Annual Meeting of the European Association of Archaeologists, Oslo, 14th-18th September 2011, Oslo, 270-271.

Mertens, J. 1957: Les routes romaines de la Belgique. Brussels: Archaeologia Belgica 33.

Mertens, J. 1964: Enkele beschouwingen over Limburg in de Romeinse tijd. Brussels: Archaeologia Belgica 75.

Opsteyn, L. - Lodewijckx, M. 2001: Wange-Damekot Revisited. New Perspectives in Roman Habitation History. In: M. Lodewijckx ed., Belgian Archaeology in a European Setting II. Acta Archaeologica Lovaniensia, Monographiae 13, Leuven: University Press, 217-230.

Roovers, I. - Lodewijckx, M. - Meganck, M. - Bourgeois, J. 2001: The HAVIK-Project, Archaeological GIS-Based Inventory for Flanders (Belgium). In: M. Lodewijckx ed., Belgian Archaeology in a European Setting I. Acta Archaeologica Lovaniensia, Monographiae 12. Leuven: University Press, 125-129.

Vermeersch, P. 1972. Un site néolithique à Assent (Brabant). Bulletin de la Société royale belge d'Anthropologie et de Préhistoire 83, 137-155.

A New Method for the Detection Validation of Architectural Remains Using Field Spectroscopy: Experimental Remote Sensing Archaeology

A. Agapiou, D.G. Hadjimitsis, A. Sarris and A. Georgopoulos

Abstract: *This paper proposes a methodology which incorporates ground spectroradiometric campaigns at a testing field in Alampra village, central Cyprus, intended to monitor the spectral signatures of crops as it is influenced by intentionally buried architectural remains. For this purpose, eight "control" square sites have been constructed. Each control site simulated a different archaeological environment. All sites were cultivated with barley and wheat crops according to the traditional practices in the region. The proposed methodology aims to monitor the phenological cycle of the crops using ground "truth" hyperspectral data in relation to the better detection of the subsurface architectural relics.*

Keywords: *experimental remote sensing archaeology - ground spectroscopy - phenological cycle - crop marks*

Remote Sensing archaeology
Introduction

Remote Sensing (RS) offers new perspectives in archaeological research. RS as a non-destructive method may be used as part of the investigation of an archaeological or historical site prior to any excavation or other intervention. On a micro scale, geophysical surveys can provide valuable information on underground monuments, while on a macro scale, aerial photography and satellite images can locate traces of previously anthropogenic residues. At the same time, the combination of RS and Geographical Information Systems (GIS) can be used for modelling past settlement trends or for monitoring anthropogenic and natural hazards for archaeological sites and their surroundings (e.g. *Hadjimitsis et al. 2009*).

Since the earliest aerial photographs used for archaeological purposes (see *Capper 1907; Riley 1987; Bewley et al. 1999; Parcak 2009*), significant technological improvements have occurred in the field of RS. For instance, the Landsat space program launched in 1972 was systematically used either to detect subsurface archaeological remains or to monitor archaeological sites. For example, Vaughn and Crawford (*2009*) used spatial models and Landsat satellite imagery to identify new areas with potential settlements of the Maya. Recently, Landsat images along with other high-resolution or hyperspectral images were used in a systematic survey of the Neolithic tells of Thessaly in Greece (*Alexakis et al. 2009*).

In the area of Cyprus, so far Landsat images have been used mostly for monitoring environmental and anthropogenic hazards in close proximity to cultural heritage sites (*Hadjimitsis et al. 2008; 2009*) and not for the detection of subsurface remains.

This continuous exploitation of satellite imagery for archaeological purposes has led to the development of so-called "RS archaeology". Over the last decades several studies have been made in different parts of the world, verifying the significance of the application of RS in archaeology (e.g. *Beck et al. 2007; Laet et al. 2007; Kelong et al. 2008; Alexakis et al. 2009; 2011; Bassani et al. 2009; Kaimaris et al. 2009; Lasaponara - Masini 2011*). The majority of these applications are focused on the detection of buried archaeological remains. Indeed, aerial photography (oblique or vertical) and satellite imagery can indicate crop marks, which in turn can be linked to the presence of underground monuments (*Bewley et al. 1999*). Studies performed by Agapiou et al. (*2010; 2012*) and Agapiou and Hadjimitsis (*2011*) have shown that ground spectroradiometers may also be used as an alternative approach for the detection of buried relics in known archaeological sites.

Nevertheless many recent studies tend to agree that the study and understanding of how crop marks are formed is a difficult task since this is a complex phenomenon with several parameters to be taken into account. For instance, Adqus et al. (*2007*), Mills and Palmer (*2007*) and Winton and Horne (*2010*), argue that crop marks are correlated with a combination of parameters such as soil moisture, soil nutrients (particularly in phases of plant growth), soil, the depth and nature of the archaeological remains, climatic conditions etc.

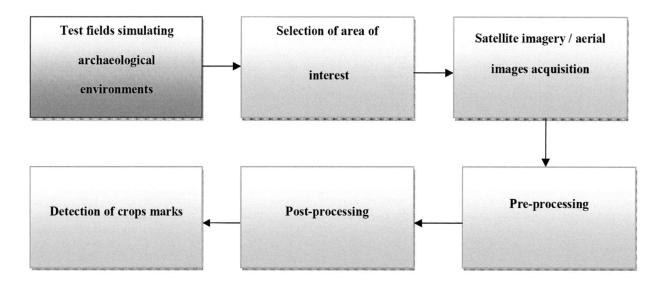

Fig. 1. Proposed methodology of experimental RS archaeology.

Limitations of RS applications

The methodology applied in all these RS investigations is briefly analysed: The boundaries of the area of interest (e.g. area under investigation) is determined either based on previous archaeological knowledge or as a result of ground measurements / observations such as geophysical or foot surveys, study of written sources, old maps etc. After the area of interest has been defined, a number of satellite images and/or aerial images are acquired. Then the necessary pre-processing procedures such as geometric, radiometric corrections are performed, and finally image analyses consisting of both spatial and spectral convolutions are applied. The results may indicate some crops marks, in the form of reflectance signatures, which are then correlated with the a-priori knowledge of the site. In some cases, archaeological investigations will follow to verify the success of the satellite image classification procedures.

This standard approach raises fundamental questions and concerns regarding the future of RS archaeology. Subsurface anomalies cannot be validated before any archaeological excavations in the area of interest. As a result, a subsurface anomaly is only an a-posteriori (after the RS application) known parameter. Additionally, in most cases, verification of the suggested features through archaeological surveys or excavations is never performed.

Proposed methodology

Despite the well-formalised methodological flow, RS archaeology does not have a complete understanding of the process of formation and modification of the crops marks. Further details of RS archaeology (e.g. the depth of subsurface targets, which crops are considered suitable for identifying architectural remains, what are the time-windows for monitoring crops through time, etc.) have not been methodically studied so far and probably will be impossible to analyse thoroughly with the usual practices.

In addition to the above, developments in space technology in the coming years are expected to be rapid. New satellite programs, from NASA, ESA and other governmental or private agencies, reflect the trend of the near future in the field of remote sensing.

This papers aims to introduce a new methodology of remote sensing for detection of subsurface remains. This methodology, named "experimental RS archaeology", aims to study the variability of vegetation in controlled and known buried targets with remote sensing data and techniques. The fundamental difference of this field compared to RS archaeology is that the subsurface anomaly is a-priori known. This can be achieved by just reversing the traditional RS archaeology process (as indicated in Fig. 1). Indeed, experimental RS archaeology can be compared with experimental archaeology in which researchers try to understand prehistoric practices through modern reproductions.

Case study area

The need for monitoring spectral signatures of crop marks created over subsurface remains with the use of RS techniques has led to the construction of a test field in village of Alampra, central Cyprus. This field simulates subsurface architectural remains, since local stone was placed at different depths and then covered with soil. The topsoil was cultivated with dense vegetation (barley and wheat) in order to study the variations of the spectral signature of the crops as a result of the presence of subsurface remains.

The main purpose of this "test field" is to explore further characteristics of the spectral signatures profiles of crops throughout the phenological cycle of vegetation and to correlate them with vegetation characteristics (e.g. plant temperature, plant height), etc. Moreover this field will be used to validate existing vegetation indices, filters etc.

which are often used in the processing of satellite images to detect subsurface remains.

Construction of the Test Field

Eight "control" sites measuring 5 x 5 sq. m were prepared in the Alampra test field. Each square simulates a different archaeological environment. These sites are located in the same area in order to minimize any differences in environmental, meteorological or soil conditions. All sites have been cultivated with barley and crops according to the traditional methods of the area. In two sampling squares (Sites 3-4) local stones were buried at a depth of 25 cm, while in two other squares similar stones were buried at a depth of 50 cm (Sites 5-6). Moreover two squares were used to simulate "tombs" at a depth of 25 cm (Sites 1-2), while the last two squares (Sites 7-8) were left untouched. Local stones used in the control field were collected from the area of Alampra.

Selection of type of Vegetation

The selection of the type of vegetation is very important for the aims of this research. Cereals crops (wheat and barley) have been selected, since these types of crops have been most commonly reported to exist as ground coverage in most RS archaeological applications for the detection of subsurface monuments (*Hejcman - Smrž 2010*). Indeed as Sharpe (*2004*) argues, cereals have a high density planting, while their root system can reach from 1.0 to 1.8 metres depending on soil type (*Canadell et al. 1996*).

In addition cereals have a high leaf area index (LAI), and therefore they are more sensitive to drought conditions. The LAI index is the ratio of leaf surface per unit area of land. In Cyprus, the phenological cycle of cereals starts in early November and lasts until the end of April or the beginning of May.

Ground RS measurements

Ground RS measurements were performed using a GER 1500 field spectroradiometer. GER 1500 can record electromagnetic radiation between 350 nm up to 1050 nm. A reference spectralon panel was used to measure the incoming solar radiation. All the measurements were taken from nadir view, from a height of 1.2 m using a 4° FOV lens. The measurements were acquired between 10.00 a.m. and 2 p.m. in order to minimise the impact of illumination changes on the spectral responses.

Hundreds of spectroradiometric measurements were taken during the phenological cycle of cereal crops (period of acquisition: 2010-2011). Spectroradiometric measurements were then catalogued according to their date of acquisition and type of cereal crop. Moreover, meteorological data were provided by the Meteorological Service of Cyprus for further investigation of the soils' parameters.

Results

The sowing period in the site took place in mid-November 2010, just before the first winter rainfalls. Barley and wheat crops were cultivated in squares 1, 3, 4, 8 and 2, 5, 6, 7, respectively. The selection of the seeding period was based on the traditional agricultural practices in the region and on previous (2008-2010) phenological cycles of crops using Landsat TM / ETM + images.

Yet, during the period of 2010 - 2011 one of the driest Novembers of the last decades was recorded in Cyprus with a total rainfall of 0.00 mm. Additionally December of 2010 was also one of the most anhydrous December months of the last years (total rainfall for the whole month was 106.00 mm). This irregularity in the climatic pattern had a direct impact on the growth of the crops.

After the first winter rainfalls on 10-12-2010, the phenological cycle of the crops began. Although the early vegetation did not indicate any signs of stress conditions, the effect of aridity began to appear both to the colour and to the height of the crops. Therefore crops were in a stress condition until late December.

Rains that fell the following month (January 2011) also had a negative impact on the plants' growth. High precipitation along with the impermeable subsoil of the region (< 0.50 m) led to further stress on the plants. This was observed in all squares except the first two (Squares 1 and 2) where the "gaps" created for the simulation of the tombs functioned as an outlet for excess water that was not necessary for the photosynthesis and evapotranspiration process. Barley crops in Square 1 continued to grow normally in contrast to wheat crops in Square 2 which showed some signs of strain, as barley tends to be more resistive to water. Fig. 2 shows the main phases of the crops' growth at Alampra site.

These stress conditions were recorded by taking several spectroradiometer measurements during the phenological cycle of the plants. From October 2010 until March 2011 over 20 in-situ visits were made (about 1 visit every 9 days) and more than 1000 ground measurements were taken. Typical spectral signatures taken on 13-03-2011 over Square 1 and healthy vegetation are presented in Fig 3. Compared to the healthy vegetation, spectral signatures over Square 1 tend to give higher reflectance values, especially in the NIR spectrum.

Some of the ground measurements taken in 2010 -2011 are summarised in Fig. 4. From this figure it is obvious that crops in some squares have not grown normally, as a deviation is noticed from the expected linear relationship between red and near infrared reflectance (namely the soil line). This observation is attributed to the stress of crops. Only in Squares 1 and 2 and in empty (non-archaeological) Squares 7 and 8, vegetation seems to follow the normal evolution of the phenological cycle. Fig. 5 shows the control area in mid-February when the stress on the vegetation is

17-12-2010: Start of the phenological cycle of crops		**26-12-2010:** Crops can be seen in the area	
04-01-2011: Crops are preserved in low height		**15-01-2011:** Stress conditions of the crops	
20-02-2011: The stress condition is again noticeable		**13-03-2011:** Phenological cycle ends	

Fig. 2. Phenological cycle of crops in the Alampra test field.

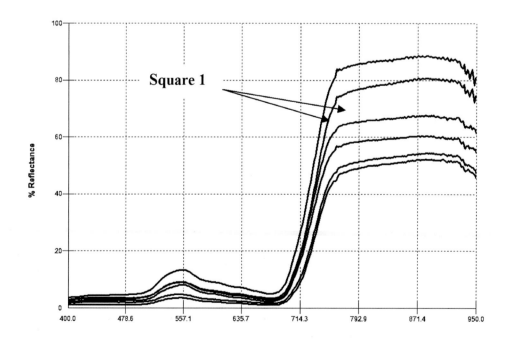

Fig. 3. Spectral signatures taken on 13-03-2011. The spectral signatures acquired from Square 1 are compared to those of the healthy vegetation.

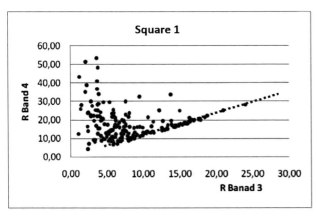
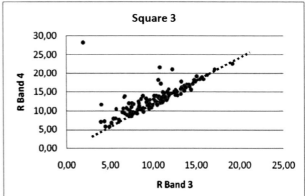

Fig. 4. NIR versus Red reflectance for squares cultivated with barley. Dashed line indicates the soil line.

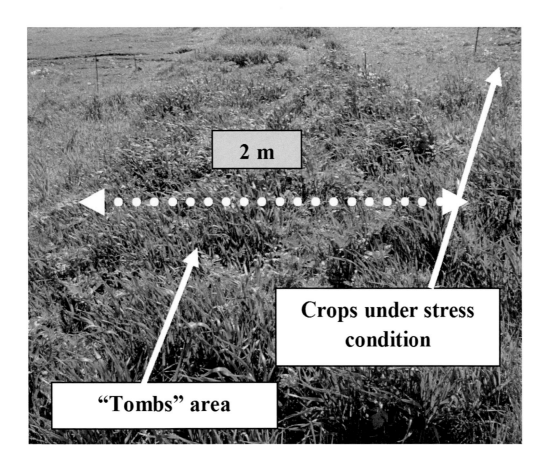

Fig. 5. Photo from Square 1, at the Alampra test field.

evident in the squares simulating the presence of tombs. The simulation is shown as a positive linear differentiation of vegetation.

Finally, the phenological cycle of barley crops at the Alampra test field was examined during 2010 – 2011 (Fig. 6). Ground spectroradiometric measurements were taken from the beginning of the phenological cycle (November 2010) until the highest peak of greenness (January 2001). The NDVI phenological cycle diagram shows that the phenological cycle over archaeological remains tends to give higher NDVI values than the non-archaeological area. The two cases studies (Square 1 and healthy site) were in close proximity in order to minimise climate changes or changes in the NDVI due to different soil characteristics.

Conclusions

This paper aims to introduce a new methodology for monitoring crop marks in relation to the presence of

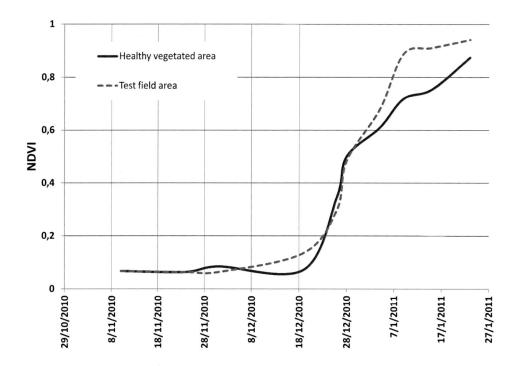

Fig. 6. The phenological cycle for Square 1 (archaeological area) and healthy site (non-archaeological area).

archaeological remains. The proposed methodology aims to explore further characteristics of the crop marks using test fields which simulate archaeological environments.

Although the results of the first year (2010-2011) were not as expected due to climatic problems that arose in the area, the experience gained and the partial results acquired from the field measurements were very important for the study of the following year (2011-2012). Indeed the authors have managed to isolate the time window (January – March) in which RS techniques were able to detect sufficient crop marks.

The preliminary results were very helpful, especially for Square 1. A linear crop mark was also made visible above the square simulating the existence of tombs. This crop mark might be a consequence of the stress period of October 2010. Crops were cultivated during September (first rainy days), while during October the total rainfall in the area was 0.00 mm. After this dry period, a high rainfall was observed all over the island. It seems that the air trapped beneath the "tomb" functioned as a gateway for the evaporation of the water.

The new phenological cycle of cereal crops is going to be investigated in the next phases of the research. Moreover a new test field will be constructed in another area of Cyprus (Acheleia) in order to examine any differences due to soil and meteorological characteristics.

Acknowledgements

These results are part of the PhD dissertation of Mr Athos Agapiou. The authors would like to express their appreciation to the Alexander Onassis Foundation for funding the PhD study. Also thanks are given to the Remote Sensing Laboratory of the Department of Civil Engineering & Geomatics at the Cyprus University of Technology for their support (http://www.cut.ac.cy/).

References

Adqus, S.A. - Hanson, W.S. – Drummond, J. 2007: A Comparative Study for Finding Archaeological Crop Marks using Airborne Hyperspectral, Multispectral and Digital Photographic Data. Proceedings of the Annual Conference of the Remote Sensing and Photogrammetry Society, Newcastle University, Oct. 11-15, 2007.

Agapiou, A. - Hadjimitsis, D.G. 2011: Detection of possible Archaeological Crop Marks in Cyprus Using Vegetation Indices and Field Spectroradiometric Measurements: Verification under area surveyed with geophysical campaigns. Journal of Applied Remote Sensing 5, 053554, doi:10.1117/1.3645590.

Agapiou, A. - Hadjimitsis, D. - Themistocleous, K. – Papadavid, G. – Toulios, L. 2010: Detection of archaeological crop marks in Cyprus using field spectroscopy measurements. Proceedings of SPIE, 7831, 78310V1 - 11.

Agapiou, A. - Hadjimitsis, D.G. - Alexakis, D. - Sarris, A. 2012: Observatory validation of Neolithic tells ("Magoules") in the Thessalian plain, central Greece, using hyperspectral spectro-radiometric data. Journal of Archaeological Science 39(5), 1499-1512. doi. org/10.1016/j.jas.2012.01.001.

Alexakis, A. - Sarris, A. - Astaras, T. – Albanakis, K. 2009: Detection of Neolithic Settlements in Thessaly (Greece) Through Multispectral and Hyperspectral Satellite Imagery. Sensors 9: 1167-1187.

Alexakis, A. - Sarris, A. - Astaras, T. – Albanakis, K. 2011: Integrated GIS, remote sensing and geomorphologic approaches for the reconstruction of the landscape habitation of Thessaly during the Neolithic period. Journal of Archaeological Science 38: 89-100.

Bassani, C. - Cavalli, R.M. - Goffredo, R. – Palombo, A. - Pascucci, S. - Pignatti, S. 2009: Specific Spectral Bands for Different Land Cover Contexts to Improve the Efficiency of Remote Sensing Archaeological Prospection. The Arpi case study. Journal of Cultural Heritage 10, 41-48.

Beck, A. - Wilkinson, K. – Philip, G. 2007: Some techniques for improving the detection of archaeological features from satellite imagery. Proceedings of the International Society for Optical Engineering, Remote sensing for environmental monitoring, GIS applications, and geology, 6749, 674903.1-674903.12.

Bewley, R. - Donoghue, D. - Gaffney, V. - van Leusen, M. - Wise, A. 1999: Archiving aerial photography and remote sensing data: a guide to good practice. Archaeology Data Service, Oxbow, UK.

Canadell, J. - Jackson, R.B. - Ehleringer, J.R. - Mooney, H.A. - Sala, O.E. – Schulze, E.D. 1996: Maximum rooting depth of vegetation types at the global scale. Oecologia 108, 583-595.

Capper, J.E. 1907: Photographs of Stonehenge as seen from a war balloon. Archaeologia 60, 571.

Hadjimitsis, D.G. - Themistocleous, K. - Agapiou, A. - Clayton, C.R.I. 2009: Multi-temporal study of archaeological sites in Cyprus using atmospheric corrected satellite remotely sensed data. International Journal of Architectural Computing 7(1), 121-138.

Hadjimitsis, D.G. - Themistocleous, K. - Ioannides, M. - Clayton, C.R.I. 2008: Integrating satellite remote sensing and spectro-radiometric measurements for monitoring archaeological site landscapes. Proceedings of the 14th International Conference on Virtual Systems and Multimedia (VSMM 2008), 124-129.

Hejcman, M. - Smrž, Z. 2010: Cropmarks in stands of cereals and winter rape indicate sub-soil archaeological features in the agricultural landscape of Central Europe. Agriculture, Ecosystems and Environment 138, 348-354.

Kaimaris, D. - Georgoula, O. - Karadedos, G. – Patias, P. 2009: Aerial and remote sensing archaeology in eastern Macedonia, Greece. Proceedings of CIPA XXII, Archives for Documentation of Cultural Heritage, Vol. XXII. http://cipa.icomos.org/fileadmin/template/doc/KYOTO/134.pdf

Kelong, T. - Yuqing, W. - Lin, Y. - Riping, Z. - Wei, C. - Yaobao, M. 2008: A new archaeological remote sensing technology. Proceedings of The International Archives of the Photogrammetry, Remote Sensing and Spatial Information Sciences 37(B7), 3-6.

Laet, V. - Paulissen, E. - Waelkens, M. 2007: Methods for the extraction of archaeological features from very high-resolution Ikonos-2 remote sensing imagery, Hisar (southwest Turkey). Journal of Archaeological Science 34, 830-841.

Lasaponara, R. - Masini, N. 2011: Satellite remote sensing in archaeology: past, present and future perspectives. Journal of Archaeological Science 38(9), 1995-2002.

Mills, J. - Palmer, R. 2007: Populating clay landscapes. Stroud: Tempus.

Parcak, S.H. 2009: Satellite Remote Sensing for Archaeology. London and New York: Routledge Taylor and Francis Group.

Riley, D.N. 1987: Air photography and archaeology. London: Duckworth.

Sharpe, L. 2004: Geophysical, geochemical and arable crop responses to archaeological sites in the Upper Clyde Valley, Scotland. PhD thesis, University of Glasgow.

Vaughn, S. - Crawford, T. 2009: A predictive model of archaeological potential: An example from northwestern Belize. Applied Geography 29(4), 542-555.

Winton, H. - Horne, P. 2010: National archives for national survey programmes: NMP and the English heritage aerial photograph collection. In: Landscapes through the Lens. Aerial Photographs and Historic Enviroment. Aerial Archaeology Research Group No. 2, 7-18.

AUTOMATED 3D-OBJECT DOCUMENTATION ON THE BASIS OF AN IMAGE SET

Sebastian Vetter and Gunnar Siedler

Abstract: *Digital stereo-photogrammetry allows users an automatic evaluation of the spatial dimensions and surface texture of objects. The integration of image analysis techniques simplifies the automation of evaluation of large image sets and offers a high accuracy (Henze et al. 2006). Due to the substantial similarities of stereoscopic image pairs, correlation techniques allow measurements of subpixel precision for corresponding image points.*

With the help of an automated point search algorithm in image sets, identical points are used to associate pairs of images to stereo models, and combine them. Points found to be identical in all images are the basis for calculating the relative orientation of each stereo model as well as defining the relation of neighbouring stereo models.

By using proper filter strategies, incorrect points are removed and the relative orientation of the stereo model is made automatically. By using 3D-reference points on an object with known distance from the camera lens, or the known focal length of the camera, an absolute orientation of the stereo model can be achieved.

An adapted expansion- and matching algorithm offers the possibility to scan the object surface automatically. The result is a three-dimensional point cloud of which the image quality defines its resolution. These partial point clouds are fitted to a total point cloud with applying an iterative closest point-algorithm (ICP), making 3D-reference points unnecessary.

By implementing a triangulation algorithm a digital surface model (DSM) can be created. The texturing can be made automatically using the images, used for the scanning the object surface. It is possible to texture the surface model directly, or to generate orthophotos automatically.

By using calibrated digital SLR cameras with full frame sensor high accuracy can be reached.

The resolution of the images defines accuracy and quality of the 3D object. For the described procedure the software metigo 3D was utilized.

Keywords: *3D-object documentation - textured surface model - orthophotos - image matching - point cloud*

Image recording

Two digital reflex cameras Canon EOS 5D Mark II were used for 3D-evaluation based on stereo models of an image set of the shown object (Katzenstein Castle). These were previously calibrated on two focal lengths (24 mm and 50 mm). (Alternatively, usable camera systems are Nikon D700 or Sony Alpha 950, digital reflex cameras with full frame sensor.)

Using a receiving rail (on a tripod), onto which both cameras were attached, a set of stereo models was taken (Fig. 1. right). In addition, three-dimensional reference points on the object were measured with a tacheometer. The measured reference points on Katzenstein Castle as well as the recording configuration on the east wall and apse are displayed in (Fig. 1). The accuracy of the evaluation is defined by the image quality and its scale.

To record plastic objects a rotation plate is utilitzed, from where single images are taken in suitable step size.

Automated model assignment and orientation

After the program is started it asks to create a new project. The evaluation accuracy and resolution need to be defined and the images are loaded into the project. The internal orientation is established for every image by linking the images to the corresponding camera.

Control points (identical points on the object) are automatically detected in the images by the evaluation software (Fig. 2 left). Based on these control points the arrangement of the images is analysed (Fig. 2 right), with the goal to detect suitable pairs of images or stereo models (parallel recording direction, a large region of overlap). The manual creation of stereo models is a possible alternative.

The calculation of the relative orientation of both images for the stereo model is made on the basis of the known control points. If there are not enough control points for the model orientation, additional image coordinates can be detected automatically or measured by hand.

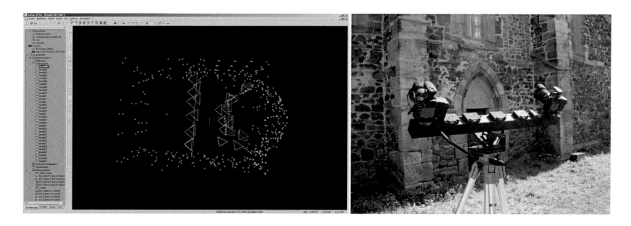

Fig. 1. Left: recording configuration at east wall and apse (Katzenstein Castle); right: used recording rail with 2 reflex cameras.

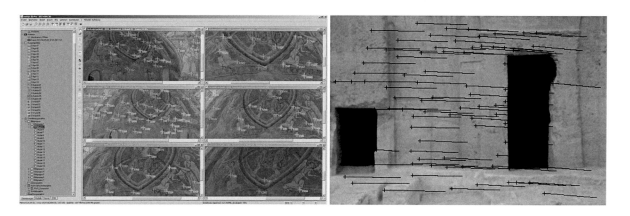

Fig. 2. Left: six images with similar image part and automatically found control points; right: result of analysing one pair of images (shift vectors of control points).

Fig. 3. Absolute orientated stereo model (green image coordinate: used control point; blue image coordinate: filtered control point; magenta image coordinate: control point was found in only one image; yellow image coordinate: not measured reference point).

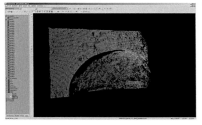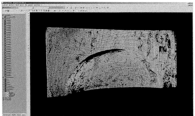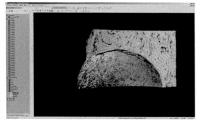

Fig. 4. Three partial point clouds in 3D window, the colouring depends on the point error.

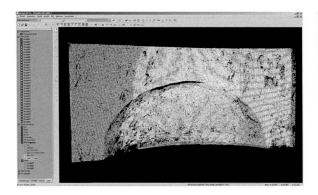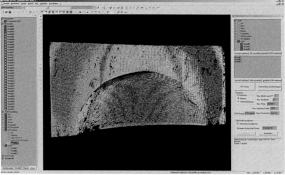

Fig. 5. Merged point cloud; right: point the colouring depends on the origin (partial point cloud).

By using proper filter strategies during the calculation of the relative orientation of the stereo model, incorrect model coordinates are detected and removed.

By measuring additional reference points, the absolute orientation of one stereo model into the overall coordinate system is made (Fig. 3). Alternatively, the absolute orientation can be calculated with the defined distance of the camera to the object .

A relation graph that describes the arrangement of the stereo models is generated using the existing control points. Therefore, it is sufficient to make an absolute orientation of only one stereo model (of one set of related stereo models) by hand. All the other stereo models of the set are automatically created in absolute orientation.

In the case of insufficient relation between the stereo models, additional reference points on the object surface can be measured to calculate the absolute orientation manually.

Automated generation of a point cloud

Due to the substantial similarities of stereoscopic image pairs, correlation techniques provide measurements of subpixel precision for corresponding image points.

In addition to the single-point measurement, object surfaces can be scanned with the appropriate expansion algorithms (*Vetter 2005*).

By considering the evaluation accuracy for every stereo model, the right step size (point distance) for matching is determined. This depends on the scale of the images. By implementing batch processing all existing stereo models can be "scanned". For every matched points the error is calculated using photogrammetric spatial intersection and the point cloud is coloured according to these errors (Fig. 4). Incorrect points are filtered automatically by an adjustable threshold.

Merging of partial point clouds into a total point cloud

With the integrated Iterative Closest Point algorithm, the partial point clouds are transformed by the identical control points and merged into a total point cloud (Fig. 5).

By implementing filter strategies, the point cloud is thinned out to the evaluation accuracy. As a consequence, these have a higher point density (*Heinrich 2010*) in overlapping areas.

Automated evaluation of a digital surface model

With a triangulation algorithm (*Bernardini et al. 1999*), a digital surface model is generated by a point cloud. In a second step, after editing the surface model, the images are mapped on it. Thus a three-dimensional digital documentation is possible (Fig. 6).

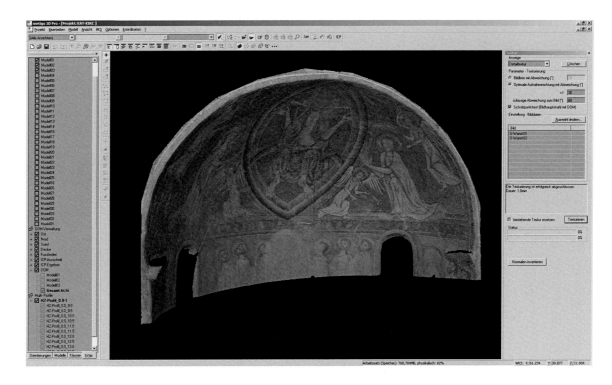

Fig. 6. 3D-surface model with image texture.

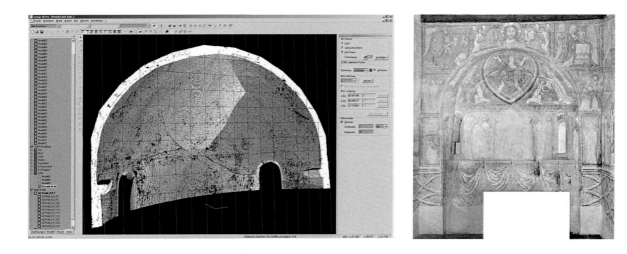

Fig. 7. Left: 3D point cloud and plane of a user coordinate system (for ortho projection); right: image plane of east wall (ortho projection to plane).

Unwrapping / digital ortho projection

For the projection of images onto a plane or another unwrapping geometry, user coordinate systems can be defined related to the overall coordinate system or with the help of a partial set of points (balancing plane).

Additional sectional profiles can be extracted and generalised from the existing point cloud or surface model.

Ortho projection onto the unwrapping geometry is made in a user-defined image scale, while image resolution is dependend on the orientated images (Fig. 7), the sectional profiles and the surface model.

These steps to generate ortho photos were processed for the vertical plane at the east wall, for the standing cylinder (Fig. 9) at the apse, and for the chalotte. Additionally, the projection geometry can be blended into the orientated images (Fig. 8).

Conclusions

The east wall with apse shown here was covered with 13 stereo models and about 100 reference points were measured with a tacheometer. The orienation and evaluation of these stereo models and the shown result were made with the software metigo *3D*. The final image processing and colour matching were made with Adobe Photoshop CS5.

Fig. 8. Left: orientated image of calotte with projection of a cylinder; right: unwrapped image plan of calotte (ortho projection onto cylinder).

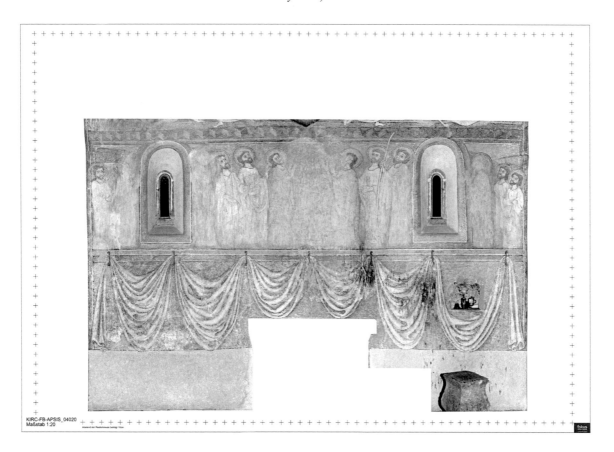

Fig. 9. Unwrapped image plan of apse (ortho projection onto cylinder).

For the described evaluation procedure for all stereo models (from loading the images to the final assembly of the image plans) nearly eight hours were required. In addition, nearly eight hours calculation time was required during batch processing for image arrangement, generation of point clouds, triangulation, and unwrapping or ortho projection. Four additional hours were needed for image processing with Adobe Photoshop.

The required time for evaluation generally depends on the number of images, the resolution of the images, and the surface model as well as the existing computing power.

The resulting orthophoto, processed in scale 1 : 10 and 400 dpi image resolution, can be used as a 2D mapping base for the documentation of the object. The digital surface model can be alternatively textured to use them for 3D mapping.

At the moment the 3D mapping is not used in restoration because of practical reasons like the amount of data, printing or data exchange with the final customer.

Acknowledgements

Parts of the here described evaluation steps were developed in a cooperation project with the Society for the Promotion of Applied Computer Science (Fig. 10) and supported by: Federal Ministry of Economics and Technology on the basis of a decision by the German Bundestag.

Supported by:

Federal Ministry
of Economics
and Technology

on the basis of a decision
by the German Bundestag

*Fig. 10. Supported by the Federal Ministry of Economics
and Technology on the basis of a decision by the German
Bundestag.*

References

*Bernardini, F. - Mittleman, J. - Rushmeier, H. - Silva,
C. - Taubin, G. 1999*: The Ball-Pivoting Algorithm
for Surface Reconstruction. IEEE Transaction on
Visualization and Computer Graphics 5(4), Oct-Dec,
349-359.

Heinrich, M. 2010: Markante Punkte und 3D- Objektkanten
in einem Oberflächenmodel. diploma thesis
(unpublished), HTWK Leipzig, Germany.

Henze, F. - Siedler, G. - Vetter, S. 2006: Integration
automatisierter Verfahren der digitalen Bildverarbeitung
in einem Stereoauswertesystem, 26. Wissenschaftlich-
Technische Jahrestagung der DGPF, Berlin, Band 15,
239-246.

Vetter, S. 2005: Generierung digitaler Oberflächenmodelle
(DOM) im Bereich der Architekturphotogrammetrie,
diploma thesis (unpublished), HTWK Leipzig, Germany.

Exploring Differences: Implications for FCVA Visibility Indices and Scales of Analyses

Mariza Kormann and Gary Lock

Abstract: *Studies of long barrows have shown that choice of location could have been based on the intended view over the landscape and may, therefore, have served as territorial markers. The question addressed in this paper relates to whether or not the quantification of changes in FCVA visibility indices can be correlated to possible choices of site location and, therefore, to hypotheses about territoriality. The FCVA indices indicate regions of high and low visibility, and the proposed method of differences can disambiguate these regions by pinpointing which scales (distances) have the most significant changes and thus, point to the optimal scale at which barrows and landscape features were visible.*

Keywords: *GIS - visibility - scale of analysis - Fuzzy Cumulative Visibility Analysis (FCVA)*

Introduction

The connection between visibility and movement is well established and has been emphasized by various authors both theoretically and within GIS-based studies (e.g. *Tilley 1994; Lock - Harris 1996; Ingold 2000; 2011; Ogburn 2006; Lock - Pouncett 2009; Lock et al. 2011 in press*). Tilley (*1994*) stated that the primary method of measuring experience and movement is through analysing visibility patterns and assigns strong significance to places and their importance that can only be appreciated as a result of movement. Ingold (*2000; 2011*) goes further and suggests that movement gives rise to a set of relations between landscape objects and their social context and can only be understood or appreciated through immersion and experience. Attempts have been made to incorporate these ideas into GIS-based archaeological analyses, Ogburn (*2006*) for example, discusses a fuzzy viewshed approach to assess clarity levels of objects over distance, taking into account the object sizes, knowledge of local environmental conditions and physical properties of the target and its settings. Lock *et al.* (*2011 in press*) introduced the concept of FCVA (Fuzzy Cumulative Visibility Analysis) in landscape analysis and related FCVA to Least Cost Path and surfaces of movement that were calculated using statistical analysis.

The use of long barrows as suitable for this type of study was first introduced by Lock and Harris (*1996*) who suggested that these monuments may have served as a kind of territorial marker for a group or groups of people. This paper continues this theme by considering the relationship between visibility, movement, and scale of analysis using the Neolithic long barrows of the Danebury region, England, as a case study together with the recently described methodology of FCVA (*Lock et al. 2011 in press*). Studies of long barrows have shown that an emphasis on choice of location could be based on the intended view of the surrounding landscape (*Lock - Harris 1996*) and their use as visible territorial markers. The implication is that the long barrows were sited to oversee a 'visual territory' and it would be useful to have a means to model the extent of such a territory. Furthermore, the issue of scale of analysis (by this we mean distance of view) has been pointed out by several authors as being significant to archaeological interpretation as one can interpret a single object in a single location or multiple objects in an entire region spanning thousands of years. Choosing the appropriate scale of analysis is a difficult task and often interpretation relies on multiple scales. While GIS have the potential for multiple scales of analyses this is often not fully utilised. This research aims to determine whether or not FCVA can provide an indication of 'optimal' scales based on visibility differences as analyses go from scale to scale.

The main question addressed here relates to whether or not the quantification of change in FCVA visibility indices (distances of view) can be correlated to possible choices of site location and, therefore, an understanding of territoriality. This approach is placed within a theoretical framework as it underlies a clear strategy to the study of visibility and movement and ultimately our research aims at providing methodologies that can help us understand the intricacies of space, visibility, movement, and scale of analyses.

This paper is organized as follows. Section two (Review of the FCVA Methodology) highlights the properties of FCVA and Section three (The FCVA Method of Differences) describes the proposed method of differences. Experimental results are described in Section four (Experimental Results) using the long barrows of the Danebury region of Hampshire and Wiltshire (England) as a case study and finally, a discussion and conclusions are presented in Section five (Discussion and Conclusions).

Review of the FCVA Methodology

FCVA simulates immersive movement in a digital elevation model (DEM) and has been introduced in Lock *et al.* (*2011; in press*). Moving from cell to cell in a digital landscape some cells are seen more often than others in a continuously changing way. These changes can be expressed by a visibility index for each cell (how many times a cell is detected as being visible or how many cells can be seen from a given viewpoint) resulting in visibility gradients due to the cumulative effects. Visibility indices are calculated using a sliding window where the size of the window defines the scale of analysis (i.e. the distance of visibility, the distance seen). As visibility indices accumulate as a result of movement, areas of high and low visibility become apparent and can be correlated to landscape features and monuments. FCVA is, therefore, a dynamic process that models different scales of visibility equating with different scales of analysis allowing interpretation of visibility and movement at multiple scales. In effect FCVA is a form of restricted cumulative viewshed.

In this section the main steps of the methodology are reviewed before the method of differences is introduced. The purpose of FCVA is to build a visibility map directly from DEM elevation data for any given scale of analysis. Thus it provides an alternative view of the DEM where each cell location contains a visibility index (i.e. an accumulated value). When the FCVA matrix is visualized and compared to the original DEM, it provides visibility information that is different from elevation; some areas of relative high and low visibility may not correspond to their high and low elevations, while some other areas may have a closer relationship to elevation data. The *visibility map* provided by the FCVA method can be a powerful tool to aid the interpretation of movement, site location and overall landscape visibility for different scales of analysis.

FCVA is based on the concept of a *sliding window* of size *rw*-by-*cw* where *rw* is the number of rows and *cw* is the number of columns (i.e. row width and column width). It is important to stress that the sliding window defines the scale of analysis. In the FCVA method the visibility index of each cell is defined by a continuous gradient between zero (never visible) and one (always visible). If the landscape DEM is defined by a matrix of elevation data with R rows and C columns, an FCVA matrix M the same size of the DEM is defined where the visibility index v at each location (R,C) is:

$$M_{(RC)} = \{v \mid v \in (0.0 \ldots 1.0)\} \qquad (1)$$

The matrix M is initialized to zero meaning that all cells are not visible by default at the start of calculations. Every time a cell is detected as visible, a small fraction f is added to the cell location (R,C) such that at the end of the calculations the values in M will be within the range of $0.0 - 1.0$. The fraction f is defined as:

$$f = \frac{1}{rw * cw} \qquad (2)$$

An important aspect of the FCVA method is that all calculations are performed within the boundaries of the sliding window. This is what binds the calculations to a chosen scale of analysis and consequently, each scale will yield a different visibility matrix M. Given that the sliding window is placed over the DEM, then from the centre cell of the sliding window lines-of-sight are evaluated to each cell covering its entire span. As each cell is detected either visible or not visible, it is marked either with a value of f or a value of 0 (zero). At the end of the calculation, the values in the sliding window are summed to represent a visibility index of its centre cell (from which the lines of sight were calculated):

$$M_{(R,C)} = \sum_{r=1}^{rw} \sum_{c=1}^{cw} V(r,c) \qquad (3)$$

Note that the visibility indices $M_{(R,C)}$ are defined in relation to a given global (R,C) location while line-of-sights and local visibility $V_{(r,c)}$ are calculated using the local indices (r,c) of the sliding window. Due to cumulative effects, cells that are visible more frequently will have higher visibility indices. Furthermore, visibility indices result in fuzzy visibility gradients with no sharp, binary boundaries between adjacent cells.

Fig. 1 shows the sliding window placed over the DEM at two different locations. At the start of calculations, the centre cell of the sliding window is aligned over the first cell of the DEM. Then it slides to the right and then down a row until all cells are visited a row at a time. The final position for the sliding window is when its centre cell is aligned with the bottom right cell of the DEM. All cells in the DEM that are covered by the sliding window will become target cells in their turn, here only two target cells are shown. A line-of-sight is indicated between the centre cell and the target. The cells on the line-of-sight are marked as grey dots and their elevation will determine whether or not the target is visible.

It is also important to note that two types of visibility indices can be calculated with the FCVA method: either *looking out* or *looking in*. An FCVA looking out map shows the count of cells that can be seen from the centre of the sliding window; it means marking (with f) the position (r,c) of every cell that can be seen. In this case, an offset of 1.60 m is added to the centre cell to simulate the eye level of a person. Then by the summation defined by equation (3), the visibility index $V_{(R,C)}$ is directly related to the number of cells that can be seen from location (R,C) within the sliding

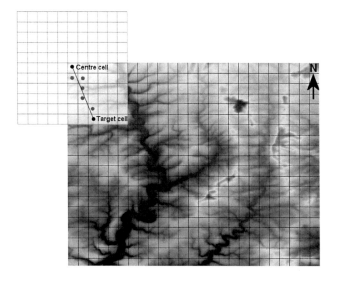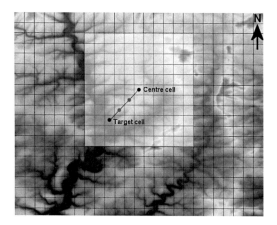

Fig. 1. Left, the FCVA sliding window placed at the initial position over a DEM; right, at an arbitrary location.

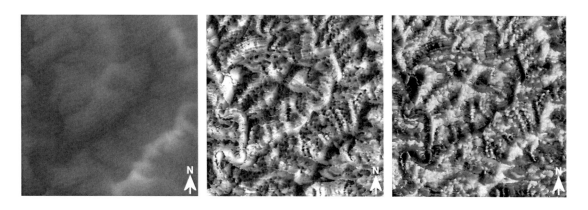

Fig. 2. Left, a topographic view of a selected area; centre and right, the corresponding FCVA maps (looking in and looking out).

window. An index of 0.9 for example would mean that 90 % of the cells within the sliding window could be seen from that location. (Fig. 2)

An FCVA looking in map is related to how many cells can actually see the centre cell of the sliding window. In this case, the offset 1.60 m is added to every cell before calculating the line of sight between that cell and the centre cell. The offset is cancelled as calculation moves to neighbouring cells. The looking out and looking in models can be usefully exploited depending whether one is interested in regions that provide maximum visibility looking out (e.g. a scenic view) or regions that are more hidden from view (looking in). These two visibility maps are not necessarily the same as discussed in Fisher (*1996*). An example of topographic and corresponding FCVA looking in and looking out map data are depicted in Figure 2. In these images, lighter areas have higher visibility indices, or are more visible. Note that there is a relationship between topography and visibility, but at some places this is not obvious especially near the ridges and can be significantly different for looking in or looking out.

The FCVA Method of Differences

The FCVA method of differences is described as follows. First, FCVA visibility maps are calculated for the landscape for several scales of analysis, these can be either looking in or looking out, similar to the ones depicted in Figure 2. Then the differences in visibility indices are calculated for each cell for all possible permutations of scale. For instance, as one goes from two arbitrary scales S_1 to S_2 the difference for each cell is calculated as a visibility matrix difference D:

$$D = M_{s_2} - M_{s_1} \qquad (4)$$

Only positive values of visibility indices are used, so that D at each cell location (R,C) needs to be adjusted to:

$$D_{(R,C)} = \{ D_{(R,C)}, if\ D_{(R,C)} \geq 0$$
$$D_{(R,C)} = \{ 0, otherwise \qquad (5)$$

The reason to keep only positive values of D is that this will indicate which areas of the landscape come into view

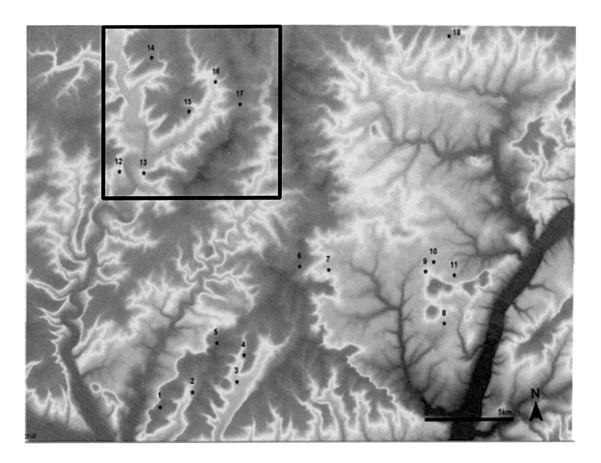

Fig. 3. The Danebury region showing topography and the study area with six long barrows (inset).

as one moves from one scale to another. Conversely, the same areas go out of view as the scales are reversed. The most significant differences are then analysed in the region around each archaeological feature of interest – this may indicate from which distance the feature was possibly designed to be best appreciated and thus, can be related to the extent of the local 'visual territory'.

However, simple differences as in equation (4) may lead to distorted interpretations; for instance, the difference between 0.8 and 0.7 is the same as between 0.2 and 0.1 but clearly the former gradient has more significance in terms of visibility. In order to recover their relative value, the gradient between cells at different scales is used to adjust current visibility indices. Assume a cell with visibility index h_1 at scale S_1 and another cell with visibility index h_2 at scale S_2. Then the visibility gradient between the two scales is $(h_2 - h_1)$ which can simply be expressed by the tangent $tan(h_2 - h_1)$. The new visibility index h_2 expressed by the method of differences is therefore defined as:

$$M_{h_2} = h_2 + h_2 \tan(h_2 - h_1) \qquad (6)$$

or, alternatively,

$$M_{h_2} = h_2(1 + \tan(h_2 - h_1)) \qquad (7)$$

The application of the method is therefore straightforward: calculate a new matrix D between two scales by applying equation (7) to each pair of cells in the original scales. Because the tangent of zero is zero and negative values are forced to zero by equation (5), the method will yield visibility indices that show an increase in visibility (or decrease if the process is reversed) that can be visualised and correlated to archaeological features and to regions in the landscape.

Experimental Results

The study area comprises the long barrows of the Danebury region in Hampshire and Wiltshire, England, Figure 3 shows the topography. The wider area has 600 km² (30 km x 20 km) and encloses all 18 long barrows of the Danebury region, while the study area used here is shown in the inset with 6 long barrows numbered 12 to 17. This area is 49 km² (7 km x 7 km), and the resolution of the DEM is 25m per cell.

FCVA data were calculated for the Danebury DEM for scales ranging from 30 to 100 cells (i.e. for a viewing distance of 750 m to 2500 m). Then the difference in visibility indices was calculated for all possible permutations of scale, following the method described in Section three (equations 4 to 7). The data have been tabulated between Scale1 and Scale2 and are depicted in Table 1. The table shows the total number of cells in the study area (281 x 281 = 78961), the increase in number of visible cells between the scales considered and their

Scale1	Scale2	Total number of cells	Increase in number of cells	Percentage increase
30	100	78961	7742	10
40	100	78961	10987	14
50	100	78961	12402	16
60	100	78961	13267	17
70	100	78961	13602	17
80	100	78961	13925	18
90	100	78961	14749	19
Average for scale 100			**12382**	**16**
30	90	78961	7966	10
40	90	78961	11415	14
50	90	78961	12905	16
60	90	78961	13866	18
70	90	78961	14173	18
80	90	78961	14157	18
Average for scale 90			**12414**	**16**
30	80	78961	8296	11
40	80	78961	11876	15
50	80	78961	13443	17
60	80	78961	14721	19
70	80	78961	15226	19
Average for scale 80			**12712**	**16**
30	70	78961	8590	11
40	70	78961	12081	15
50	70	78961	13729	17
60	70	78961	15250	19
Average for scale 70			**12413**	**16**
30	60	78961	8749	11
40	60	78961	12336	16
50	60	78961	13475	17
Average for scale 60			**11520**	**15**
30	50	78961	9194	12
40	50	78961	12936	16
Average for scale 50			**11065**	**14**
30	40	78961	8833	11

Table 1. Statistics for different scales of analysis.

relative percentages. A statistical summary is provided for each scale by averaging the increase in number of cells and their percentages.

While summary statistics for each scale of analysis are provided in Table 1, these relate to the whole of the selected study area and thus do not relate to any archaeological feature in particular. In order to focus on a feature, statistics need to be calculated for the region or for the visibility patch that may exist around the feature. For example, consider barrow 15 at the centre of the study area as depicted on the top left of Figure 4. The topographic map shows that the barrow is at the edge of a slope, possibly overlooking the valley below. The method of differences was applied and visibility changes that happen around this barrow were

tracked at every scale of analysis. It turns out that the larger increase in visibility happens between scales 50 and 100 (viewing distances of 1250 m and 2500 m). At FCVA scale 50 as depicted on the top right of Figure 4, the barrow is located in a narrow area of low visibility (dark grey), and one could say that it is hidden from view. At FCVA scale 100 depicted at the bottom left of Figure 4, the same location becomes of a higher visibility (lighter grey) and it suggests that at this scale Barrow 15 overlooks large areas to the east and south, and that this barrow is located to be seen from further away.

The bottom right of Figure 4 shows several regions (patches of light grey) of different sizes overlain on the topographic map. These patches quantify the area where an increase in

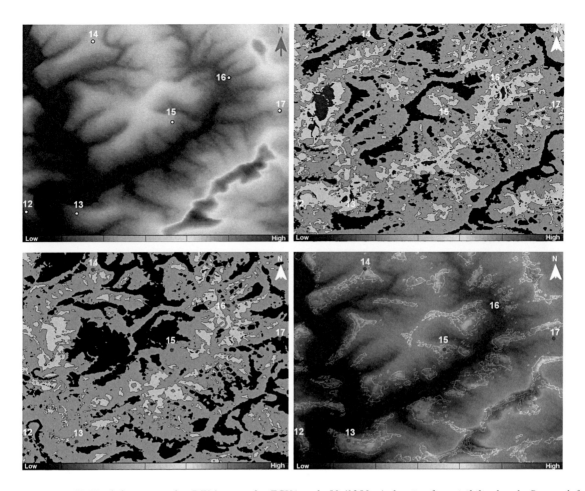

Fig. 4. Barrow 15. Top left: topographic DEM; top right: FCVA scale 50 (1250 m) showing four visibility bands. Bottom left: FCVA scale 100 (2500 m) showing four visibility bands; bottom right: FCVA difference between scales 50 and 100 overlaid on the topographic map.

visibility between the two scales of analysis is observed and it can be seen that it increases considerably around long barrow 15 from the smaller scale. This suggests that Barrow 15 was located to be visible from the greater distance, 2500 m, and supports the idea of it being a marker overlooking a 'visibility territory'. It is not known however what is the optimal scale of analysis, although the method of differences gives an indication as in Figure 4 bottom right. Certainly one cannot make strong statements regarding the extent of territory but by analysing changes in scale it is possible to conjecture the statistical minimum and maximum sizes of a particular territory and in which direction it extends.

Figure 4 also introduces visibility bands with three being depicted at top right and bottom left. Dark, medium and light grey correspond to areas of low, medium and high visibility respectively. Assuming that regions of high visibility indices suggest optimal scales for the long barrows, scales were selected based on their highest band around the archaeological feature. Based on these criteria, Barrow 15 is scale 70 (1750 m), which yields the largest region with medium visibility (the region has no high visibility). For the other barrows the optimal scale of relative high visibility are: scale 30 (750 m) (for barrows

16 and 17), scale 60 (1500 m) (for 12 and 13), and scale 100 (2500 m) (for 14).

Figure 5 depicts increase in visibility indices from scales 50 to 100 for Barrow 13, which is the optimal scale of analysis for this barrow. Note that for other long barrows this is not the scale that provides the highest increase in visibility, consider barrows 16 and 17 for instance which both lie in areas where visibility has not increased. This shows that each landscape feature or monument is associated with its own optimal scale and this can be calculated using FCVA differences. The optimal scale can be interpreted as the distance from which the monument attains maximum visibility.

Comparing Barrows 13 and 15 in Figure 5, it is clear that Barrow 13 has a larger area of increased visibility. Thinking of long barrows as territorial markers sited to overlook their local 'territory', it is possible to suggest that the territory associated with Barrow 13 might have been larger than the territory associated with Barrow 15.

Discussion and Conclusions

The work presented in this paper has focused on visibility, movement and scale of analysis. The FCVA methodology

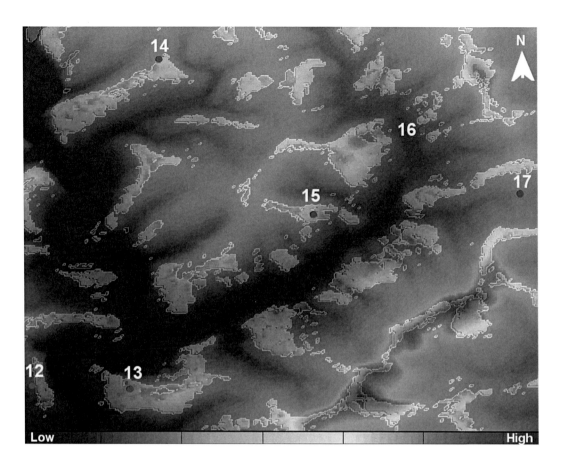

Fig. 5. Patches of increased visibility for scale 100 around Barrow 13.

has been highlighted and a method of differences applied to FCVA visibility maps is proposed as a tool to analyse visibility changes from scale to scale (i.e. at different distances). By simulating a virtual walk in a landscape defined by a digital elevation model, FCVA visibility maps are constructed for any desired scale of analysis. At the end of FCVA calculations, the visibility map shows areas or regions of high and low visibility, which can be directly correlated to landscape features or monuments. The changes to FCVA maps are thus, related to movement and their corresponding scales of analyses, defined by the size of the sliding window.

The FCVA method of differences brings out a number of issues related to the interpretation of visibility maps:

1. Changes in FCVA indices and scale of analysis can be correlated to areas of changed visibility as a result of movement. FCVA directly shows for each scale of analysis which areas have higher visibility and this can be a useful measure to aid interpretation shedding light on the role of visibility and movement regarding natural and cultural features;

2. The method of differences can pinpoint significant visibility changes from scale to scale; it can disambiguate regions by scales with their most significant changes and thus point to the optimal scale in which features are to be seen;

3. Assuming the notion that the optimal scale of analysis equates to high visibility, it is possible to tentatively conjecture that local 'visual territories' may be defined by the scale of analysis. The optimal scale is the one that would yield the highest increase in visibility for a particular landscape feature;

4. Visibility changes are multi-scalar for multiple features – each feature may have its own optimal scale.

Our previous work has demonstrated the use of FCVA for Least Cost Path analysis and their relationship to surfaces of movement. Here we have shown that the method of differences can pinpoint areas of increased or decreased visibility as a result of movement and some implications to landscape analysis at multiple scales. A full validation of the methodology to landscape analysis is work in progress. Future work includes statistical analysis to determine the correlation between extent of territory and visibility. The plausibility of the relationship needs to be tested for all barrows possibly using Kolmogorov-Smirnoff and related techniques.

References

Fisher, P. 1996: Extending the Applicability of Viewsheds in Landscape Planning, Photogrammetric Engineering and Remote Sensing 62(11), 1297-1302.

Ingold, T. 2000: The perception of the environment. Essays in livelihood, dwelling and skill. London: Routledge.

Ingold, T. 2011: Being alive. Essays on movement, knowledge and description. London: Routledge.

Lock, G. - Harris, T.M. 1996: Danebury Revisited: An English Iron Age Hillfort in a Digital Landscape. In: M. Aldenderfer – H.D.G. Maschner eds, Antropology, Space, and Geographic Information Systems, 214-240.

Lock, G. - Pouncett, J. 2009: Walking the Ridgeway Revisited: The Methodological and Theoretical Implications of Scale Dependency for the Derivation of Slope and the Calculation of Least Cost Pathways. 37th Annual International Conference on Computer Applications and Quantitative Methods in Archaeology (CAA), "Making History Interactive", Williamsburg, Virginia, USA, 192-203.

Lock, G. - Kormann, M. - Pouncett, J. in press: Visibility and Movement: Towards a GIS-Based Integrated Approach. In: S. Polla - P. Verhagen eds, Berlin Studies of the Ancient World, De Gruyter Excellence Cluster Topoi, Berlin, Germany.

Ogburn, D.E. 2006: Assessing the level of visibility of cultural objects in past landscapes. Journal of Archaeological Science 33, 405-413.

Tilley, C. 1994: A phenomenology of landscape. Oxford: Berg Publishers.

Invention and Innovation Processes in Prehistoric Societies

François Djindjian

Resume: *L'invention dans les sociétés humaines implique généralement la convergence de plusieurs processus socio-cognitifs différents et indépendants, dont certains sont accessibles à la méthode archéologique. Nous nous intéresserons plus particulièrement ici à ceux liés à un processus de serendipité, qui met en évidence un grand nombre d'inventions, passagères ou durables, connues en Préhistoire, dont nous donnons des exemples : taille du silex, emmanchement, gestion du feu, terre cuite, maîtrise de la température, agriculture, domestication, métallurgie. Nous développons ensuite une approche basée sur la désynchronisation entre l'invention, qui est un processus cognitif, et l'innovation dans le cadre d'un changement socio-culturel, qui est un processus systémique (et qui, en cas de succès, est à l'origine de nombreuses autres innovations). Nous appliquons cette approche à l'étude de la transition entre le Paléolithique moyen et le Paléolithique supérieur en Europe, ainsi qu'à l'étude de quelques régressions au cours du Paléolithique supérieur.*

Abstract: *Invention in human societies generally involves the convergence of many different and independent socio-cognitive processes, of which several are accessible to archaeology. Here we will be particularly interested in the serendipity process, which lies at the origin of many inventions known in prehistory, short lived or durable, for example: stone knapping, hafting, control of fire, terracotta, fire temperature control, farming, domestication and metallurgy. We have developed an approach based on the desynchronization between the invention, which is a cognitive process, and the innovation within society, which is a systemic process (and which, if successful is the origin of many other innovations). We apply this approach to the study of the transition between the Middle Palaeolithic and the Upper Palaeolithic in Europe, and also to several cases of regression during the Upper Palaeolithic.*

Keywords: *socio-cognitive processes – serendipity – Middle-Palaeolithic Upper Palaeolithic transition.*

The mechanisms of the invention process

In human societies invention generally involves the convergence of many different and independent socio-cognitive processes, in particular the following:

1. A cerebral cognitive capacity of invention.
   This is certainly a critical point when working in the earliest periods of mankind. They are based on analogies with the cognitive capacities of actual apes known through experimental approaches or on the evolutions of the morphocranial characteristics of the hominoids. For example, it applies to the emergence of language, attributed at the earliest to *Homo erectus* or at the latest to *Homo sapiens*. Here we will consider that, since the emergence of modern man, in the majority of cases discussed here, there is no cognitive limitation of invention for mankind.

2. A serendipity process (analogy, random event, casual correlation, error).
3. A need or a utility (functional explanation).
4. A capacity for investment (in time and means or their equivalent).
5. An internal or external constraint (social, economic or environmental), implying a change.

The mechanisms of the invention process and archaeology

Most of the very early processes cannot be investigated with the archaeological method, but some of them may be estimated indirectly from artefacts or ecofacts.

A. Leroi-Gourhan (*1943*), in his book "*L'homme et la matière*" developed an ethnographic classification of tools. For the same tool, the worldwide kaleidoscope of different technologies of manufacturing and the cultural variability confirms the universal rule of "the need is creating the function" in the history of mankind (process no. 3). Fortunately for the archaeologist, the material culture is partially preserved (unlike organic materials in most cases), and an artefact analysis can reveal much information and particularly the purpose (by statistics measuring the repetition of the manufacturing process), the use (by microwear analysis) and the technology (by experimentation) which may trace the cognitive ability of humans to find a solution to their functional needs.

In archaeology, we have also numerous examples of process no. 5 in which a huge change is due to environmental constraints (revealed through palaeo-environmental reconstruction), to economic constraints (revealed through determination of food resource management, manufacturing production system, raw material procurement, trade, etc.), or to social constraints (either given by the material culture revealing the social structure of the society or by events like migrations, wars, infiltration of the population, social collapse or epigraphy).

Finally, process no. 2, or the serendipity process, which associates natural events (analogy, random event, casual correlation) with a human attitude that is open and ready to see the inventive potentiality, which is particularly interesting because it seems possible to deduce from the identification of the different parts, that process that lies at the origin of the invention. This is the reason why we have particularly focused on it in the following paragraphs.

Serendipitous inventions in prehistory

Many inventions in prehistoric times cannot be considered as complex technical revolutions like in modern times. They are simple ideas resulting from the observation of casual events.

Certainly generally speaking, the limited technical background of archaeologists lies probably at the origin of a systematic overestimation of the technical difficulties that should be overcome for the development of know-how or to make an invention, supposing often the origin of some external contribution. Many examples are characteristic, such as:

- The question of lighting in caves and consequently the question of the antiquity of palaeolithic cave art (see the polemic on palaeolithic lighting with the first lamp in the cave of La Mouthe, until the results of a chemical analysis by Marcellin Berthelot),
- The hunting of large animals (mammoth, rhinoceros),
- The erection of megaliths,
- The building of the pyramids in Egypt.

Our suggestion is to say that technical inventions are, most of the time, the results of very simple invention processes and we will try to demonstrate this with several examples.

The sequence of inventions in stone knapping techniques

The sequence of inventions in stone knapping techniques may be summarized as follows:

- From the pebble to the chopper, by a casual removal of a flake during the use of the pebble as a hammer,
- From the chopper to the chopping-tool, by a casual bilateral removal during the use of the chopper,
- From the chopping-tool to the handaxe, by bilateral circular removals to give a morphology (more precisely a longitudinal axis of symmetry and sometimes a sharpening) and a thinning down for attaching a handle (for the invention of hafting, see below),
- From the handaxe to the Levalloisian technique, by a

casual removal of a "Levalloisian" flake in place of a thinning-down flake on the butt of a handaxe,
- From the Levalloisian technique to the volume prismatic technique, by pivoting by 90° the lateral edge of a Levallois nucleus which is then the crest edge of a future prismatic nucleus.

The summary in so few lines of the sequence of inventions in stone knapping techniques could seem a caricature to the reader, in particular to those who are not familiar with flint, and that the technological jargon and the typological variability of stone tools may be off-putting by their apparent complexity.

To be more complete, we must add other parallel know-how which is also important:

- The ability to recognize the quality of the raw material and to find suitable outcrops (if there is a need for that), which appears to be the case from the beginning of the Upper Palaeolithic due to the need for thinner and longer, and lighter blanks (cf. below for the question of mobility in palaeolithic times);
- The progressive control of the quality, the regularity and the precision of percussion (hard hammer, soft hammer, knapping by pressure (Solutrean), heating, etc.). The development of the soft hammer technique in the beginning of the Upper Palaeolithic is an invention associated with the development of the industry made on hard animal material (bone, ivory and antler).

Everybody always remembers the famous diagram by A. Leroi-Gourhan (*1964*, 194, fig. 64) showing the evolution over time, from the pebble culture to the Mesolithic, of the increase in edge length of flint blanks from 40 cm to 100 cm (Fig. 1). Of course, the diagram is used much more to produce a visual effect than to compute a real quantitative curve, obliging us to point out here some kind of manipulating evolutionism. In fact, the diagram clearly shows three different systems which are not comparable: the handaxe system, the flake/blade manufacturing system, and the microlith manufacturing system. Nevertheless, the diagram may be applied usefully to the flake/blade system, showing the major change in the edge length from the Middle Palaeolithic (MP) system to the Upper Palaeolithic (UP) system. The reason for such a change will be explained in section 6, with the introduction of the concept of mobility of hunter-gatherer groups, which obliges them to develop a light toolkit for travelling. The underlying explanation of the diagram is then no longer some kind of evolutionism (following G. de Mortillet) but a systemic change due to a functional need (mobility) caused by climatic variations.

The invention of hafting

The innovation of hafting is the result of the association of the wooden shafted arm with a handaxe in order to realize a stone hafted weapon. This technology was first applied to

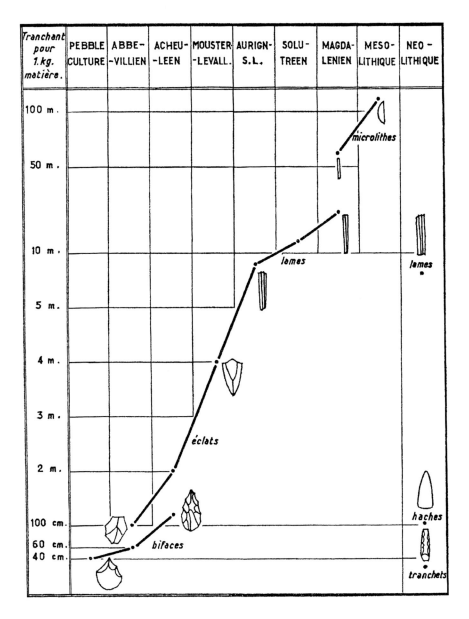

Fig. 1. Leroi-Gourhan's diagram of Palaeolithic blank production.

weapons and later to tools (to obtain lighter tools that were easier to transport).

The efficient hunting of large mammals has induced naturally the need for both a hafted weapon (French "arme de hast") and a projectile weapon (French "arme de jet").

The first weapons we know, dated to around 400 000 years ago, are the wooden hafted weapons of Clacton (England) and Schöningen (Saxony), with their points hardened by fire. The change from the wooden weapon to a composite weapon made with a flint point and a wooden shaft is due to an improvement in the hunting technique (to obtain a better perforating or bleeding power), necessitating finding a solution to affix the point to the shaft (fixing of a handle with tendon, fibre or glue).

The fining down of a flint point has been a long technological process since the Lower Palaeolithic (handaxes), the Middle

Palaeolithic (Mousterian handaxes, Micoquian points, leaf points), transition industries (leaf points on blades), Aurignacian (Font-Yves points), Gravettian ("fléchettes", Font-Robert tanged points with axial hafting, Gravette points and Microgravette points with lateral hafting), Solutrean (leaf points, stepped points, etc.), Magdalenian (Teyjat points, Laugerie-basse points), Hambourgian (Cresswell points, Hambourgian points), Epipalaeolithic (Lingby points, Ahrensbourg points, etc.), Mesolithic (microliths, triangles and trapezes), and Neolithic until the Bronze Age. Such a continuous morphological evolution lies at the origin of the application of the Theory of Evolution by G. de Mortillet (and Gaudry) to prehistory and their mistaken consequence during thirty years (negation of Aurignacian *sensu lato*) until the corrections by Breuil in 1911.

Several different processes are probably interfering here, particularly:

- The mechanism of hafting (axial, with or without a tang; lateral, straight or with a step),
- The weapon (hafted weapon; projectile weapon, by hand or with a propeller; arrow of the bow) which implies a progressive but not continuous fining down and a more and more perfect symmetry and stability of the point. Certainly, we must imagine the handaxe for a shafted weapon, a leaf point for a projectile weapon (end of MP, MP-UP transition, UP), a microlithic point for an arrow point (Epipalaeolithic, Mesolithic and later, even if it could be possible to discuss the evidence of the innovation without future of the arrow during the Solutrean),
- The weapon morphologies are also specialized for hunting different kinds of animals in different kinds of environment (cold steppe, shrub valleys, Holocene forest, etc.). But they may also identify a group.

The invention of fire

The discovery of fire and its properties is associated with repeated natural phenomena (thunderbolt, volcano). More innovative is the acquisition of the know-how on how to obtain fire, which may be associated with indications of heating which were observed when working wood. And finally, solutions for conserving a fire are also simple. Ethnographic comparisons furnish enough examples of people conserving a fire by transporting charcoals in wooden or leaf containers (the ember pot of our grandmothers).

More difficult are solutions to produce fire, either by friction, by rubbing dry wood on dry wood, or by percussion, producing sparks by striking iron sulphur minerals of marcasite (found readily in flint chalk layers) or pyrite which may fire up tow, tinder (a dried mushroom) or dried herbs (*Collina-Girard 1998*). Leroi-Gourhan (*1943*) affirms that people adopted metal lighters and renounced wood heating techniques, which are more time consuming.

Mythology has often preserved the traditions of keeping a fire (sacred hearths). They have also kept alive the memory of these important innovations by making them sacred them: Zeus produced natural phenomena including fire (thunder bolts), Prometheus gave humans fire; Hephaestus (Vulcan) god of fire and metalworking.

The invention of terracotta

The first invention of terracotta is a serendipitous result of the long-time use of hearths located on a loess soil in the semi-sedentary Pavlovian dwellings of Moravia (around 27 000 BP). The temperatures obtained in such hearths can measure up to 800°C, high enough to produce terracotta (500 to 600°C).

Here is also found the first use of terracotta with impressions of basketry, likely to form and reinforce elements for building huts (and not as the first basketry clothing as proposed by Soffer (*2004*) in Dolní Vestonice where the very cold climate and the very large number of carnivore bones is indicative of the use of furs to fabricate clothing). The Pavlovian innovation of terracotta produced only female and animals figurines.

In the early farming period of the Middle East, the emergence of terracotta pots is known between 7000 and 6400 BC, while terracotta figurines appear earlier around 9000 BC. The production of terracotta is known thousands of years before they found a social and industrial use such as for storing seeds and meats during the development of farming, after the use of stone dishes around 9200 BC and of plaster dishes around 7500 BC (*Aurenche - Kozlowski 1999*).

But the terracotta discovery is only the beginning of a long list of technical innovations which are outside the scope of this paper:

- Extraction and preliminary processing of raw clay,
- Addition of mineral or organic matter ("*dégraissant*") for obtaining more elasticity of the terracotta during the decreasing temperature,
- Controlling the temperature above 600°C (increasing, stability, decreasing) and the atmosphere (reducing, oxidizing),
- Realizing the first kilns,
- Designing the piece (moulding, casting, turning) which is a revolution volume,
- Ornamentation (plain ware, painted ware, incised ware, impressed ware, etc.),
- Colouring,
- Glazing,
- Etc.

The technical control of increasing the temperature of fire

The technical control of increasing the temperature of fire may be associated with the serendipitous observation of the positive action of the wind on a hearth, or the breath of air expulsed from an empty animal-skin water bottle, prototyping future bellows. The use of open air hearths allows reaching temperatures of up to 650°C, while the use of semi-subterranean hearths allows reaching temperatures of up to 850°C. The use of a potter's kiln easily allows reaching temperatures of the melting point of copper at around 1083°C.

The invention of colouring (ochre)

The first invention of colouring is to notice the ability of charcoal to give a black colour.

The second invention of colouring is the serendipitous convergence between a hearth installed on a soil rich in iron oxides (for example loess, the temperature transforming the yellow goethite into a red hematite), giving all the colour spectra between yellow and red purple. We effectively know that during the Upper Palaeolithic, oxide of manganese and hematite were procured by prehistoric people. On the other hand, it has been impossible to find traces of vegetal colouring, which could also have been used as body, clothing and other artefact colouring.

The invention of farming

The invention of farming was in fact a long series of inventions, starting with the properties of seeds, gathered and lost near the dwelling, resulting in new growth of the same plant. The repetition of such a casual event has involved an unexpected experience plan that agronomists developed much later and in a more formal and mathematical manner.

Of course, the properties of seeds are not the only revolution of farming, which has known repeated technical revolutions from the 9th millennium BC to the 20th century AD. The main parameter for the technical progress of farming is the per-hectare yield (*Djindjian 2011*, chapter 10).

The invention of domestication

The invention of domestication has also been a long series of inventions, starting with the casual adoption of very young animals, some of them being able to adapt themselves to life with humans. The first animal to be domesticated was probably the dog. Of course, adopting a baby animal is not domestication, which has known a long series of evolutions by crossing breeds and by selection.

The invention of metallurgy

First came the development of an interest in collecting ores: hematite for colouring and marcasite for making fire, resulting in collecting also native metals like copper and meteoric iron. The native metals were worked by cold hammering to manufacture the same tools produced before in stone, like for example since the 6th millennium BC by the Sumerians and Egyptians. It is highly likely the development of ceramics which allowed the discovery, in the potter's kiln, of the properties of metals to become liquid at a given temperature (smelting), but also roasting which transforms metal sulphurs into metal oxides.

The invention of glass

Glass is the result of melting silica at 1700°C. But mixed with soda or potash and a stabilizer like lime, the melting point is reduced to 850°C, a temperature easily obtained by ceramists and metallurgists. According to Pliny the Elder (23–79 AD), the discovery is due to Phoenician traders, who during a bivouac on a sandbank of the Belus river (near Saint Jean d'Acre), cooked their pot on natron (natural soda) stones and obtained a viscous liquid. If the legend is true, it would be a pure serendipitous event.

Invention and innovation

There is generally a more or less timely desynchronization between the invention process and its development in society, which we will call the innovation process.

The source of innovation is the consequence of a process of communication, either internal or external to the society considered:

1. A capacity of internal communication or mirroring discussion with others and an easy transmission of inventions between people (this is generally the case with hunter-gatherer societies),
2. An external contribution (acculturation, contact, cross-fertilization, etc.).
   And the development of the innovation is the result of an acceptance or a resistance to its development:
3. A social context more or less favourable to the acceptance of the invention in society, and starting the process of innovation: absence or presence of crises, social organization (family, tribe), customs, obstacles to change, taboo, mental block, believes in progress, unions or trusts, financial interests, loss of power or social dominance, etc.

We can say that the development of an innovation is generating a systemic process, which can see a stagnation, a fast development, a regression, a resilience and a comeback or a definitive abandoning.

Process no. 3 is so immaterial that it is difficult to validate by other means than by ethnographic comparisons or texts from historical archaeology.

The limitations of such an approach are well known. For example, remember the paradigmatic proposals of M. Sahlins (*1972*) for palaeolithic economies arguing the low charge of hunter-gatherer food resource management compared with the high charge of farming systems (even with the consequence of increasing demography), which are now generally refuted (*Kelly 2007*).

We have numerous examples of first contacts between prehistoric tribes and European ships exploring the world from the end of the 15th century, showing the high level of curiosity and the ability concerning the recovery of raw material of metals, fragments of tools or tools (for example, Emperaire, 1955 for the Alakalufs in Tierra del Fuego). On the other hand, we also have examples given by ethnologists concerning the very traditional life of tribes which have been studied by Europeans since the 17th century which may appear certainly as an obstacle to change (for example, Levi-Strauss, 1955 in Amazonia). This point has been questioned by Levi Strauss (*Hénaff 1991*, 301), who was wondering if the "primitive" tribes were a representative sample of all the ancient civilizations or at the opposite the continuity through time of very particular closed systems. The proposed explanations are generally sought in the evidence of a more or less stable socio-economic environment, but could be also found in a reaction against the dangers of contacts with another population (for example the Amazonian tribes and the arrival of Europeans). Such a question may be more globally analysed as a classic opposition between history and structural anthropology (from a systemic point of view). Contemporary examples are nevertheless showing that all societies have both engines to change and brakes to change which are a component of their own evolution.

The example of the transition from the Middle Palaeolithic to the Upper Palaeolithic

The blade and bladelet technology appears much earlier in the Middle Palaeolithic (OIS 7, OIS 5, OIS 3), but the development of this technology, which is the definition of the Upper Palaeolithic when it completely replaces the Middle Palaeolithic flake technology (Levallois, Discoid, Quina), appears much later in OIS 3. The change in the development of the technology is associated with the change in the mobility and the subsistence strategy of hunter-gatherer groups during the period 40 000 – 35 000 BP (*Djindjian 2012*). It means that blade technology was already known 250 000 years ago, and has seen several periods of development and regression before the Upper Palaeolithic.

The transition from the Palaeolithic to the Neolithic

Many features are essential for the emergence of farming: gathering of cereal plants, sedentary dwellings, food storing, grindstones, storage dishes (stone, plaster, terracotta). These did occur already during the Upper Palaeolithic, thus the change in the food subsistence strategy happened much earlier. In Central Europe, during the Pavlovian (Early Gravettian of Central Europe in Moravia), semi-sedentary dwellings, food storing in deep permafrost pits and terracotta figurines are known for a short period between 27 000 and 26 000 BP, associated with a food subsistence economy based on mammoths. In Eastern Europe, during the Eastern Gravettian, grinding, which was in the early days of archaeology the definition of the Neolithic period, is known around 24 000 – 22 000 BP (Kostienki 4, Molodova V), used mainly in making stone and ivory female statuettes and grindstones. It is thus possible to find situations in which only part of the process is present, which would prevent a proper transition to farming.

A systemic analysis of the transition from the Middle to the Upper Palaeolithic

A systemic analysis of the transition between the Middle to the Upper Palaeolithic may be developed by first defining the initial system (MP) and the final system (UP) and then the rational succession of inventions, innovations and changes to make the transition from the MP to the UP (*Otte 1996; Djindjian et al. 1999*).

An attempt to define the Middle Palaeolithic System

*   Knapping techniques
    *   Flake knapping ("discoid", Levallois, Quina)
    *   Blade knapping (Levallois)
    *   Blade and bladelet knapping (prismatic)

*   Variability of the tool assemblages
    *   Sidescrapers versus notches and denticulates
    *   Levallois, discoid and Quina knapping
    *   Handaxes, bifacial points, Mousterian points, Levallois points
    *   Knives
    *   Small percentage of Upper Palaeolithic tools

*   Small diversity of tools: Sidescrapers, notches and denticulates, knives, points (in contradiction to the number of tools in the list of F. Bordes & M. Bourgon).
*   Small diversity of point morphology (probably used with wooden hafting).
*   Impossibility to define "cultures" (i.e. time and space techno-complexes). Then, at a given time, there is no territory occupied by a network of hunter-gatherer groups circulating, meeting each other and exchanging technical know-how. Each group has his own small territory.
*   No bone industry.
*   Local procurement (circulation within 20 km around the dwelling).
*   Small territory (less than 1000 km^2).
*   Food resource management.
*   Food resource management is local and opportunistic inside the territory. The hunting strategy is an itinerant hunting; when the hunting territory is exhausted, the group moves on and the dwelling is abandoned for a long time.
*   The social relationship between groups is limited by the fast circulation of groups, resulting in a weak network organization.
*   The absence of dwelling structures is due to continuous habitation of rock shelters, limiting the preservation of structures (palimpsest).
*   Burials are often found in the dwellings (built when they were occupied or when they were deserted?).
*   Absence of art is due to no intra-group or inter-group individualization because there is neither a group nor a territory to mark.

An attempt to define the Upper Palaeolithic System

*   Cultures: a network of hunter-gatherer groups inside a delimited territory (*Djindjian 2009, in press*).
*   Blade and bladelet knapping technology: innovation of the prismatic core which is a "mobile" core. The strategy involves the preparation of the cores from flint pebbles directly at the outcrops, and to transport and to store them more easily throughout the territory.
*   Production of small blanks (blades and bladelets) which involves development of tool hafting.

- Higher variability of tools: endscrapers (scraping), retouched blades (side-scraping), burins (chiselling and cutting but also cores), hafted retouched bladelets (cutting), hafted points (projectile element).
- Equivalence between Middle and Upper Palaeolithic tool functions (and morphology): only the blank has changed: sidescrapers and retouched blades; notches and denticulates (ditto); points (ditto); knives and bladelets; sidescrapers and endscrapers.
- Bone and ivory industry: a change from the wooden spear and the flint spear to the bone or ivory point.
- Various household tools: needles, awls, picks, hammers, choppers, axes, etc. The reduction in size is a consequence of the specialization in tools.
- The diminution of the tool size involves a new generalized system of hafting: hand/handle/tool and hand/shaft/point.
- Dwellings are seasonally re-occupied sites. There is a case known of semi-sedentary dwellings associated with a mammoth economy during cold and dry periods.
- Distant raw procurements are occurring up to several hundred kilometres, implying a good knowledge of outcrops and good territorial control.
- Burials are associated with long-term occupied or seasonally re-occupied sites. But the presence of isolated human bones remains to be clarified: "mobile burial" or particular ritual?
- Art indicates identification (at an individual, intra-group or inter-group level) and allows the perception of territory.

The transition between the Middle and the Upper Palaeolithic

Mobility is the main factor of explanation for the systemic change from the MP to the UP, and lies at the origin of the change in material culture (*Djindjian 2012*).

From the Middle Palaeolithic . . .

The food resource strategy is opportunistic and diversified in a local territory of about 1000 m^2 around the dwelling. Thus, the mobility is weak, and does not favour light tools. Local stone procurement consists of various qualities (good-quality flint if local but generally poor-quality flint, quartzite, calcareous flint, etc.). The variability in the tool assemblage is correlated with the quality of the raw material, used preferably for certain tools (good-quality flint for scrapers, poor-quality flint for notches and denticulates). If the food resources are exhausted, groups are obliged to leave the dwelling and to move on to a new territory. The dwelling is deserted and the tools are abandoned on the site.

. . . to the Upper Palaeolithic

A systemic sequence of rules is given here as a preliminary draft:

- Climatic change (interpleniglacial),

- Changes in the herbivore zoocenoses,
- Limits of local opportunistic food resource management and interest in changing to a planned food resource management,
- Obligation to survey a larger space,
- Opportunity to survey landscapes newly opened up by the climatic change,
- Interest in acquiring knowledge about new zoocenoses,
- Adaptation of hunting techniques and arms,
- Solving the constraints of travelling in a larger territory during the annual cycle,
- Travelling easily with tools and arms,
- Need to reduce the weight of tools and arms to be transported,
- Development of bladelet and blade knapping to obtain more and smaller blanks from the same core,
- Development of hafting which allows the recovering of the active part of the tool or arm with a lower weight,
- Need for quality flint to improve the lightness of knapping,
- Survey of the landscape searching the outcrops for good-quality flint,
- Better knowledge and control of the landscape,
- Emergence of the concept of territory,
- Emergence of the concept of "cultures" by identification of intra-territorial groups and differentiation of extra-territorial groups,
- Organization via a social network of the intra-territorial groups and exploitation of the territory (meetings, people exchanges) by the group network,
- Emergence of art: perception and representation of the territory and its zoocenoses, transmission of knowledge about the territory and its zoocenoses, communication and "sacralization" of the critical processes of life (fertility, food resource management), personalization (at individual, intra-group, inter-group levels),
- Demographic growth of the group and, by subdivision of a group, demographic growth of the group network,
- Conquest of new uninhabited territories,
- Systematic occupation of all the available territories,
- Geographical and climatic partition,
- Climatic crisis of the Last Glacial Maximum (LGM) stage of OIS 2.

Regression processes in the Upper Palaeolithic

It is interesting to wonder if there is some kind of example during the Upper Palaeolithic of regression processes. During the LGM, since 22 000 BP, the European population is progressively flowing back to the southern Mediterranean parts of Europe: Solutrean in the western part, Early Epigravettian in the central part, Molodovian and Steppe Area industries in the eastern part. In south-western Europe, the Solutrean from 21 000 to 19 000 BP and the Badegoulian from 18 500 to 17 000 BP are revealing several unexpected features:

- Reappearance of poor-quality raw material (quartzite

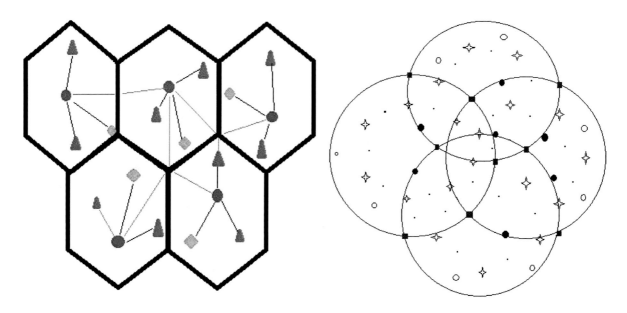

Fig. 2. Landscape management strategies. 2a: local opportunistic strategy (MP during OIS 4, UP during the LGM of OIS 2). 2b: extended planned strategy (Aurignacian, western Gravettian, Magdalenian).

and others), indicating loss of the traditional outcrops due to the abandonment of previous territories,

- Reduction in the size of the territory, with summer travels to the north (for quality flint raw material procurement and food resource management),
- Flake knapping reappears,
- Bifacial points are reappearing (they have been compared to Aterian tanged points, a Mousterian culture of North Africa which disappeared 20 000 years earlier),
- Reduction of the bone industry,
- Absence of portable art (in comparison with the Gravettian and Magdalenian),
- Open air rock art development in areas where there are no caves (Portugal, Spain).

The Mousterian-like component of the Solutrean stone industry has led several specialists to propose a direct evolution from the Aterian to the Solutrean in the Iberian Peninsula or from the Mousterian to the Solutrean in the Rhone valley, or more generally as a hypothesis of the origins of the Solutrean.

Such features are demonstrating a huge change in the system from the last Gravettian around 22 000 BP to the first Solutrean, due to the change of territories, both in location and in size, then modifying the raw material procurement system, the food management system and the mobility system.

Conclusions

This short initial paper must be seen as a preliminary approach to a very complex question which concerns invention, innovation and change in prehistoric societies. Most of the time, in archaeology a change in the material culture is seen as the arrival of new populations rather than a cultural change within the same population. Nevertheless, it has already been proven that civilizations may collapse on their own, without any role of other neighbouring civilizations (*Renfrew - Cooke, 1979*). The same argumentation may be used for transitions.

It is clear now that the so far undemonstrated association of a human type with a culture type (*Homo neandertalensis* with the Middle Palaeolithic, *Homo sapiens* with the Aurignacian) has confused the issue. In the Middle East and in North Africa, *Homo neandertalensis* and *Homo sapiens* manufactured the same Middle Palaeolithic industry, while in Western Europe they manufactured a similar Upper Palaeolithic industry (Castelperonnien and Gravettian). We have tried to demonstrate that the culture change from the MP to the UP may be shown by a systemic process which is independent of the population concerned.

References

Aurenche, O. - Kozlowski, S.K. 1999: La naissance du Néolithique au Proche-Orient. Paris: Errance.

Collina-Girard, J. 1998: Le feu avant les allumettes, Expérimentation et mythes techniques, Collection Archéologie expérimentale et Ethnographie des techniques XIV. Paris: Éditions de la Maison des Sciences de l'homme, 150 p.

Djindjian, F. 2009: Le concept de territoires pour les chasseurs cueilleurs du Paléolithique supérieur européen. In: F. Djindjian - J. Kozlowski - N. Bicho eds, Le concept de territoires pour les chasseurs cueilleurs du Paléolithique supérieur européen. Actes du XV° Congrès UISPP, Lisbonne, septembre 2006, Session C16, vol. 3. BAR Intern. Series 1938, 3-25.

Djindjian, F. 2011: Manuel d'Archéologie. Paris: Armand Colin.

Djindjian, F. 2012: Is the MP-EUP transition also an economic and social revolution? In: *L. Longo ed.*, Middle to Upper Palaeolithic Biological and Cultural Shift in Eurasia. International congress EAA, 15-20 September 2009, Trente. Quaternary International 259, 72-77.

Djindjian, F. in press: Contacts et déplacements des groupes humains dans le paléolithique supérieur européen: les adaptations aux variations climatiques des stratégies de gestion des ressources dans le territoire et dans le cycle annuel. Colloque de Liège "Modes de contacts et de déplacements au Paléolithique eurasiatique", 29-31 mai 2012.

Djindjian, F. - Kozlowski, J. - Otte, M. 1999: Le Paléolithique supérieur en Europe. Paris: Armand Colin.

Emperaire, J. 1955: Les nomades de la mer. Paris: Gallimard.

Hénaff, Cl. 1991: Claude Lévi-Strauss et l'anthropologie structurale. Paris: Belfond.

Kelly, R.L. 2007: The foraging spectrum: diversity in hunter-gatherer lifeways. New York: Percheron Press.

Leroi-Gourhan, A. 1943: Evolution et techniques. L'Homme et la matière. Paris: Albin Michel.

Leroi-Gourhan, A. 1964: Le geste et la parole. Techniques et langage. Paris: Albin Michel.

Levi-Strauss, Cl. 1955: Tristes tropiques. Paris: Plon.

Otte, M. 1996: Le Paléolithique inférieur et moyen en Europe. Paris: Armand Colin.

Renfrew, C. - Cooke, K.L. eds 1979: Transformations: mathematical approaches to culture change. New York: Academic Press.

Sahlins, M.D. 1972: Stone Age Economics. Chicago: Aldine.

Soffer, O. 2004: Recovering Perishable Technologies through Use Wear on Tools: Preliminary Evidence for Upper Paleolithic Weaving and Net Making. Current Anthropology 45, 407-418.